EMILIO COMICI

EMILIO COMICI

ANGEL OF THE DOLOMITES

DAVID SMART

RMB

For information on purchasing bulk quantities of this book,
or to obtain media excerpts or invite the author to speak at an event,
please visit rmbooks.com and select the "Contact" tab.

RMB | Rocky Mountain Books Ltd.
rmbooks.com
@rmbooks
facebook.com/rmbooks

Cataloguing data available from Library and Archives Canada
ISBN 9781771604567 (hardcover)
ISBN 9781771604574 (electronic)

Printed and bound in Canada

We would like to also take this opportunity to acknowledge the traditional
territories upon which we live and work. In Calgary, Alberta, we acknowledge the Niitsítapi (Blackfoot) and the people of the Treaty 7 region in
Southern Alberta, which includes the Siksika, the Piikuni, the Kainai, the
Tsuut'ina and the Stoney Nakoda First Nations, including Chiniki, Bearpaw,
and Wesley First Nations. The City of Calgary is also home to Métis Nation
of Alberta, Region III. In Victoria, British Columbia, we acknowledge the
traditional territories of the Lkwungen (Esquimalt, and Songhees), Malahat,
Pacheedaht, Scia'new, T'Sou-ke and W̱SÁNEĆ (Pauquachin, Tsartlip,
Tsawout, Tseycum) peoples.

We acknowledge the financial support of the Government of Canada
through the Canada Book Fund and the Canada Council for the Arts, and
of the province of British Columbia through the British Columbia Arts
Council and the Book Publishing Tax Credit.

Also for Katrina.

"I embrace you, in the sixth grade."

—EMILIO COMICI

CHAPTERS

ACKNOWLEDGEMENTS

Any errors or insufficiencies in this book are my own, but I have many people to thank for their contributions. Thanks to Elena Turro at the Fondazione Giovanni Angelini – Centro Studi sulla Montagna in Belluno for her patience with obscure research. Without Shayle Kilroy's research and translation assistance, some of the best parts of this book would not have been written. I relied heavily on Brian McKenna for Italian translations of climbing texts and owe much of what is referred to here to his expertise. Thanks also to the Italian Studies Department at the University of Toronto. Reinhold Messner keeps the history of the Dolomites alive beautifully, and I thank him for answering my emails. I also thank Joanna Croston at the Banff Mountain Film and Book Festival for encouraging my work. Katrina Kilroy, to whom this book is dedicated, read manuscripts and made my work as a writer possible over the last two years. Finally, I wish to acknowledge the one thing without which this book and the research it represents would have been impossible: the unique spirit of history and philosophy that suffuses the Italian climbing world and particularly the Club Alpino Italiano: *Excelsior!*

CHAPTER ONE

CITY OF WIND AND STONE

Emilio looked down between the heels of his basketball shoes, 400 metres to the talus of the north face of the Cima Grande. In the cool, permanent half-dusk of the north face, the outrageous dream, his obsession, had almost killed him twice that morning, once with a broken hold and once with a mishap with a rope. Inspiration from the ghost of his hero Paul Preuss would have been welcome, although unlikely here, in the realm of the pitons Preuss rejected. Up here, Emilio only had himself to depend on, but that was all he had ever wanted anyway. Let his *squadristi*, the intellectuals in the alpine club or the ancient local guides in Cortina d'Ampezzo, look at him askance. Up here, on the north face of the Cima Grande, it was Leonardo Emilio Comici of Via Bazzoni in Trieste, and none of those men, such as they were, who was *la cosa vera*, the real thing.

How did he come to find himself here, on the hardest rock wall in the world, alone?

***

In 1915, Emilio followed his mother, Regina, into the Bora headwind that blew from the Carso's limestone highlands and down through the streets of Trieste. A black mantilla hid her face. On one side, she held the hand of Emilio's lanky brother, Gastone, and on the other, the hand of his 8-year-old sister, Lucia. They had been to mass at the church of Our Lady of Providence, who guided the ships across the wild oceans and brought the sailors home.

In Austrian-ruled Trieste, the Italian majority viewed the church with suspicion, and there were rumours that the priests were government spies, but Regina Cartago had been born on Italian ground in Verona and had faith. How she arrived in Trieste is lost to history. Tourists came no closer than Venice, a hundred kilometres west. Pretenders to thrones, poets, writers, lovers, criminals, sailors and the nationless continued east to Trieste, where Regina had fallen in love with the handsome shipwright, Antonio Comici.

Emilio inherited Regina's strong brow, dark narrow eyes, and a head always tilted a little as if amused or skeptical. Antonio was lantern-jawed, broad nosed, tall and muscular. Fourteen-year-old Emilio was pudgy, sickly, slow to show signs of puberty and given to melancholy.

A gust blew Emilio off balance, and his hands caught the rough hemp rope strung along the sidewalk between steel staves. To show the wind his strength, he dropped down and ran into it towards his mother. He wished his father were there to see him, but since the war had begun – a year before, in 1914 – Antonio had worked every day of the week at the Österreichischer Lloyd and Cosulich Società Triestina di Navigazione shipyards. But he wanted his mother to see him beat the wind even more.

Emilio was something of a *mammone*, devoted to his mother and in awe of the sacrifices she made for her family. For his whole life, she would cook for him, advise him and do his laundry in her fortress and temple, a modest apartment in the safe, humble neighbourhood of San Vito. They were at number six, Via Bazzoni, not too far from the docks for Antonio to walk to work.

Via Bazzoni took its name from the crenellated villa of Palazzo Bazzoni, the headquarters of the Glanzmann family, who had enriched themselves as shippers and importers in service of the hungry empire to the north. Emilio and his friends had often stopped games in the street as one of the Glanzmanns' shiny automobiles carried women in mink stoles and men in top hats to the opera or smart restaurants on the Corso.

At home, Regina took off her mantilla and shook out her long black hair. Emilio followed her to the kitchen, where she hummed as she broke the dried salted stockfish into a pot with a few unpeeled and wizened root vegetables. Emilio grew up on dishes that were lessons in how, just barely, to survive winters, wars and famines.

Emilio took the mandolin, with its neck worn smooth from his father's hands, off its hook. He couldn't remember when he could not play. He sang a tune he had learned with his father and the sailors at the harbour. Regina hummed along until her favourite part, then joined in. Emilio loved how they sounded together, and her Veronese accent with its lilt at the end of each word made even her curses sound like poetry.

"Trieste sleeps," sang mother and son, "the sea is still, the shining stars make me dream."

The music was redolent with his love for his grey city, that sad prisoner of Austria. His parents had taught him to long for reunification of all the Italian lands, the goal of those who called themselves irredentists. For Emilio, even as a boy, the tragedy of his city resonated with the sadness inside him he found so hard to escape. Like Trieste, Emilio had a certain *distacco*, or aloofness without indifference or cruelty, and *lontananza*, a sufficiency unto himself kept pure of any arrogance because it was fated, not chosen.

***

In the early summer of 1914, Russian-backed Serbians had assassinated Archduke Franz Ferdinand in Sarajevo. Like most *Triestinos*, young Emilio blamed the event and the Great War that followed on the brutality of the Austrian government. Even Italy seemed to have lost its way and joined in an alliance with Austria and Germany. The war seemed far away and unlikely to benefit Trieste until, in May of 1915, a miracle happened: Italy forsook its alliance with Austria and Germany and declared war on Austria to reclaim ethnically Italian lands.

In Trieste, the Austrians acted swiftly to suppress Italian nationalism and thus inadvertently turned many young people into irredentists. The Austrians mined the harbour because they feared a British amphibious invasion, which they expected the Italian population of Trieste to support. The police shuttered the coffee shops said to breed irredentism, and, for good measure, closed the Italian boys' clubs. Expressions of Italian sympathy were brutally crushed. Young Italians drafted into the Austrian army were sent to the Russian Front because most of them would desert if forced to fight the Italians. Emilio felt a rush of pride and excitement when he heard of the young heroes who risked death to cross the Austrian lines on the Carso to enlist with the Italian army.

For much of the conflict, the Austrians held the Italians back 30 kilometres west of Trieste, at Duino. The Italian aerial bombardment of Trieste, reinforced with aircraft and pilots from other allied countries, was limited in scale but sustained and indiscriminate. Irredentists risked death or arrest to stand in the streets and cheer on the Italian aircraft.

The imperial ship works were moved south to Pula in Croatia, where the Slavic workers inspired more trust from the Austrians. Austria-Hungary's greatest saltwater port and railhead became almost unusable when the British blockaded the narrow mouth of the Adriatic between Brindisi and Otranto. Antonio sat for days at the kitchen table, playing the mandolin or the guitar. Money became literally scarce, as cash from the banks and maritime insurance companies had been sent north to Gorizia, further from the front. Rationing kept the population on the edge of starvation. Austrian mines in the harbour made fishing dangerous. Boredom and hunger bred anger. Unemployed Italian youths joined students from Emilio's school to clash with the police in the Piazza Grande. Even as the Italian army suffered a series of defeats, irredentist author Scipio Slataper swore that Trieste's youth "would be happy to die in [Trieste's] blaze."[1]

After the first Italian victories, German troops were sent to the Italian front in the Dolomites and introduced poison gas, air warfare and a new level of brutality to the war. Germany, once seen as an ambivalent nation by Trieste irredentists, now shared in Austria-Hungary's infamy.

Too young to work or fight, Emilio spent many days entertaining himself. His *lontananza*, or natural aloofness, drew him away from the city to the solitude of the Carso. In the broken bone-white limestone wilderness split by gullies full of red sumac, he explored and daydreamed.

"My Carso is a landscape of limestone and junipers," wrote Slataper. "A fierce cry, turned to stone. Grey boulders stained with rain and lichen, twisted, split, jagged. Dry junipers. Long hours of limestone and junipers. The grasses are all bristles. Bora. Sunshine. The earth is without peace, without continuity. It doesn't even have any field to spread itself in. Every attempt it makes is all fissured and cloven. Cold caves, lying dark. The water-drop, carrying with it all the soil it has stolen, falls regularly, mysteriously, for a hundred years, and another hundred years."[2]

One day in the hot, hungry first week of August 1917, Emilio walked along the dusty road between the Carso and the blue Adriatic, lost in his thoughts. At first, he thought that the figures to the west were a mirage, but then he heard distraught voices. Dozens trudged towards Trieste. Peasant women in kerchiefs cajoled goats or cows. Mothers carried small children. Some pulled donkeys laden with bundles or furniture. The only men were a few unarmed soldiers in dusty uniforms, with crutches or bandaged limbs.

He found a woman carrying two infants and followed by three children. Stress and exhaustion lined her face. The children's tears made lines on their cheeks.

"What's happened?" Emilio asked. "Who are all of these people?"

"General Cadorna took Duino, but first he shelled it. We are lucky to be alive. There were many, many dead."[3]

She told Emilio that she had no family in Trieste and intended to seek the charity of the church or the authorities.

Emilio concealed his joy at the thought of the Italian army closing in on Trieste, but he feared for the woman and her children. Trieste already sheltered 10,000 refugees from the northern Carso. Food and shelter were hard to come by. But what if his own mother had been in such a plight? He did the only thing he could, and brought them home.

"Mama," Emilio said, "these are refugees, they have nowhere to go and they're hungry, we must take them in."

Antonio and Regina already had five mouths to feed. Food, fuel and medicine were strictly rationed. And yet, in the old Mediterranean way, the stranger was seen as a second self, never to be cursed or rejected. The woman and her children stayed with the Comicis until the end of the war, in the autumn of 1918. There was no time limit on the ancient pact of hospitality. Emilio was proud of himself. Life could be sad, but there was hope for Italy, and there were moments, even for a boy in the Carso, to be a hero.

***

Emilio left school at 15 and became a junior clerk at the Port Authority's Magazzini Generali, the warehouses of the Punto Franco Vecchio.

Every day he strode purposefully to his job, dressed in grey trousers and an open shirt. He always ate lunch in the same restaurant. He was a serious young man. When he went out with his friends to bars in Castello di San Giusto on the weekends, he drank only orange juice and went home to his mother at ten p.m.[4]

Despite his social reticence, Emilio craved excitement and contact with other young people. In 1916, he joined the Trieste Gymnastics Society. In addition to gymnastics, the society offered track and field activities, calisthenics and strength and endurance workouts like rope climbs and horizontal ladder traverses. At 15, Emilio still had plump cheeks and dark, almost girlish eyes. After a year at the society, Emilio grew into the physique of his father, not tall, but muscular, handsome, with high cheekbones.

The Trieste Gymnastics Society club set out to harden both its members' bodies and their political views. Before the Great War, the irredentist politics of the society were usually tolerated by the police to prevent ethnic unrest. The police stood back, however, when in 1915, Austrian sympathizers burned down the society's building to end the publication of *La Piccola*, an irredentist newspaper published on the premises. Young Emilio knew the society's reputation and embraced its commitment to sport and Italian nationalism.

Out of the earshot of police and informers, between bristly boat rope climbs and calisthenic routines, Emilio learned of Italian victories at the front and the legends of Trieste's irredentists, many of whom now fought on the Italian side. Inevitably, the name of Napoleone Cozzi, a founder of the society and Trieste's greatest irredentist and climber, came up.

Cozzi's climbing partner Antonio Carniel described Cozzi as "small, enthusiastic, volcanic and agile as a squirrel."[5] He was best known to the public as the artist who had painted the murals in the Caffè San Marco, where he and other irredentists had plotted against the Austrian government. Cozzi, however, did not limit his political action to chats over coffee.

In 1904, the Austrian secret police searched the headquarters of the Trieste Gymnastics Society and found several Orsini bombs, home-made grenade-like devices popular with anarchists. Cozzi was taken into custody on charges of high treason and imprisoned in Vienna to await trial. The Italian government intervened on his behalf, and, on the unlikely premise that the bombs had not been intended for an attack, Cozzi was acquitted.[6]

Cozzi was a more successful revolutionary as a climber. He surprised alpinists in the Eastern Alps with his aggressive skills honed on the Carso at Val Rosandra on the eastern outskirts of Trieste, where he created the first *palestra*, or practice climbing area, in Italy.[7] With Trieste climbers Alberto Zanutti, Giuseppe Marcovig, Antonio Carniel and Tullio Cepich, he formed the group of climbers who became known as the Flying Squad.

The squad made numerous first ascents in the Cridola and Carnic Alps and tried to equal or outdo Austrian climbers like the great soloist Paul Preuss or the guideless climbing pioneers Eugen Lammer and Emil Zsigmondy. In 1910, Cozzi and Zanutti climbed a prominent rock spire in the Civetta group in the eastern Dolomites and named it Torre Trieste to proclaim their city's arrival on the stage of alpinism.

In 1902, Cozzi solved one of the great rock climbing problems of the Eastern Alps when he led a vertical crack on the unclimbed Campanile di Val Montanaia. Zanutti, however, quailed at the thought of a struggle with even harder cracks and walls higher on the pillar, so they retreated. Before Cozzi could attempt the climb a second time, he indulged in a night of drinking with Austrians Victor Wolf von Glanvell and Karl Günther von Saar and shared details of his route. Glanvell and Saar promptly used the information to snatch the first ascent, an act that provided Cozzi with more proof of Austrian treachery.

When Italy joined the allies in 1915, Cozzi was one of the first *Triestinos* to enlist in the Italian army and risk exile from his hometown if Italy lost the war. He served with the *alpini*, or mountain infantry, on the Alpine Front, where the lines stretched over high passes, across glaciers and rock walls. Both sides blew up mountaintops, forged trails with explosives, bombarded peaks and strafed them with machine guns and filled valleys with poison gas. The mountains themselves inflicted heavy casualties. On a single day in 1916, later known as White Friday, 2,000 soldiers from both sides combined were killed in avalanches. Although the war ended with an Italian victory, 600,000 Italians had lost their lives and a million more had been wounded.

The nation made the *alpini* into heroes for their defense of the Alps against the Austrian and German hordes. Cozzi, however, never got to enjoy these honours. In 1916, he died in exile of complications from syphilis. Nonetheless, in death, as in life, his legendary status among irredentists in Trieste continued to grow.

At Cozzi's Trieste Gymnastics Society, teenage Emilio could not help but learn that to become a hero for the motherland, and Trieste, was not a duty but an adventure.

***

News of Austria-Hungary's surrender reached Trieste on October 30, 1918. The Italians of Trieste, despite years of malnutrition, celebrated with bonfires, danced and drank in the streets. The "Marcia Reale d'Ordinanza," the anthem of the Kingdom of Italy, banned by the Austrians, was sung: "The Italian Alps will be free / angelic speech will reign, the hated barbarian / will never set foot here / as long as our fervent patriotic love lasts / as long as our civilization reigns." Pictures of King Victor Emmanuel III of Italy and flags hidden away for years were draped from windows. Church bells rang. Despite years of military incompetence and the staggering waste of Italian lives, irredentists claimed the war as proof of Italian prowess.

The Slavic and Austrian citizens were less festive. Amidst the anarchy of the open city, there was no one to stop the mobs who looted their homes and businesses.

On November 4, before Trieste had even been ceded to Italy by treaty, a ship full of Bersaglieri troops arrived from Venice. Emilio was ecstatic. The expedition had been inspired by the intervention of Dr. Paolo Jacchia, a Jewish doctor and irredentist.[8] Despite the cold weather and a strong Bora wind, the crowd cheered.

The 500-year-long Austrian occupation of Trieste came to an end to the sound of the Bersaglieri brass band as they marched double-time through the streets. In the eyes of Emilio, the city's faith that it would one day overthrow the oppressors had contributed to the victory.

There was a notion older than the church that the wronged eventually take their revenge against the oppressor, not in love and understanding, but in a *vendetta*, the Italian word for vengeance. Overnight, Italian became the official language of the whole region. German, Slavic and Austrian institutions were vandalized and suppressed. Many Slavs and German-speakers Italianized their names to avoid persecution.

The world outside of Italy, however, remained wary. The post-war restoration of sea trade was slow. Worse still, Trieste had been the chief saltwater port of Austria-Hungary. Now Trieste competed with all of Italy's ports, including the modern port of Venice, 150 kilometres to the west. The warehouses of the old port filled slowly with imported goods. Few new ships were laid at Antonio Comici's shipyards. Emilio filled the idle hours in the warehouse with door jamb pull-ups and deadlifting the silent adding machines. His physical strength grew, but like many nationalists, he was impatient for the longed-for liberation to bear fruit.

In 1920, the Trieste National Hall, a centre of Slavic life in the city, was burned by blackshirts, a new group of extreme nationalists who followed war veteran and political firebrand Benito Mussolini, whom they called Il Duce, or the leader. The blackshirts' numbers grew as liberal governments in Rome failed in 1920 and 1921. Their uniformed presence in the street added a sense of the discipline and glamour that young nationalists like Emilio craved enough to ignore the street violence that killed 1,500 Italians and injured 40,000 more, brought down municipal governments and led to the burning of dozens of liberal and socialist newspaper offices.

In 1922, Emilio's 14-year-old sister, Lucia, was diagnosed with a brain tumour. There was nothing to be done except to relieve her pain with morphine. Emilio spent every spare moment at her bedside, ashamed that he could not protect her and yet reverent of her heroic capacity to suffer. On the day before she died, she gave him her bracelet, a four-strand, gold-dipped steel chain. It became a symbol of Emilio's *vendetta* against death. He would bide his time, but one day, he would avenge his sister by defeating death in his own way. Emilio never believed in accidents, even when the transgressor was a force of nature. He would later wear the bracelet when he climbed. Partners said that all they could hear as he led the hardest pitches in the Alps was the occasional ghostly tinkle of Lucia's bracelet.

Emilio avoided church, but he was moved by the music at his sister's funeral mass. "De profundis clamavi ad te, Domine" (out of the depths, I call to thee, O Lord), words he knew from the school chapel, had a new poignancy.[9] His sister became the first name in a necrology that was to grow quickly once he became a climber.

In 1921, Emilio saw a flyer for the XXX Ottobre (30 October) Society, named after the day Trieste became part of Italy. The society called on brave local youths of both sexes to meet in the nearby neighbourhood of Pitteri for gymnastics, marches and dances. On weekends they would venture into the Carso to camp and explore caves. Emilio was the 26th card-carrying member of the society, but he had little time to join in their activities before he had to perform his compulsory military service.

In late October of 1922, while Emilio was in the army, Mussolini's fascists orchestrated the failure of the elected national government in Rome, and King Victor Emmanuel III approved of a government led by the Partito Nazionale Fascista, or PNF. Fascism became the law of Italy. The choice faced by the majority of Italians was stark. "On the one side," said fascist Mario Carli, "the cowardly, the soft, the hysterical, the effeminate, the cry-babies, the mommy's boys; on the other the strong, the aware, the idealists, the mystics of danger, those who triumph over fear and those who are courageous by nature, the hot-blooded heroes and the heroes of the will."[10]

Mussolini proclaimed that reunification of Italian territory was only the first step towards a fascist future. Italy must expand and found a new Roman empire in the Mediterranean and Africa. In the fascist economy, workers, management and capital would all work together for the betterment of the nation. The economy would be nationalized. To young people like Emilio, fascism offered the progress and hope that had not been realized by the liberation. Mussolini and his second-in-command, *alpino* and aviator Italo Balbo, became Emilio's heroes. When Emilio was released from military service, he became a party member and joined the *squadristi*, or blackshirts, and the XXX Ottobre Society became the centre of his social life.[11]

The Trieste Gymnastics Society's cloak-and-dagger irredentism seemed feeble and surreptitious next to the rigours of the XXX Ottobre. Romantic nationalists in suits and top hats led the Gymnastics Society. The Roman characters "s. XXX. o" emblazoned on Emilio's new club's uniforms had a stylish, up-to-date fascistic aesthetic. Military-style trumpeters called members to order. Marching was compulsory. Lean, idealistic, in search of adventure and fond of uniforms, Emilio fit right in.

The XXX Ottobre encouraged the healthy relations between sexes that were the precursors of the reproductive duty to create more citizens. In the dancehall, Emilio easily learned the steps of the waltz. His outward grace hid from teenage girls his lack of self-confidence. The girls who were attracted to his smile and handsome looks did not know that they could not match the sacrificial heroism of the women he idolized: his mother, his sister, the refugee he took in on the Duino road. Emilio preferred women who were more reticent towards him, as if their aloofness reflected their intuition that there were hidden obstacles to gaining his love.

Mussolini embodied the state's aspirations and destiny as a man of action and adventure. The XXX Ottobre Society took Mussolini's lead and emphasized the moral benefits of caving and hiking.

Some of the most famous caves in European speleology were within 20 kilometres of Trieste. The XXX Ottobre cavers, however, were equipped with handheld lanterns and had to restrict their explorations to caves accessible without ladders or ropes. Emilio soon found out that real cavers recorded the depth of their exploration below the surface. This information, which had originally been collected for geological purposes, had transformed cave exploration into a sport. Cavers competed to go deeper and further and mapped their explorations, although accuracy was elusive with the available instruments.[12]

Emilio and the more intrepid, and, as yet, unequipped cavers of the society dabbled in the exploration of deeper, more technical caves. In the Grotta dei Pini, Emilio and his friends reached a depth of 270 metres, after which Emilio decided technical equipment of some kind was required, not principally for safety but for deeper and longer expeditions. "We will sacrifice a few of our own lira," he wrote in the xxx Ottobre newsletter, "to buy the necessary tools." These included ropes, army surplus wire stepladders once used for the war in the Alps, carabiners, pitons, hammers and carbide lamps screwed onto army helmets. Armed with this gear, and expressions of determination, the cavers of the xxx Ottobre looked much like a squad of *alpini* ready for a raid on an alpine redoubt.[13]

Now they could explore the caves accessed by long vertical drops, such as the Abisso di Semi, Abisso d'Lune and the Abisso Selva di Pirro. Emilio reported on many of their expeditions in the society newsletter, and soon, accomplished adult cavers like Severino Culot and Cesare Prez joined these trips.

General Italo Gariboldi, commander of the Italian troops in the newly established province of Trieste and an ambitious fascist, saw the xxx Ottobre as a school for young heroes. He ordered his troops to drive the xxx Ottobre and their gear to the caverns. Unfortunately, the antiquated army trucks often broke down before they arrived at their destination, and the cavers had to get out and push them.[14]

The xxx Ottobre Society founded a chapter devoted to serious caving, which, like all fascist institutions, soon had a rule book to be followed in detail. Emilio had wandered into the society after his military service to alleviate the boredom of his job at the Magazzini Generali. Now he dreamed of setting world depth records for the glory of Italy.

In 1924, Emilio joined a team set to achieve a new depth record in Bus de la Lum cave. In 1902, a world depth record had been set in the Bus de la Lum by Luigi Marson, who had estimated the depth at 450 metres. Emilio's party would bring a plaque to commemorate Marson's achievement at his low-point and try to venture deeper into the cavern.

They descended for 24 hours without rest. The down-climbs, traverses of horizontal shafts, dampness and narrow squeezes exhausted their bodies and nerves, but the lure of a new record beckoned them deeper. At the place where Marson had claimed his record, their instruments, which were more modern than Marson's, read a mere 225 metres, half of his supposed record.[15] The team was neither equipped nor mentally prepared to repeat the effort they had already made and go on even deeper. They left the now-inaccurate plaque in the cave and started the long, weary exit. A legend about Emilio claims that after this painful first lesson in the elusiveness of glory, he made his way straight from the mouth of the Bus de la Lum to the summit of Cimon del Cavallo in the Carnic Pre-Alps. There, he forsook the caves and pledged himself forever to the world of mountains and climbing.

It's a good story that played to climbers' aversion to caves. The Cimon del Cavallo was a legendary and symbolic landmark, visible from the Adriatic. It was also the first peak climbed in the region, by Giovanni Girolamo Zannichelli and Domenico Pietro Stefanelli in 1726 – not to reach the summit, but to pick wildflowers. Unfortunately, Cimon del Cavallo was more than 45 kilometres from the Bus de la Lum, too far to hike after 30 hours in a cave.

Emilio explored many caves after the Bus de la Lum. In 1925, he had his greatest and most tragic caving adventure. A sudden rainstorm that flooded the lower reaches of the Raspo cave trapped a team of cavers deep in the cavern. Emilio volunteered for the rescue team.

After two days of attempts, the rescuers finally reached the edge of a hundred-metre waterfall, above the place they believed the victims had been trapped. The yellow light of the rescuers' carbide lamps showed the lines around their eyes darkened by dirt and fatigue, and their hollow, stubbly cheeks. The leader was Severino Culot, a master of the world beneath the Carso. The battered trumpet he wore around his neck to communicate with cavers higher up made him look a little like he was leading a raid. Emilio had been trained as a radio-telegrapher in the Army, but communications in the cave were still medieval.

The third rescuer was Giulio Benedetti, a dark-eyed and gaunt youth from Pitteri who Emilio had met on the rescue. His hair was parted into two upturned horns that licked the brim of his battered helmet and gave him a satanic appearance.

They were deafened by the flood waters filled with dirt and stones that thundered over the edge of their passage. Culot pointed upwards to signal the end of the attempt. Even if one of them made it down through the waterfall, the dangerous climb back up would take almost superhuman strength. Emilio looked at Benedetti, whose lips were drawn back to expose his white teeth in a grim smile. They both pointed downwards, and risked expulsion from the xxx Ottobre Society for insubordination. Culot thought for a second and then unexpectedly nodded his assent.

Emilio took a bag of food and climbed down into the waterfall, belayed by Benedetti. The trapped men had left a wire ladder, but the rungs were little wider than a hand, the flow of the water tangled it and the bottom half had been torn off by debris. His only link with safety, Benedetti's taut belay rope, might be broken by a falling rock at any moment, but Emilio moved onto the cold slick rock to climb downwards. Frigid water poured over his shoulders and down his neck, but he reminded himself that the men below must be even more terrified than he was.

After 30 metres, Emilio reached down with his foot and couldn't find a hold. He slipped the haversack of food off his shoulders and threw it down the cavern. His heart beat faster when he heard a faint voice below. In this contest with death, he had been a victor, but there was nothing else his team could do alone. At the very least, they would need a longer rope. "It's Comici, from the xxx Ottobre!" he shouted. "We'll be back with more help!"[16]

Culot was too exhausted to join the second rescue team, so veteran caver Cesare Prez took the lead. Benedetti and Emilio had bonded in the cave, but to Emilio's disappointment, Benedetti had to return to work in Trieste. Emilio, however, was prepared to forsake his job to go right back into the cave.

Benedetti, Culot and even the victims were emotionally and existentially closer to Emilio now than the men he worked with in Trieste. In the caves, Emilio discovered a bond that could only be forged in strife and danger with men who respected his own *lontananza*, unlike the hearty but superficial bonhomie men shared in bars and offices. This realization resonated with Mussolini's image of himself as a leader who emerged from the masses in the fire of war. Duilio Durissini,

Emilio's fellow xxx Ottobre caver, wrote that "the harsh, unnerving, tiring hours spent in the abyss strengthened [Emilio's] mind and body. The patient search and the cautious proceeding in the darkness, developed in him the measured calm and absolute mastery of himself that served him later… in the blazing solitude of the starry universe… these [caving days] must have prepared him for the Alps."[17]

Emilio's reunion with the victims was bittersweet. Only two had survived. Two brothers had been separated from the rest of their party and drowned in a chamber that filled with water before they could escape. The Raspo rescue had been one of the most technical rescues in caving history.

On the day that the silver medal for civic valour was awarded to Culot and Prez (but not Emilio) for their part in the rescue, Emilio wrote "*DELUSIONE!*" (disappointment) in his diary. Emilio wanted to receive recognition. He wanted the world's honours. He wanted respect. The atmosphere of the xxx Ottobre and fascism, with its emphasis on awards and titles, played on this desire. To Emilio, the lack of recognition was an insult, not an oversight – and an insult not from men but from fate. And the old way was that no insult, big or small, whether it was from an enemy, a friend or death itself, could be left unanswered.

Emilio tried even harder and more notorious caves. In 1927, two years after he had started climbing, he did his last and most gruelling caving trip, the Medjame cavern in Croatia. Its 30 underground bodies of water, long hard chimney traverses and narrow passages were threatened by rain and rockfall from crevices that led to the surface. There were other caves to explore, and Emilio might well have continued caving if he had not discovered climbing. Emilio craved an all-consuming devotion to a single person or activity, and if he had felt that way about caving, he never would have tried climbing. Once he had begun to climb, the caves simply could not compete with his new love: climbing the cliffs of the Carso and the mountains of the Julian Alps.

CHAPTER TWO

VAL ROSANDRA

In 1924, Emilio's caving mentors, Culot and Prez, introduced Emilio and Benedetti to the Società Alpina delle Giulie (Julian Alpine Society) in Trieste. The society took its name from the Julian Alps, the closest mountain range to Trieste, and had eccentric and nationalistic associations. Its main project in the 1920s was to make first post-liberation ascents of peaks formerly in Austrian provinces and wave the Italian flag on the summits. Its members dabbled in freemasonry.[18]

The society was the centre of Trieste mountaineering. Its founders included Napoleone Cozzi and his partner, Alberto Zanutti, who still led climbing trips to the *palestra* at Val Rosandra. Julius Kugy, who had introduced Cozzi to alpinism, was the society's, and indeed Trieste's, most eminent mountaineer. Kugy's fame had recently spread beyond Italy with the publication of his mountaineering memoir.[19]

Kugy and Emilio came from opposite ends of Trieste society. Kugy had been born to a rich merchant clan of ethnic Slavs and inherited an importing business. Although his fortune was depleted by the war, there was enough money left for Kugy to spend his life mostly as a philanthropist. He sponsored the Trieste choral society. He also paid to replace the Hermann Findenegg hut in the Madre dei Camosci group, which had been destroyed in the war. Although he had served on the Austrian side and had loved the cosmopolitan empire of Austria-Hungary, he acquiesced when the Club Alpino Italiano (Italian Alpine Club, or CAI) renamed it after an Italian infantry captain named Corsi, who died on Monte Grappa. After the Great War, Kugy spent much of his time in pursuit of the elusive *Scabiosa trenta* flower, of which he wrote in his memoir:

> And thus you, the long sought and passionately desired
> miraculous flower of my heart, will rise some time from the

dreams of my yearning, from the strength of my trust, from the mysterious gloom of your origin, of your blossoming and vanishing, and you will come and join me in the late evening of my life... Scabiosa Trenta! Never did my belief in you die, though you seemed to be beyond my reach. And though you were far away, I have never been unfaithful to you. I have been on the lookout for you all my life, anxiously listening to any news about you.[20]

Cozzi, the bomb maker, represented hard climbing and revolution, but Kugy had a Mitteleuropean bourgeois world view and went to the mountains not to climb hard but to appreciate nature. As Kugy's friend Paul Kaltenegger tactfully put it, Kugy "preferred the [easier] Aiguille Verte to the [harder] Dru."[21]

In 1880, Kugy took his classical alpinism to the Julian Alps and made the first ascent of Škrlatica (2740 metres), the third-highest peak in the Slovenian Julian Alps, and followed it up with dozens of other first ascents in the range. He named the mountain group that included the Ago di Villaco, Jôf di Montasio (2752 metres) and Jôf Fuart (2666 metres) the Madre dei Camosci (Mother of Chamois) and proceeded to explore and record it in some detail.

In the Western Alps, Kugy climbed with the Englishman Albert Mummery. They shared no languages, but Kugy nonetheless absorbed from Mummery the ethos of the golden age of alpinism, which frowned upon pitons. Many of the most famous adherents of the anti-piton school were bourgeois climbers from Vienna. The Vienna school's greatest proponent, the brilliant soloist and intellectual Paul Preuss, eschewed pitons and rappelling. Preuss's breathtaking solo first ascent route on the east face of the Campanile Basso in 1911 had been repeated for the first time only in 1925 by a party with a rope and pitons. Kugy was a climber in Preuss's Viennese tradition of style before difficulty.

Kugy's fame was such that it attracted modern climbers as well as traditionalists. Emilio and Benedetti imbibed climbing tradition from Kugy, but they learned to climb from modern experts like the studious Fausto Stefenelli and the experienced Alberto Zanutti. Stefenelli and Zanutti were followers of Hans Dülfer, the German who climbed the east face of the Fleischbank with pitons and rope tension after he had inspected the route on rappel, and his Italian counterpart, Tita Piaz. Piaz, a guide from the Fassa valley, used pitons on his revolutionary 1908 first ascent of the west face of the Totenkirchl in Austria. Italian guide Angelo Dibona adopted pitons as well and used them on his new route on the Croz dell'Altissimo.

Technical climbing in the Eastern Alps was curtailed in the Great War, when the front between Italy and Austria cut through the Dolomites. Famous mountains like the Rosengarten group and the Marmolada became the sites of bloody industrial warfare. The war on the Western Front claimed the lives of many young climbers, including Dülfer.

After the war, the borders reverted to their pre-war informality. The physical remains of the war on the alpine borders, however, remained and became a popular attraction. Even the cultured Venetian guidebook writer and editor of the CAI journal Antonio Berti delighted in the Marmolada, the highest peak in the Dolomites, not only because of its alpine beauty but also because there one could see "tattered remains of clothing, shell casings and shrapnel, battered wooden beams, rusted bayonets, stockless rifles, petards, bomb shells, crushed canteens, harpoons, loaders, cartridges."[22] Berti's fascination with this post-war wreckage is all the more intriguing as he, himself, was a veteran of the Alpine Front.

The Touring Club Italiano, an offshoot of the CAI, compared battle-worn Dolomite peaks to "the face of a mutilated brother," asserting that "the ravaged face of the mountain is even more beautiful."[23] Amidst all of this detritus and nostalgia for destruction, the pre-war objection that pitons, even used in quantity, would destroy the spirit of climbing and the fabric of the mountains themselves seemed banal.

In the mid-1920s, when Emilio made his first climbing trips in the Julian Alps and Val Rosandra with the Julian Alpine Society, the mood in Italian climbing was right for the great age of the piton to begin.

***

Rosandra River cut a steep-sided valley, 40 to 90 metres deep, into the pith of the Carso as it flowed the last 15 kilometres to the Adriatic at the Bay of Muggia. The air in the valley smelled of limestone, the gnarled pines that hung from ledges, and by season, sumac, wild carnations, gentians. The valley was quiet except for the gurgle of the river, the cries of birds that echoed from the cliffs, and the wind in the dry grass.

Val Rosandra had roughly sheltered men and animals since the Stone Age, but attempts to civilize it had left only a broken Roman aqueduct, a couple of tiny mill hamlets reached by a narrow-gauge railway and a hermit's chapel. Trieste had grown towards the western rim, but the valley itself remained a small patch of unspoiled and ancient southern Europe.

Since Napoleone Cozzi first visited Val Rosandra, climbers had taken the liberty to name the valley's rocks and cliffs that were mostly too small to warrant the attention of map-makers. Montasio, like many such names, was meant as a joke. It was only 30 metres high and nothing much next to its namesake, Jôf di Montasio, at 2752 metres the second-highest peak in the Julian Alps. Individual climbs had also been given names that were sometimes merely descriptive, like Diedro (Dihedral), or fanciful, like Nottambuli (Night Owls) and Pazzo Volante (Crazy Flight).

Climbing in Val Rosandra was backward compared not only to the Alps but to comparable local climbing areas like Fontainebleau, near Paris; Peilstein, close to Vienna; and Buchenhain, near Munich. In 1926, German climber Willo Welzenbach created his grade system, which could be applied to any climb, anywhere. Its simplicity added to its popularity. Roman numerals I through VI described ascending levels of difficulty. The basic standards for each grade, regardless of the region, were:

I. Easy. The simplest form of climbing, holds can be chosen both for feet and hands and holds are only used for balance.

II. Slightly difficult. It is necessary to move each limb separately and to know the correct motions. Holds, however, are numerous.

III. Quite difficult. The mountain is steep or even vertical. Holds are less numerous and may be hard to use.

IV. Difficult. Holds are rarer, good technique and some training is needed.

V. Very difficult. Holds are very rare, climbing requires training and is physically demanding. Examining the passage before the climb is usually necessary.

VI. Extremely difficult. Holds are rare and their position requires a specific combination of well-studied movements. The climbing can be very delicate or particularly strenuous and overhanging. Requires training and significant strength in the arms and hands.[24]

At Val Rosandra, there were no climbs of grade VI (the hardest grade), and only a few of grade V. Trieste climbers nonetheless took seriously the pursuit of difficulty on the 50-metre walls of Val Rosandra. Many climbed only in Val Rosandra and had no aspirations to travel to the Alps. Some invented their own climbing gear and techniques. A few carried grappling hooks, others free soloed. Local cavers practised their ropework there. One local wore a shaving-brush plume on his Tyrolean hat.[25]

A full rock climbing kit comprised half a dozen carabiners, ten pitons, 30 metres of ten-millimetre manila rope, a few rope slings, a hammer for the leader and a lighter hammer for the second. Pitons were mostly manufactured by blacksmiths, and the popular ring pitons were just spikes with rings manufactured for hauling tree trunks. Everything else, with the exception of the carabiners, was stocked by hardware merchants. For footwear, most climbers in the Alps still wore rope-soled *scarpette*, although a few had begun to experiment with crepe-rubber-soled roofer's slippers. The urban craggers of Val Rosandra preferred footwear from city gyms and playing fields, the American-style, canvas-topped, rubber-soled basketball shoes. Whatever the footwear of choice, the whole climber's kit cost a fraction of the price of a bicycle.

Zanutti taught Emilio and Benedetti, who already knew how to rappel from caving, how to use pitons, carabiners and running belays.

Stefenelli showed them how to swing across blank rock on the rope, or stand in a sling attached to a piton. Along with technique, they learned the legends of their new sport: how Dülfer had mastered the piton, the difference between free and aid climbing, the great solos of the Austrian Paul Preuss and the singular status of the Italian Dolomites in world climbing.

Emilio and other Italian climbers in the 1920s considered pitons and other hardware necessary. Piton use, in their minds, segued with the historical development of climbing and pointed to the future. The piton did not eliminate adventure. Climbers on overhanging walls of limestone, equipped with manila ropes from the local hardware store and carabiners and pitons from a blacksmith, risked just as much, or more, than they did soloing on lower-angled rock with many holds.

Piton usage became complex partly because the selection of available pitons was largely unimaginative. There were some different thicknesses and lengths of blades, but none were specialized for aid climbing, and many still fit only in the specific type of crack they were designed for. Emilio realized that the best and most versatile piton was made for vertical cracks, because the eyelet for the carabiner was at a right angle to the blade, so it could be used in corners or offset cracks without blocking the carabiner.

Emilio improvised on what Zanutti and Stefenelli had taught him and what he had learned in caves. He extended the use of the piton into even more dangerous situations with the deliberate use of pins strong enough to hold body weight but too weak to support a fall. He fell, dropped pitons, ripped them out of the rock when he weighted them and often backed off, but he persevered.

With his new rock climbing techniques, caving experience, a quirky, low-commitment environment and as yet unfocussed ambitions, Emilio was free to experiment with new techniques. Most climbers had deployed a simple loop of rope to use aid from a piton. That worked well when aid climbing was an occasional emergency technique, but Emilio wanted something more versatile. He tied three loops in a sling to form rungs and make a miniature version of the wire ladders he had used in caves. These slings became known to Anglophone climbers as *étriers*, the French word for stirrups, but

Italian climbers called them *staffe*, or ladders, hearkening back to their derivation from caving gear. Emilio always climbed with two *staffe*, one for each foot.

He discovered that two ropes were preferable for aid climbing because the leader could hang from one line and clip the free rope to the piton above and haul himself up. Most climbers tied the rope around their chest, but Emilio found that the waist tie-in gave him better leverage and a few more centimetres' reach. Climbing with two ropes at the same time had been a technique used to increase safety and to enable the leader to decrease rope drag.

Emilio used pitons in a radical new way. He hung from one rope clipped to a piton, clipped the slack rope into a piton overhead and had his belayer put tension on that rope and pulled himself up on it. The lower rope would catch him if the upper piton tore out. Traditionally, the majority of pitons were placed for the utmost security and left behind as permanent fixtures for subsequent parties. A few might be placed on long climbs by an individual party, and of these, most would be left behind for subsequent parties. Fixed pitons on climbs were slowly increasing in number, although few climbs sported more than a few on each pitch. In situ, pitons rusted and weakened over a few seasons, since they were made of soft steel or iron. Climbers could not rely only on fixed protection.

Mountain guides at the time were born with a claim to the mountains that was almost aristocratic in its authority, although it carried none of the material advantages of class. Urban workers had to conquer the peaks with the piton rather than a pedigree. Emilio made an extensive, almost absurdist study of the outer limits of piton use. The deliberate use of pitons that would only support body weight rather than the greater load of a falling climber was unknown. Emilio taught himself how to place pitons which would hold no more than his body weight in tiny pockets and cracks. He would intersperse strings of these dubious pitons with more solid "base" pitons to catch him if he ripped out the weaker ones. This required an extensive arsenal of pitons, carabiners and slings, and Emilio towed a thin line to haul up more pitons from the belayer if required. The extra line also allowed him to haul up the second climber's pack to make it easier for the second to climb. On aid sections the second did not prusik or use the still un-invented mechanical ascenders, but went strenuously piton to piton, like the leader.

Cavers relied on the rope to rappel and climb, but most climbers held that the leader should not fall. Emilio embraced the active use of the rope. He practised leader falls to discover the perfect stance to lessen the impact. His hard free climbing and aid climbing on poor pitons made occasional unexpected falls inevitable. After he had climbed the hardest established routes in Val Rosandra, Emilio set out to make his own routes on vertical bulges and steep walls that had never been considered climbable.

For all of this piton work, Emilio saw free climbing as the basis of rock climbing and applied himself to the systematic improvement of its basic techniques and movements. In the Eastern Alps, where the rock was often unreliable, climbers were exhorted to weight each hold equally in case one broke. Emilio, however, studied the movements in free climbing and developed a semi-dynamic style of movement much emulated by his peers.

The CAI used its new political powers to assume the Julian Alpine Society into the club. Within the new Julian Alps Section of the CAI, Emilio and his friends founded the Gruppo Alpinisti Rocciatori Sciatori (Rock Climbing and Skiing Group), or GARS, for ambitious climbers. The GARS became synonymous with the energetic group of mostly young people who changed the scene in Val Rosandra and saw themselves as an integral, if small, part of the Italian national climbing scene.

Giani Stuparich described the Sunday-morning eight a.m. bus from Trieste to Bagnoli, the closest stop to Val Rosandra: "A company dressed in corduroy trousers and short canvas jackets... everyone, men and women, had tanned faces and the same casual air of risk and joy. The same lively way of communicating with each other. Age was irrelevant despite differences. Young girls of seventeen were in brilliant agreement with men of fifty... a summer dream made of sheer stone and sky... in the eyes of some of the young girls, an exaltation barely contained."[26]

In Trieste, the Slavic and Italian communities were wary of one another, partly as a result of the racial violence and unrest in the city in the early 1920s. In Val Rosandra, Italian and Slavic climbers ignored the past and shared ropes and friendships. Emilio, who never had the anti-Slavic tendencies of many Italian nationalists in Trieste, enjoyed the company of his Slavic friends and learned their songs in après-climbing drinking sessions.[27]

In this atmosphere redolent with idealism, adventure and fellowship, Emilio's technique and training had dimensions of spirituality and aesthetics as well as athleticism. Climbing partnerships were more than friendships. They were bonds that transcended mundane concerns and enmities through which ropemates could transmit intangible moral resources.

"Not only do [belayers] constantly follow the leader with their eyes," said Emilio, "but almost step-by-step, live with his spirit, cooperate in his advance, silently transmit all of their willpower to the leader. They desire his success, suffer with him when he climbs the crux. Only with this spiritual foundation, this communion of spirits, can a rope proceed safely."[28]

The intensity of the bond between climbers did not preclude moments of youthful languor. When it was too hot, or climbing did not appeal to them, Emilio and his friends lounged by the river, suntanned and drank wine, while Emilio played the guitar and sang.

Emilio developed an almost childlike trust in partners who were *Triestino* and had learned to climb as he had, in Val Rosandra. Giulio Benedetti, Fausto Stefenelli, Claudio Prato, Albano Barisi, Giordano Bruno Fabjan, Cesare Tarabocchia, Mario Premuda and Ovidio Opiglia and dozens of other Val Rosandra climbers shared more than climbing with Emilio. They spoke with the same accent, had starved together during the Great War and grown up blasted by the Bora and eating bacalao. For the rest of his life, with a few exceptions, Emilio preferred partners from Trieste, even if he hardly knew them, and occasionally even turned down climbing opportunities when there were no *Triestinos* available.

They all shared a longing to climb that was greater than their free time, location or income allowed. They had to transform themselves into climbers not by climbing in the famous ranges but by weekends and a few evening hours on the cliffs of Val Rosandra, practising hammering pitons into disused masonry during lunch break at work, bouldering on buildings and training in the gym. To become a climber without mountains is to develop a kind of mental toughness that, in Emilio's case, imbued him with the idea that he was almost invincible.

Many of Emilio's early forays into the mountains were based on the notion that drive would overcome the most basic practical concerns. As soon as he became serious about climbing, he began to explore the Julian Alps on foot, sometimes with the other young members of the GARS and sometimes alone. These impromptu, underequipped forays taught Emilio how to survive in the mountains with little equipment, food, maps and plans but sometimes led to missed trains and shifts at work.

Once, while he searched for water, Emilio unwittingly trespassed into Yugoslavia, where he was arrested by the border patrol. A Yugoslavian judge sentenced him to a month of hard labour. Emilio, a fastidious eater who looked after his clothes and personal grooming, would have made a very unhappy prisoner. Luckily, the Yugoslavians released him after a visit to the jail by the Italian consul, and he made it back to Trieste in time to attend a dance.[29]

On his first climbs in the Julian Alps, Emilio was often accompanied by Benedetti and Giordano Bruno Fabjan. Unlike most of the GARS members, Fabjan came from a middle-class family. He was a superb climber and an experienced caver as well as a national golf champion. Fabjan's calm, analytical approach to climbing complemented Emilio's more obsessive and emotional devotion to the rock.

As the Julian Alps became Emilio and his friends' main object of desire, Val Rosandra's walls were reduced to a weeknight and poor-weather training ground. This new passion for the mountains, however, proved expensive. Even the fares of Mussolini's improved, low-cost "People's Train" service added up to a major weekly expense on a working man's budget, and unexpected bivouacs made for even more missed trains and Monday shifts at work.

Train travel maintained old Europe's order of time and status with its expensive tickets, printed schedules and segregated classes of carriages. The Great War, however, had produced a more versatile, proletarian option soon to become popular with climbers: the mass-produced motorcycle.

In 1921, the first Normale machine rolled out of the Moto Guzzi factory in Lecco and put motorized travel within the reach of the Italian worker willing to risk a dangerous, proletarian, modernist reputation and, possibly, death on the roads.

For the illegal climbing guide and political agitator Tita Piaz of Pera di Fassa, the so-called Devil of the Dolomites, the motorcycle became both a means of transportation and a calling card. Piaz recorded that on an all-night trip from his hometown of Pera di Fassa to the Totenkirchl in the Kaisergebirge to make the first ascent of the west face in 1908, he had run over a dog and two chickens and collided with a turnip cart. Alpine aesthete Guido Rey sneered that the machine branded Piaz as a "modern," a reputation that Piaz and many motorcycle enthusiasts would gladly embrace.[30] Climber and writer Domenico Rudatis rode hard and was taken out of climbing by an accident on his motorcycle in the mid-1930s. Motorcycles were one of the many passions that propagandists attributed to Emilio's hero, Mussolini, publishing photos of the frowning dictator astride late-model machines.

Emilio's first bike cost him 5,000 lire (about us$2,500 today), an enormous sum for a man who often made less than 1,000 lire a month.[31] The investment would be recouped in train and bus fares and shifts at the docks that would have been lost without the freedom to drive home from the mountains through the night.

There was, however, some doubt as to whether or not Emilio's motorcycle would last long enough to make good on his investment. It was an army surplus machine made by the Birmingham Small Arms Company in Britain. BSA machines had a poor reputation in Italy, and motorcycle enthusiasts transformed its initials into a joke in Italian, that went something along the lines of: "we should know how to get there ourselves [without the motorcycle]."[32] A long history of motorcycle accidents, falls and repairs to his first machine and its successors ensued, all of which Emilio suffered gladly in exchange for the freedom to travel to the mountains whenever he liked.

During these costly repairs and injuries, Emilio began to wonder whether he might be better off living right in the mountains instead of commuting every weekend. He was, by nature, impatient. With only weekends to climb mountains, his progress as an alpinist who could undertake long routes was slower than he wished. He confided in Kugy that he wanted to quit his job at the Magazzini Generali and move to the Dolomites to be a mountain guide. In the mountains, he thought, he would work only a few days a week and spend the rest of his time climbing new routes with friends from Trieste.

Kugy discouraged him. Kugy knew the guide's trade from the patron's point of view and had even trained two Slovenian woodsmen, Matije Kravanje and Osvaldo Pesamosca (the latter also reputed to be a highwayman), to act as his guides in the Julian Alps. He explained to Emilio that guiding was seasonal work and guides were mountain people who took farm work, road building and mining jobs when there were no clients. He also told Emilio that, unlike most city workers, guides had no pension. Even the famous Angelo Dibona, who had guided royalty and conquered some of the hardest unclimbed faces in the Alps, had to take a menial job filling in sitzmarks on a local ski hill after failing health forced his retirement in his late 60s.[33]

Kugy also warned Emilio against hard and dangerous climbing. He had watched Emilio emerge as the leader of a group of young climbers in basketball shoes who were handy with pitons but lacked Kugy's romantic reverence for the hills. If Emilio moved to the mountains, they would follow, bringing their new approaches. Unlike so many places in the Alps, the Julian Alps had remained a preserve where what the golden age alpinists would have considered mere gymnastics had not been pursued as an end in itself. Kugy sincerely believed that walls such as the north face of the Riofreddo, one of the biggest unclimbed faces in the Julian Alps, were impossible, and therefore any who tried them both spoiled the reverential atmosphere and risked their lives for nothing.[34]

Emilio, however, was an ambitious young man who could not help but wonder if Kugy had judged him as something less than the *cosa vera*, the real thing, when it came to both guiding and exploratory climbing. For the present, Emilio took Kugy's advice and gave up on the guiding idea. Soon, however, he would defy Kugy's attempt to stand, fortified by alpine tradition, between Emilio and the unclimbed walls of the Julian Alps.

The tension was inevitable. Kugy's nostalgia for the days before pitons and carabiners, when the mountains had been part of Austria-Hungary, was irreconcilable with the dreams of Emilio, who had grown up poor and hopeful of that empire's demise. For Emilio, the alpine tradition was not a possession of the old guard, or a caveat and a warning, but a wild invitation to new experiences. If anything, Kugy's warning fanned Emilio's desire for the unclimbed faces of the Alps, and few had ever desired unclimbed walls as ardently as Emilio.

CHAPTER THREE

THE MOTHER OF CHAMOIS

The summer of 1925 was busy at the Trieste docks. Emilio's irredentist views had been guided by propaganda and the XXX Ottobre towards fascism. Emilio was now a member of the PNF (the National Fascist Party) and a *squadrista* who wore his blackshirt uniform at fascist public functions. His trust in the party was validated by lavish fascist spending on Trieste: a new soccer stadium, shipbuilding contracts and an aircraft factory. The warehouses were even busier than they had been under the Austrians. Prosperity, however, had an unexpected disadvantage for Emilio. The national transformation to which he was pledged restricted him to climbing on weekends. Weekday nights, he trained in the gym or went to Val Rosandra on his motorcycle for a few hours of climbing.

On Friday night, Emilio usually loaded his gear on his motorcycle, which was made even less stable by Benedetti or Fabjan riding pillion, and rode from Trieste to the Julian Alps, a couple of hours to the north. The Madre dei Camosci group was their usual objective, a favourite of the GARS because of its dense grouping of rock peaks and steep walls.

From Sella Nevea, they usually hiked up the path to the Corsi hut, beneath Austrian gun placements that made black sockets in the silver rock walls, and bivouacked in the meadow beside the hut. When they eventually got to the rock the next morning, because Emilio was no earlier riser, they usually enchained a couple of routes in a single day. If necessary, they would go until benighted without bivouac gear. Exhausted, but not sated, they returned to Trieste late on Sunday night or early Monday morning, by the light of Emilio's motorcycle headlight.

It was a harsh, joyous alpine initiation. Riccardo Cassin, the great Lombard alpinist who later came to know and climb with Comici, said, "When, in the Julian Alps, [Comici] found himself face to face with the north walls of the Modre dei Camosci [*sic*], his innate passion, which he had never felt before, exploded with such a force that it changed his life."[35]

"All that the mountain gives us," Emilio wrote of his early experiences in the Madre dei Camosci, "is beautiful and great, both the joy and the bitterness. We come to her with devotion, and with devotion we accept everything that comes to us through her."[36]

***

In the August Ferragosto holidays of 1925, the citizens of Verona, Gorizia and other eastern Italian cities crammed onto Mussolini's People's Train service to the Adriatic coast or Lake Malcesine. Emilio and Benedetti joined the hardy and idealistic young people headed inland for the Alps, where the meadows around the Corsi hut were dotted with tents hung with guitars, accordions and a few climbing ropes. Emilio was naturally shy and a light drinker, but he loved to sing, and on the night of August 4, 1925, he and Benedetti stayed up late to carouse with some students.

The next morning, they got out of bed late and decided to wander up into the peaks and look for a short climb. At 11 a.m. they stood at the foot of a snowfield beneath the 300-metre pillar of the Ago di Villaco, which stood between the hut and the wall of the Campanile di Villaco. Emilio traced his finger up a line on the southeast ridge, which started out easily angled and reared to vertical for the last half. They had only climbed technical rock for a couple of seasons, but the Ago di Villaco looked like a perfect candidate for their longest climb yet. "The climbing," Emilio wrote, "was too beautiful not to attempt it."[37]

After a scramble, they entered wet, narrow cracks too wide for pitons. When these ran out, a steep wall slowed them down. They were "two tiny pygmies up on the wall," wrote Emilio, "whom a breath could send into the abyss."[38] On the Ago di Villaco, Emilio noticed for the first time that climbing made the difference between himself and those who merely watched or read about mountaineering. On a wall, the *lontananza* had always felt beautiful. The heights represented "the silent poetry of verticality, of which Guido Rey writes, or that sense of loss and fear that paralyzes our will and makes us doubt ourselves."[39]

As they climbed, the sunshine gave way to dark clouds. Retreat down their route, by this point, was more onerous than to continue and descend the col between the Ago di Villaco and the Campanile di Villaco.[40] The storm, however, held off. Emilio left a note in a crack on the summit, and they rappelled.

The Ago di Villaco was Emilio and Benedetti's first apparently new mountaineering route. Emilio's account shows a young man taken by his own creativity, the thrilling environment and the commitment. It also revealed Emilio's inexperience and lack of background knowledge about climbing in the Julian Alps. Despite Emilio's commentary about the closeness of death, their route was later downgraded from grade IV to grade III. Much later, they found out that it had already been climbed by Germans H. Klagl and H. Stagl in the war year of 1917.[41]

In 1925, however, Emilio and Benedetti believed the route was their own and returned to Val Rosandra as the first ascensionists of a substantial alpine climb. Emilio's respect for Kugy, tinged as it was by his need for the older climber's assistance with his guiding plan and Kugy's potential patronage in mountaineering circles, was diminished by the ease with which he had climbed a new route. The unclimbed walls of the Madre dei Camosci were not so deadly after all. Kugy himself, however, would have known about the previous ascent of the Ago di Villaco. In the light of traditional men's-club mountaineering, Emilio and Benedetti's claim was not a mistake but a déclassé impulse to prove themselves at the cost of others.

In the spring of 1926, Emilio and Benedetti chose a bona fide unclimbed route to the summit of a rock pillar in the Madre dei Camosci that Kugy had named the Kleinspitze. Emilio and most Italian climbers, however, continued to call the pillar L'Innominata. Their proposed climb started in the steep northeast gully and struck out up the steep north wall of the pinnacle. The climbing appeared to be less sustained than the Ago di Villaco, so despite the rain, they set off up the opening gully. Rockfall, although gradual at first, escalated to a barrage and forced them to retreat.

Even as they rappelled, the waterfalls roaring in the hidden depths of the faces, the broken light in the clouds, and the clatter of falling rock inspired a feeling of ecstasy in Emilio. "I struggled with the desire to touch these faces," he wrote, "to possess them, to penetrate their mysteries to obtain unspeakable and unimaginable emotions."[42]

By the end of the 1926 climbing season, Emilio still only had one notable new route to his credit, and he was determined to double that number before the season ended. On August 17, 1926, he was back beneath the northeast gully of L'Innominata, this time with young *Triestino* and Val Rosandra climber Gino Razza. They had packs full of extra pitons, provisions and enough clothing to continue in bad weather.

The sky was clear, rockfall in the gully was light, and they climbed quickly up to the steep rock on the north face. Their heavy packs made the climb slow, strenuous and awkward. Emilio felt his pack pull him backwards on a face-climbing traverse. He decided to hang it from a piton so that Gino, who would have a rope from above, could tie it to the extra rope and Emilio could haul it up to the belay.

When Emilio got the second shoulder-strap off, the pack slipped from his grasp. At the belay, Razza stuck out a hand and plucked the falling rucksack from the air as it flew past. Razza had saved them from Emilio's mistake. Without the pack that contained most of their pitons, they would have had to retreat.

Emilio resolved to take less gear with him the next time, and, despite his subsequent reputation as a climber who relied on equipment, he was known throughout his career to take fewer pitons and less bivouac gear and food than his partners and preferred speed and safety over comfort.

From the summit, Emilio got his first close-up view of the 750-metre-high vertical north face of the Riofreddo, the most famous unclimbed north wall in the Julian Alps. The grey, shadowy face had only a few continuous cracks and none that went all the way to the top. Kugy considered it impossible, but Emilio spied a snaking chimney that ended at a steep pillar on the left and vertical cliffs on the right. Emilio could not see an obvious way to continue from that point, but the whiff of impossibility excited him.

Razza shared Kugy's impression of the wall and had no interest in an attempt. After all, Emilio was still practically a beginner on big routes and had dropped their equipment on a comparatively easy climb on a second attempt, after he was driven off it once by misreading rockfall conditions.

Other climbers from the GARS doubted that the wall was possible. The only climber Emilio could find to try it with him in 1926 was 19-year-old Stanislaus Strekeli, a Slav from Gorizia, on the border with Slovenia. Emilio had anti-German views based on his experiences of Austrian imperialism, and never tied in with a German or Austrian on a hard climb, but he was not biased against Slovenians. The majority of fascists distrusted Slavs, whom they branded as a secret vanguard of Bolshevism, but forgave the Germans their part in the Great War. Emilio's enmity was reserved for Austrians and Germans.

In the last week of August, Emilio and Strekeli attempted the face. Emilio led as they climbed roped together at the same time up the broken, cold, grey rock. Gradually, the wall reared up towards the vertical, the holds became fewer and smaller, and they stopped to belay every 30 metres. Pitch after pitch of free climbing, each harder than the last, intimidated Emilio, who wasted time and strength placing too many pitons. For all his practice at Val Rosandra, he struggled to apply his new techniques efficiently on a big climb.

It was one thing for Emilio to climb at his physical limit on the crags of Val Rosandra, or on the shorter walls of the Madre dei Camosci, like the Ago di Villaco. It was another to climb at his limit and also battle the psychological oppression he felt on a wall like the Riofreddo. About 380 metres up the wall, the prospect of several hundred more metres of vertical climbing overwhelmed Emilio. Strekeli was not skilled enough to take the lead, so they retreated. Emilio left his hammer and pitons at their last rappel station, a gesture that suggested he might return, although he said he would never again attempt the wall, or another like it.[43] He never climbed with Strekeli again.

Back in Trieste, Emilio had time to consider why he had failed on the Riofreddo. At a distance, it was easier to dissect the wall and to reduce it to discrete problems. Emilio concluded that his blend of free and aid climbing, although rightly based on the piton, had been inefficient. Climbing a big wall is more than a technical problem, but not less. He refined his lead climbing in Val Rosandra and mastered climbs with a mix of aid and free climbing on a single pitch. He also became a faster, more elegant free climber.

The isolation of the Madre dei Camosci from the mainstream of alpinism afforded Emilio the freedom to work on his projects and to improve. Further west, any climbs like the north face of the Riofreddo that had not been completed by pre-war aces like Paul Preuss, Tita Piaz, Hans Dülfer and Angelo Dibona would now be on the agenda of a new cadre of talented German and Austrian climbers.

The lack of competition in the Madre dei Camosci also allowed Emilio to bask in the conceit that he possessed personal rights to unclimbed routes, or in some cases, entire faces. If other climbers took an interest in a climb on Emilio's roster, he saw them as interlopers in a matter of the heart between himself and the wall and either rushed to complete the climb as quickly as possible in an act that never truly satisfied him, or entirely gave up the project. He rarely compromised on this point.

Emilio, however, was a methodical rather than a natural climber, and even by 1928, two years after his first attempt on the north face of the Riofreddo, he still made mistakes, and most of his first ascents were of purely local interest. In early June of 1928, with *Triestinos* Giorgio Brunner and Riccardo Deffar, for example, Emilio made the first ascent of a route pointed out by Kugy as a potential unclimbed classic: the snow-and-ice-filled northeast gully of the Forcella Berdo on Jôf di Montasio, the highest peak in the Madre dei Camosci and the second-highest peak in the Julian Alps. Rain had melted the ice and softened the snow. Rockfall was even heavier than it had been on his first attempt on L'Innominata. Emilio had neither crampons nor an ice axe and chopped steps with a rock. They finished the route, but from then on, Emilio avoided steep snow and ice.

***

Climbers like Emilio, who lived far from the mainstream of alpinism, kept up with the climbing news through columns in the newspapers *La Stampa* and *Lo Sport Fascista*, sensationalized mountaineering reports in the magazine *La Domenica del Corriere*, the newsletters of the CAI sections and the CAI's monthly journal, the *Rivista Mensile del Club Alpino Italiano*, known among climbers as the *Rivista Mensile*.

The *Rivista Mensile*'s cover, with its sleek, futurist illustrations of skiers, mountains and climbers, published reports on new climbs and political pieces from CAI headquarters in Rome. Action photographs showed climbers clinging by their fingertips to vertical faces, swinging across blank rock on ropes or athletically grappling with overhangs as they hung from pitons. Climbing was portrayed as an athletic, adventurous and aesthetic pursuit for (mostly) men armed with modern tools and politics.

British expeditions between the world wars affirmed and benefitted from imperialism; Germans politicized climbing; the Italians, however, brought their mystical and philosophical preoccupations to the mountains.[44] Many journalists, like Vittorio Varale, could report on climbing with the breathless detail and enthusiasm of a cycling hack following the Giro d'Italia but also pen deeply philosophical treatises on mountaineering. Italian magazines and newspapers provided a platform for the musings of journalist-intellectuals like Dino Buzzati, who praised climbing because of "the spiritual foundation of mountaineering... the contempt for the awards of applause, for its essence, which is boldness, for the spirit of sacrifice."[45]

Climbers who hungered for more profound philosophical insights into mountaineering could follow the writings of right-wing intellectual Julius Evola, who claimed that the Aryan Solar race were the best practitioners of alpinism and that there was no mountaineering without risk.[46] Publisher Domenico Rudatis (who used the pseudonym "Rud" when he wrote in Evola's literary magazine, *Krur*), wove together mysticism, politics and technical climbing.

To Rudatis, hard rock climbers were the successors of Vyasa, who engraved the 200,000 verses of the Mahabharata on a wall, and also the successors of the *alpini* of the Great War.[47] In the Dolomites, his three main interests, fascism, mysticism and alpinism, converged.[48] He promised that a new, "spiritual-athletic" type of climbing would supplant the old, "bourgeois-sentimental" school, to fight "the mechanical rationalism of modern civilization."[49] Rudatis believed that just as superficial, bourgeois Western civilization had gone into decline, what he called "Western Alpinism," with its fascination with long, less technical routes, had become decadent, and "Eastern Alpinism," as practised in the Dolomites, was exciting, vibrant and spiritual.[50]

The climbing press kept Emilio and the GARS up to date in their techniques, their attitudes and even their style of climbing clothes. Emilio tentatively drew national attention to the activities of his climbing community with his first submissions to the *Rivista Mensile*, in the form of short reports on his routes on the Ago di Villaco and L'Innominata.

The newspapers were preoccupied with the goings-on in the Dolomites. Although 18 peaks in the Dolomites rose over 3000 metres in height, they were less popular for mountaineering than they were for rock climbing. The vertiginous limestone walls and ridges had been the crucible of rock climbing history and technique since climbers discovered them in the 19th century. Munich soloist Georg Winkler, Preuss, Dülfer, Piaz, Dibona and many others had all added to the legacy of legendary routes there. They had made the Dolomites' Tre Cime di Lavaredo, the Sassolungo, the Vajolet Towers, the Antelao, Sorapiss, Marmolada and the Campanile Basso shrines to hard climbing.

As a nationalist, Emilio was happy to follow the climbing press's lead and call aid climbing and the use of pitons, carabiners and rope tension the Italian style. German and Austrian climbers, however, had invented these techniques and were still their masters, as the most recent hard Dolomites climbs revealed.

The climbing writers of Italy declared that a new battle was being waged against Italian pride in the Dolomites. The Austrian and German invaders were brave, determined and armed with pitons. Their objective was to climb the hardest routes in the Dolomites and to claim them as proof of the prowess of their national alpinists at the expense of native Italian climbers. Italian mountain writers entreated their fellow mountaineers to beat the Germans to the top of the walls of their homeland.

Welzenbach's universal grading system fuelled the rivalry. Before the 1920s, grades in the Alps had mostly been used in guidebooks as an aid to visiting climbers. Practice areas like Peilstein in Austria had their own systems, as did the sandstone rock climbing area of the Elbsandsteingebirge. Italian alpinist Renato Chabod objected that Welzenbach's system failed to take into account weather, rockfall and loose rock. Welzenbach responded that his system was supposed to take into account prevailing conditions. A rock slab that was grade iv when dry might be grade v when wet. Welzenbach, one of the world's best ice climbers, claimed that his system applied to both rock and ice climbing, but he provided no adjectival descriptions of each ice climbing grade.[51]

Welzenbach's system was not intended to be limited to free climbing. He allowed direct aid from slings, the use of pitons as handholds and rope tension. He deemed that any route which required the sustained use of aid was to be awarded the sixth grade. Aid and free techniques were not yet always separated into distinct styles.

Welzenbach presciently enjoined climbers to remove their pitons to preserve a route's quality as well as its challenge. In a couple of decades, the sheer number of pitons would overcome concerns about the strength of individual pins, but in the 1920s and '30s, the dubiousness of pitons was still top-of-mind for Dolomite climbers.

Aid climbing itself was strenuous and athletic and required so many pitons that climbers used it only as a last resort, so entire pitches of aid climbing were rare. Photographs, illustrations and guidebook descriptions from the time show that grade vi climbing pitches often had free climbing interspersed with short sections of aid.

Climbers added plus and minus to each of the roman numerals and so created a 12-grade system. In 1911, Paul Preuss could only describe the climbing on the upper slopes of the Mont Rouge de Peuterey by comparing it to the similar Führerweg on the Fleischbank. If he wanted to describe the east face of the Campanile Basso, he said it was harder than the west face of the Totenkirchl. After Welzenbach, those relationships seemed arbitrary and aristocratic in their attachment to places. The literal, folkloric and even strictly geological memories of mountains faded to the background of climbers' consciousness. Little roman numerals appeared beside the lines drawn on illustrations of peaks in guidebook illustrations. The Alps became a matrix of numbers and lines.

***

Welzenbach's system was not open-ended, so a special value was given to grade VI, the *sesto grado*. The sixth grade did not simply define a climb that was harder than a grade V+, it defined climbing at the absolute limit of human ability. Julius Evola decried the concept that mountains are principally locales for romantic idylls, and promoted them as places where humanity tested itself.[52]

Italian climbing writers saw the *sestogradiste*, or grade VI climber, as an athlete in the classical Roman sense, as well as a member of a spiritual avant-garde. Young climbers at every practice area in Europe, including Emilio and his friends, aspired to become grade VI climbers.

In the 1920s, however, more Germans and Austrians than Italians had climbed grade VI. Worse still for proud Italian climbers, their former enemies expressed their status as climbing's champions on the same Dolomite peaks where they had fought the Italians less than a decade before. First ascents of new grade VI routes won international climbing prestige for the Germans and Austrians and cast a shadow of inferiority on Italian climbers, who had not defended their country's climbing honour on their own mountains.

In 1924, Felix Simon of Leipzig and Rolando Rossi of Innsbruck made the first ascent of the 1100-metre-high north wall of the Pelmo and graded it VI-. It was the hardest route in the Dolomites, but it had not demanded enough of the climbers for the sixth grade. That step would be taken by the remarkable Emil Solleder of Munich.

In 1925, Solleder was a 26-year-old veteran of a hard working-class upbringing and the Great War, but looked none the worse for it with his blond hair, suntan and craggy good looks. He chose the life of a *Bergvagabunden* (mountain vagabond), like many other Munich inter-war climbers, and earned the few comforts he required in the mountains by repairing hut roofs, chopping firewood and other manual jobs. To save money, he made his own pitons and climbed in cheap roofer's shoes that often fell apart as he climbed.

In the first week of August 1925, accompanied by the skilled Saxon rock climber Fritz Wiessner, Solleder made the first ascents of the

1100-metre north face of the Furchetta, likely the first VI in the Alps, and the north face of the Odle, at the same grade. Solleder said he led the crux of the Furchetta, a 220-metre headwall of steep climbing on friable rock, with only poor pitons as protection. Wiessner, however, later claimed to have led it himself. The discrepancy added to Solleder's reputation as an incredibly skilled and yet also arrogant man. When Wiessner was struck on the head by a rock Solleder knocked off when he was leading, Solleder blamed him for sticking his head out from under an overhang at the wrong time. "Now the longed-for, hotly contested wall has fallen!" said Solleder after the Furchetta. "I don't want to boast, as the proud, intoxicated winner, but I want to say that the north face of the Furchetta was conquered in good climbing style."[53]

A few days later, on August 5, Solleder, accompanied by German climbers Franz Göbel and Gustav Lettenbauer, attempted the 1200-metre-high northwest face of the Civetta in the northern Dolomites. The mountain took the ancient Venetian name for owl.[54] The broad northwest face, with its central summit with spurs on each side and walls that spread like giant wings, gave the mountain the appearance of a monstrous raptor about to take flight. The wall was vast, devoid of weaknesses and split only by narrow, discontinuous vertical crack systems. The Civetta's snowy ledges and icy cracks reminded Rudatis of arcane priests who stood ready to sacrifice climbers.[55] Any attempt to climb it would be complicated by the cold, since the wall was one of the highest above sea level in the Dolomites and never saw the sun. Retreat from the upper wall would require numerous rappels and dangerous downclimbing.

The wall had attracted the attention of all of the legendary climbers of the Eastern Alps. Paul Preuss had dreamed about it. Angelo Dibona, Hans Dülfer, Luigi Rizzi and brothers Guido and Max Mayer had tried it but were overwhelmed by the thin cracks, rockfall and cold. Austrian big wall expert Hans Fiechtl, who had invented the modern piton, warned Solleder to "keep his fingers off" the northwest wall of the Civetta for his own good.[56]

On Solleder's first attempt, snow covered the ledges and holds and the cracks ran with water. Göbel and Lettenbauer held their packs over their heads to absorb the impact of falling rocks as they belayed Solleder, who continued up through barrage unscathed. After 30 hours on the wall, Göbel took the lead but was injured in a fall that ended the attempt.

Solleder and Lettenbauer left the injured Göbel in the Coldai hut and, after a single day of recuperation, renewed their assault on August 8. The face still ran with water and falling rock. The pair made an all-out effort and placed 15 of Solleder's homemade pitons, some of which they used for aid. They reached the top hungry and disoriented by hypothermia. Their bare toes stuck out of their tattered roofer's slippers.

One of the greatest problems in the Alps had fallen to a German party. With hard modern free and aid climbing on untravelled rock, relentless verticality, a tough bivouac in bad conditions and the party's complete self-reliance enforced by the height and remoteness of the face, the Solleder-Lettenbauer redefined extreme climbing. In an open-ended system, the climb would have received a new grade, but on the Welzenbach scale, it simply made the sixth grade even harder. The big wall concept was born.

Giusto Gervasutti, a university student from Cervignano del Friuli, not far from Trieste, already had a reputation as a specialist in big alpine routes. He summarized the general sense of awe at Solleder and Lettenbauer's achievement: "Solleder tackles the wall where the height is highest, where the line of ascent is aesthetically perfect in its verticality from the base to the summit, where the wall is more daring and more arduous."[57]

Solleder and Lettenbauer did not promote their climb as a German victory. Solleder could barely share the credit with his partners, let alone an entire country. Italian climbing intellectuals like Rudatis, who claimed to have introduced the term *sesto grado* to the Italian public, however, framed this German grade VI on Italian rock as an affront that required a response in kind by Italian climbers.[58]

The academy of the CAI had moved its headquarters to Rome in 1929, far from the mountains but close to the corridors of power. In the words of fascist mountaineer Augusto Turati, the academy's mission was to help bless Italian climbing with "the vivifying breath of fascism."[59]

The academy believed that German mountaineers in the Dolomites must be surpassed, and kept an eye out for young talent that might rise to the challenge. By 1928, through the *Rivista Mensile*, Kugy's contacts throughout the climbing world and the gossip chain, news of a handsome, hard young *Triestino* had spread beyond Val Rosandra and the Julian Alps. Important climbers wanted to meet Emilio to see him climb and assess his potential.

Rudatis asked Emilio to team up with him for a new route in the eastern Dolomites on the Cima del Bancon. Emilio, who kept a certain *distacco* with other climbers, and especially those who did not come from Trieste, had never quite mastered the "contempt for the awards of applause" that Buzzati saw as a cardinal virtue of mountaineers. He met Rudatis at the Vazzoler hut as soon as he could, and Rudatis kept him from his usual pre-climb early bedtime to chat about climbing.

Rudatis had accompanied many talented young climbers. A current favourite was yogi Pino Prati, who Rudatis said followed a "mystical way of liberation, of naked power, of absolute existence."[60] Rudatis also followed the dark-eyed and intense veterinary student Renzo Videsott, with whom, three weeks before, he had climbed the demanding northeast ridge of the Pan di Zucchero.

On the morning of September 4, 1928, Emilio found himself belayed by Rudatis as his friend, Felice Franceschini, looked on. If it had been an audition for Rudatis's patronage, Emilio should have passed with top marks. In one day, he had led every pitch on a new route up the 300-metre-long Cima degli Aghi, and then a traverse to their new route to the top of Cima del Bancon.

Rudatis, for the moment at least, was unimpressed, and Emilio subsequently rarely climbed with him. Rudatis published his manifesto on the state of *sesto grado* climbing, *Das Letzte im Fels* (*The Latest on the Rocks*), in 1936. Although Rudatis had been on the first ascents of many of the routes he listed as expressions of the *sestogradiste* philosophy, Emilio's routes were overlooked.[61] Emilio, however, didn't relate to Rudatis or other philosophers and preferred partners who saw climbing not as a mystic practice but as a trade with spiritual benefits.[62]

Through Rudatis, however, Emilio met climbers who would play a role in his life, including Mary Varale (née Gennaro), the outstanding female alpinist who had made an arduous first ascent on the rock peak of Punta Sant'Anna. Varale's husband, Vittorio, was a well-read sports journalist who Emilio knew from the papers, and an advisor to the fascist government.

These contacts gave a new context and impetus to Emilio's efforts. He still aspired to become a mountain guide, but now he added a desire to use his climbing skills to "show that Italian rock climbers can go where Germans considered [it] impossible for them."[63]

To do so, however, he would have to draw attention to his efforts and, in the process, measure both his vulnerability to criticism and his appetite for attention. Some who knew Emilio saw him as averse to publicity. "Keeping out of the limelight," said Riccardo Cassin, "was Comici's style."[64] Cassin, however, mistook Emilio's fear that the limelight would compromise his privacy for a fear of publicity itself. In the spring of 1928, Emilio could have returned to the Magazzini Generale, pursued his hobby quietly and never discovered whether the rewards of applause that Buzzati spoke of were anything more than the applause itself. Instead, he made plans to conquer an old enemy, the only wall in his home ranges big and famous enough to make the world take notice: the north face of the Riofreddo.

***

On Tuesday, August 7, 1928, Emilio and Fabjan, one of his most trusted friends and partners, hiked slowly up the trail to the Corsi hut. The silver rock walls of the Madre dei Camosci were free of snow, and the sky deep blue. They would soon be up there, picking their way, handhold by handhold and piton by piton, on rocks never touched by climbers before, towards glory, retreat or possibly an early death.

Emilio had long lived in the psychological shadow of the wall, and now that he entered its physical realm, he felt a new energy that was part anticipation and part foreboding. Kugy's warning about the north face of the Riofreddo had turned out to be prescient. In 1928, two parties had already failed on the wall.

Slovenian Mira Pibernik (nicknamed Marko), was one of the best women climbers in the world. Her favourite partner was Stane Tominšek, a prominent Slovene intellectual and a bold alpinist. Together, they had made the first ascent of the 900-metre north face of the Jôf di Montasio (in Slovene, Špik nad Policami), one of the last great problems of the Julian Alps and, with its long sections of V+ rock climbing, one of the hardest climbs east of the Dolomites.

Pibernik and Tominšek had passed Emilio and Strekeli's high-point and were partway up the steep chimney system in the middle of the wall when it started to rain. They improvised a bivouac site at a hanging belay in a chimney, beneath a chockstone that protected them from the rockfall that continued throughout the night. Dawn came clear but cold and found them weary and shivering, their legs numb from hanging in rope slings all night. After their hard bivouac, the chimney became known as the Black Room. Their resolve was broken and they descended.

In late June, Friulan teenagers Celso Gilberti and Riccardo Spinotti tried the wall. The weather was still bad, however, and the wall ran with snowmelt. Wet rock made even easy climbing treacherous, and a rainstorm forced them to bivouac in the Black Room. They had passed the chockstone that had protected Pibernik and Tominšek and they were both struck by rockfall in the night.

At first light, bruised and exhausted, they retreated. They slowly and arduously downclimbed as much as they could to conserve pitons for rappel anchors. Spinotti became listless from exhaustion and hypothermia. Gilberti worried that Spinotti might lose his grip on the rappel rope or lose consciousness while downclimbing, so he took over setting the rappel anchors and did what he could to keep Spinotti alert, given that he, too was exhausted. They reached the snowfield at the base in the early evening. After Gilberti had pulled down the rope from the last rappel, he turned around to congratulate his friend on their escape from the wall, but Spinotti's body had finally given up and he lay dead in the snow.

***

Emilio arrived at the Corsi hut before Fabjan. The door was unlocked and the hut was vacant. The custodian had gone down to Valbruna to pick up supplies because there were few visitors on Tuesdays. Emilio sat on his pack to watch the sunset. The shadows crept from the north face of the Riofreddo to the northeast ridge he had climbed a year ago with Gino Razza. Emilio knew Spinotti and Gilberti and described the view of the face that evening as a waking nightmare made bearable by his sense that Spinotti's spirit interceded on Emilio and Fabjan's behalf with the mountain, pleading his own sacrifice so that these new and worthy climbers could have safe passage.[65]

Emilio loved to sleep in, which sometimes led to late starts, but the reason they slept in the next morning was that he had forgotten to wind their alarm clock. Late in the morning, they roped up where Spinotti had died. Spinotti "would always remain near us," said Emilio, "and in the most difficult places, he would support us and in the moments of discouragement, he would infuse us with strength and courage. We knew in our hearts that we had his tacit consent. He was there with us, with benevolence he looked upon us. He urged us to climb." Emilio's intuition about the supportive presence of the departed reflects the theory that supernatural experiences of participants in high-risk pursuits are "agency detection mechanisms" that have evolved to protect them.[66]

Although the spirits of the deceased supported and warned Emilio, he often saw the mountains themselves as antagonists in the spiritual battle of alpinism. He referred to mountains as goddesses who demanded victims.[67] Although Emilio conceded that this was the goddess's prerogative, it was the duty of climbers to respond with a *vendetta* in the form of a successful completion of the climb. For Emilio, there was no such thing as an accident, and every mountain tragedy or failed attempt demanded a response.

On the wall, Emilio felt "intense, natural, wild joy."[68] He and Fabjan quickly passed the place where Emilio had left his pitons and hammer and entered the chimney. Much of the wide crack was either too slippery with water or too wide to bridge with their legs, and they had to climb the walls on either side. The higher they climbed, the longer these sections of wall climbing became, until they had to detour from the chimney for several pitches at a time.

From Gilberti and Spinotti's high-point in the Black Room, they anticipated the hardest climbing yet, but after ten metres of vertical face climbing on the chimney's side wall, they reached easier rock. Spinotti and Gilberti had retreated a few metres from where the face relented. If they had continued to the summit instead of retreating, Spinotti might have lived. Emilio learned something that became a tenet of his climbing: there was no way to know whether the wall above had holds or cracks, except by trying it.

On the summit ridge, they watched the sunset turn the clouds over the black valleys red and orange. The dark north face of the Riofreddo fell away beneath their feet. They embraced. Fabjan had been an outstanding partner: calm, fit, competent, able to share the lead on hard terrain. The credit for the climb belonged to them equally, but for Emilio, it had been more than a feat of alpinism. It was the settlement of a score with the mountain on behalf of Spinotti, and the first big wall where he had failed but then returned with a new approach and succeeded.

Spinotti and Gilberti and Pibernik and Tominšek had retreated after hard bivouacs on the inhospitable wall, Strekeli had been too weak to do his part in 1926 and Emilio had climbed too slowly. Now, two years later, Emilio and Fabjan made a team of almost equal partners. They climbed the wall in a day partly because they used a minimum of pitons and only occasional rope tension. It was a well-planned and executed victory, their first climb that had significance beyond the Julian Alps.

The summit, said Emilio, was a "moment which God does not let pass into oblivion. Feeling it, recalling it as it was, divinizes the memory and strengthens the desire to equal it." But it was not God but Spinotti's ghost whom Emilio credited with the supernatural support of their climb. Spinotti, said Emilio, "led us through the most difficult and dangerous passages, an invisible hand supporting us above the void."[69]

They began the complicated descent of the southeast ridge right away, but it was slow work for the exhausted climbers. They had left behind the heavy bivouac gear that had slowed down Emilio and Razza on L'Innominata, but darkness made it impossible to continue safely, and they bivouacked in a chimney. They had no extra clothes or food, but they babbled all night through chattering teeth about their new climb, the biggest and hardest route in the Madre dei Camosci.

Before they left for Trieste, they made a pilgrimage to the cemetery in Valbruna. "Under a small wall," wrote Emilio, "we found a mound of fresh earth, decorated with a rough wooden cross and a yellowed laurel wreath. It was Spinotti's grave. He was in a coffin in a humble grave, too far away from home for anyone who knew him to come and shed a tear over… a valiant but unfortunate comrade who made the final sacrifice of his life on the mountain."[70]

They gathered some pink rhododendrons and laid them on the grave. Up on the wall, where climbers approached the realm of the dead, the fallen alpinist had spiritual power. In the valley, he occupied a lonely grave.

The climb was rated V+, an easier grade than the best climbs made that year in the eastern Dolomites. It was, however, a major breakthrough in the Julian Alps. Kugy had not anticipated such a bold move from Emilio, and predictably, he did not seem to welcome it. He stood outside the Corsi hut not long after the first ascent of the north face of the Riofreddo and stared at the wall through his pince-nez and mumbled, "Colossal, colossal."[71]

The newspapers and the alpine press reported on the Riofreddo climb, and Emilio saw his picture in the newspaper for the first time. His fame, along with Trieste's good reputation with the fascist government, encouraged the Opera Nazionale Dopolavoro (the National Recreation Club, or OND) to charter the informal GARS rock school in Val Rosandra in 1929. The OND saw good potential for fascist leadership in the GARS, but Kugy and some of the older mountaineers thought of the school as something of a joke. The only cadre of climbing instructors in Italy were mountain guides in alpine villages, most of whom were neither fascists nor *palestra* climbers. For guides, Rome's enthusiasm for dock workers who fooled around on small cliffs and played at climbing instructors on their days off was understandably difficult to understand.

The philosophy of the newly named Val Rosandra School of Rock Climbing, however, was not to guide tourists up easy routes but to teach the Italian way to climb, with pitons and efficient free and aid climbing movements. The signatories of the school's constitution were all members of the GARS. Some of them had not climbed for long, but Emilio trusted them anyway.

The rules of the school, which were informal at first, were eventually put in writing.[72] Courses would be held in the spring and autumn (it was hot in Val Rosandra in the summer) and on weekends, since most of its students would have weekday jobs in the city. The school would provide ropes and pitons, and instructors would bring their own *scarpette* and other personal equipment. It was up to the instructors to collect fees from their students, which remained a challenge for Emilio, who often felt too shy to ask for his pay.

The school would utilize the names climbers had given the rock walls of Val Rosandra. The signatories of the constitution became the head instructors, and Emilio was named the director. The instructors were required to attend the annual general meeting of the Trieste section of the CAI, which was now the party's instrument of control over the climbing community.[73]

On a typical fall weekend course, the instructors went to six different stations, one for each grade. At each station, techniques likely to be demanded at the grade were taught. At the Crinale Piccolo, Stefenelli taught basic first-grade methods of movement. At the Montasio, caver and engineering student Mario Premuda and alpine specialist Carlo Cernitz taught slightly more complicated methods for the second grade. Claudio Prato, one of the oldest and most traditional instructors, paired with ambitious new router Albano Barisi to teach free climbing at grades IV and V at the Montasio, and included the famous Cozzi Crack in their itinerary. Emilio, Benedetti and Fabjan, assisted by Barisi and Val Rosandra expert Ovidio Opiglia, taught grade VI rock climbing on the arêtes of the Montasio and the Benedetti Overhang. Duties at this last station would have involved as much demonstration as hands-on instruction.[74] It was an impressive display of local climbing interest and expertise that would have drawn many students and crowds of onlookers as well.

The school's success led to more official approval, in this case from the CAI in Rome and from Angelo Manaresi, Mussolini's extraordinary commissioner to the National Alpine Association. Manaresi was well known for a popular Alpine Front war memoir and some unsophisticated poetry, and he was a powerful patron as Bologna's undersecretary of war to the Kingdom of Italy and a *podestà* (an appointed fascist civic leader). Manaresi gave the Val Rosandra school the title of National School of Alpinism.[75]

Some thought that the title was too grand for a school based in humble Val Rosandra. In fascist Italy, however, names were often more impressive than the institutions they described. The National School of Alpinism of the Italian Alpine Club in Val Rosandra was staffed by amateurs who earned small fees, but it did not offer full-time employment. The changes in the school's status did not afford Emilio any extra freedom, time or money to climb.

Emilio wanted to devote himself full-time to climbing, but as long as he lived in Trieste, he needed his job at the Magazzini Generali. He and Fabjan returned to the Riofreddo and climbed the beautiful north arête, but the Julian Alps themselves seemed a little too familiar to Emilio now. He needed somewhere else to go, where the mountains might be his whole life.

His dream of becoming a mountain guide was continually rekindled by trips to the Dolomites, where the world's greatest climbers proved themselves and the mountain guides lived and worked in the shadows of the mighty rocks.

***

In late August of 1929, the day after the first ascent of the northwest face of the Dito di Dio in the Sorapiss group, Emilio and Fabjan chinned the rafters of the Vandelli hut. After all, at grade v, their new route had not been much of a workout.

A tall, balding man recognized Emilio from his picture in the *Rivista Mensile* and introduced himself. Severino Casara, despite his well-pressed climbing clothes, was not an ordinary tourist. He was both a frequent contributor to the climbing papers and a man with a reputation in the climbing community. Casara, a lawyer from Vicenza, was accompanied by his friends Mario Salvadori and Emmy Hartwich-Brioschi, a beautiful middle-aged woman who wore a gold necklace and a fashionable artificial wave in her black hair.[76]

Casara introduced Emmy to Emilio and compared him to Paul

Preuss, Emmy's former lover and the greatest climber in the Alps until he fell to his death soloing the Mandlkogel in 1913. The climbing leg injury that had prevented Emmy from meeting Paul in the week before he died still gave her trouble. She smiled and leaned on her ebony walking cane, a proud veteran of that lost, romantic world of Austria-Hungarian climbing before the Great War. For Emilio, who never learned how to take even modest compliments, the moment must have been awkward. Casara's comparison to Preuss was premature.[77]

Preuss had railed against the piton, but Emmy had had a soft spot for piton users ever since Hans Dülfer secretly told her that she climbed better than his girlfriend, Hanne Franz. Emilio's fascist views would not have given Emmy pause, even though both she and Paul were Jews. Many high-ranking fascists still opposed anti-Semitism, and rank-and-file fascists like Emilio never suspected that the party would ever persecute Jews. Catholic and Jewish *squadristi* had struggled side by side against Slavic nationalists in the streets of Trieste in 1919 and 1920. Emilio had seen no contradiction between the fiery speeches of Paolo Jacchia, the leader of the Trieste blackshirts, and the fact that he was Jewish.[78]

The next day, Fabjan, Emilio, Casara, Salvadori and Hartwich-Brioschi hiked up the Croda di Vilaco. It was the first time Emilio played the role of guide in the Dolomites, and Emmy took a special interest in him, as did Casara, who needed friends.

In 1925, although he was a climber of evidently only average abilities, Casara had claimed the first ascent of the north overhang of the Campanile di Val Montanaia, solo, shod in socks. After the route was published in Antonio Berti's encyclopedic and authoritative *Guide to the Eastern Dolomites*, more skilled climbers tried the route and failed.[79] Doubts about Casara's claim circulated. Berti had been a university lecturer in Casara's hometown of Vicenza, where he and Casara had become friends, and Berti likely sponsored Casara's application to the Academic Section of the CAI. Berti had exposed himself to criticism by publishing the climb, but his credibility was such that he convinced some climbers of the veracity of Casara's claim. After a few years of failed attempts, however, detractors outnumbered believers. Emilio knew the story, although he never publicly gave his opinion about it.

Whether or not Casara consciously set out to improve his own reputation by his association with the pure, strong and idealistic Emilio Comici, he did much to deepen and prolong the friendship. When Casara returned to Vicenza, he began a frequent but often one-sided correspondence with Emilio. Emilio neither snubbed nor especially encouraged him. He did not try to make friends, but he had them anyway – men like Casara who did not understand him but befriended him for their own purposes.

Casara had searched for a young climber to satisfy his fulsome appetite for admiration in exchange for avuncular advice and some patronage. Casara tried to befriend the young Giusto Gervasutti (who would make the second ascent of the Comici-Fabjan on the Dito di Dio) by loaning him a copy of the unedited proofs of the latest version of Berti's guidebook. Gervasutti took little interest. He came from a solid bourgeois family, was popular with his friends, had his own contacts in society and the CAI and needed no patrons.

On the Croda di Vilaco, Casara gossiped with Emilio about climbing controversies and the notions of Rudatis and Evola. Emilio was bored by climbing philosophy. Casara, however, read his silence, "steely eyes" and impassive expression as the reflection of deep inner values that ran parallel to his own. From that day forward, Casara wrote himself into Emilio's story. He claimed that day to have shown Emilio the line up the northwest face of the Sorella di Mezzo (Middle Sister) on the Sorapiss massif that would later become one of Emilio's great climbs in the range.[80] Emilio, however, never mentioned Casara's advice on the climb and said he had chosen the line himself, a skill for which he was widely renowned.

Emilio and Emmy became friends. Mussolini famously wanted men to be overbearing towards women, but Emilio had always been passive and respectful towards the opposite sex.[81] He was as hurt when a woman he admired ignored him as he was when the goddess of the mountains spurned him.

Emilio's desire to win the approval of Emmy, who was married and therefore not physically available, was no less powerful for not being sexual. Emmy had been Preuss's lover. The breath of his life lived on in her. Her history, rather than her marriage to Otto Brioschi, made her a woman apart for Emilio. His preoccupation with Emmy in his correspondence and her warm manner with him, evident in photographs, show that he shared something rather more than a friendship with her, although they were not lovers. When Emmy smiled at Emilio and put her hand on his shoulder to help her walk when her leg injury was bad, he could not help but remember that she had also smiled upon the fallen heroes Dülfer and Preuss. For Emilio, Emmy was much more than a friend from Vienna. Her smile concealed the sultry, intoxicating, pitiless gaze of a dangerous tradition choosing a champion.

***

Those few days in the Sorapiss group became Emilio's mental image of mountain guiding. He imagined a lifetime of relaxing climbs with paying friends from the city, interspersed with forays on new routes with strong partners from Trieste. To real guides, however, clients were not friends but city folk in need of constant supervision, whose main roles were to obey and pay. Guides did occasional hard routes, partly for their own pleasure, but mostly to establish their credentials and gain publicity for their skills.

The party, the CAI and tradition held that the best guides were drawn from the racial stock of the Alps, which had evolved to be brave, hardy and practical. In the minds of party social theorists, an ideal guide had the mental and physical resources of an effective miner or infantryman.[82] Emilio, a sensitive, creative, city-raised proletarian, wanted to guide principally to be able to climb hard routes on his days off. He hoped that his climbing reputation would make up for his lack of alpine pedigree, although he also knew it would be a challenge. In the eastern Dolomites, top climbers from all over Europe competed for new climbs.

The needs, experience and inspiration that pushed Emilio to choose his next challenge in the Sorapiss massif had many sources. His ambition to build his reputation in the Dolomites near Cortina, the centre of Italian guiding, was the strongest.[83] The northwest face of the Dito di Dio would have been a good calling card for a hard climber's first serious visit, but Emilio had in mind something that would turn heads in the cities and earn him some respect from the guides of Cortina.

***

On August 26, 1929, the day after the scramble up the Croda di Vilaco, Comici and Fabjan stood in the permanent dusk of the north walls of the Tre Sorelle (Three Sisters) of the Sorapiss and stared in wonderment and fear.

"My gaze settled," wrote Emilio, "...on the gloomiest and most vertical wall, [the northwest face of the Sorella di Mezzo] and for some time I could not look away. That wall was for us! The more vertiginous, crazy, far-fetched, frightening and bewitching, the more immense the attraction these walls exert upon us. Why are we so anguished in front of such walls? Why are we unable to free ourselves from that oppression and drive away the ugly idea of confronting them?... To the naked eye, the wall was so vast and complex that details were lost, here a huge wall, there protruding black ceilings or perfectly smooth walls... What worried me most, in addition to the perpendicularity and height of more than 500 metres of the wall, was its black and blood-red colour, streaked by long lines and some cracks. Was it passable by man, or only by water?"[84]

Here was a wall that almost rivalled the Civetta in scope, difficulty and danger. It was scored by shafts and cracks as damp and dangerous as caves and portentously splotched with blood-coloured stone.

"The next morning," Emilio wrote, "very early on, when the sky was still strewn with stars, armed with everything we had, we headed for the attack. The first gleam of dawn found us panting as we crawled up the talus to the glacier. With crampons, we climbed up to the place that we had already identified for the attack: a rock step that extends down towards the glacier. Both on the left and on the right, the base [of the wall] is eroded by the millennial glacier, which scarified the mountain, forming huge blood-red caverns. We passed the step and climbed slabs under a great black roof to a gravelly terrace. Nearby, water roared in a huge gully that divided the Terza Sorella from our face on the Sorella di Mezzo."[85]

Emilio's description of the ascent had its closest literary parallel in

Dante Alighieri's *Inferno*: "The vision of that horrible beauty cannot be expressed in words, because words are always the same and may sometimes seem exaggerated: that picture was simply fantastic and seemed to be brushed by colours so varied and contrasting, now fused together now completely detached, they left us surprised, confused," Emilio wrote.[86] After 100 metres of nerve-wracking loose rock, a yellow roof only succumbed to slow and exhausting aid climbing. More hard aid and free climbing brought them above another overhang. At the sinister red rock they had seen from the base, they knew they had reached the centre of the wall. They crawled across a ledge to avoid an overhang. A chimney took them to a smooth slab that could only be climbed with the aid of a piton, and the last of the hard climbing.

They rated the climb vi-, a grade that they had previously only climbed on the crags of Val Rosandra. They stopped short of giving it a full grade vi because the hard sections were separated by easier climbing that they guessed made it easier than Solleder and Lettenbauer's climb on the Civetta. Emilio and Fabjan had, nonetheless, almost made the first new grade vi climb by Italians in the Italian mountains.

On the same day Emilio and Fabjan climbed the north face of the Sorella di Mezzo, Casara and Salvadori made the first ascent of a tower in the Zurlon cirque via an approach pioneered earlier in the season by Emilio and Fabjan. Casara named the tower Cima Emmy, after his muse.

Casara was ecstatic about his new friend's triumph on a climb he claimed to have pointed out himself, and wasted no time in hailing it as the first Italian grade vi. It was the first time, but not the last, that Emilio would have his achievements exaggerated by well-meaning boosters. He soon understood that his climbs could serve the goals and needs of others in ways he did not intend. Emilio was insecure about his lack of education and did not always speak up when more educated climbers spoke erroneously about his climbs. For now, he did little to correct Casara's mistaken appraisal of the climb.

Despite the minus sign, the Sorella di Mezzo broke the barrier to grade vi. Within 12 days of the first ascent, three more grade vis were completed by Italian climbers. The Austrians and Germans had been served notice.

The Sorapiss excursion with Fabjan was the most successful climbing trip Emilio had ever made. His two hard new routes strengthened his reputation. He had new friends who might even become clients in the future. It was a bittersweet motorcycle trip back to Trieste, loaded down with rucksacks and Fabjan, back to the job at the docks and weekend trips to Val Rosandra, and the now less glamorous Julian Alps.

***

Emilio's successes inspired other *Triestino* climbers to try their skills on the unclimbed faces and pinnacles of the Julian Alps. In early August of 1929, while Emilio was in the Sorapiss group, Mario Orsini, a local youth who Emilio had singled out for his talent, and fellow *Triestino* Dario Mazzeni attempted the Torre degli Orsi, a 300-metre-high rock pillar in the Montasio group. Halfway up, they bypassed the most obvious but daunting line up a smooth wall. While Mazzeni led, a single rock fell and killed him. Orsini was understandably traumatized by the task of rappelling and lowering his friend's body, pitch by pitch, to the ground.

Emilio responded to the first fatality from the GARS of Val Rosandra with a statement of his philosophy of death in the mountains. The mountain, Emilio wrote, is "a beautiful goddess who sometimes takes her victim, and we should not be discouraged."[87] "When the mountain wants its victim, when a lover leaves us, when a dear brother disappears from our alpine family, tears do not flow from our eyes to alleviate bitterness: pain constricts the chest. After the first moment of anguished stupor, which tightens the throat and cuts off our speech, rebellion seizes us, but against whom? Against the mountain? No, we venerate it too much! Perhaps it is against adverse destiny. But destiny? Tomorrow it will be our turn. What do we care? Precisely because of the inevitability of our deaths we challenge destiny. We do not need to desert [climbing] or lose heart. We want to be worthy of our [fallen] partner, and, like him, to face everything serenely."[88]

The climbing dead consoled and admonished. "What would our [departed] partner say," he wrote, "if we were overwhelmed by discouragement, if we deserted the mountain, if we feared the difficulties and the dangers? No, dear Dario, no! Even though we know what our fate will be, we will never quit and that's why we launched the challenge against the [mountain] that struck him, against the very difficulties and dangers. We had to climb with iron will to win, at any cost."[89]

Masculine strength, Roman virtue, iron will, victory at all costs and sacrifice are fascist clichés that occasionally show up in Emilio's accounts of his climbs, although they are at odds with his usually self-absorbed and anguished tone. These clichés are largely absent from Emilio's private correspondence, so he may have felt the need to express his political views only when speaking to a wider audience. The dissonance between the slogans and the rest of his writing shows that fascism was not integrated fully into his view of climbing. If he had not added at least occasional fascist statements, someone in the censorship process would have done it for him. Censorship in fascist Italy was extensive and arbitrary, and no document was too insignificant for revision. This is not to imply that Emilio disagreed with the fascist sentiments in his articles, regardless of whether or not he was their author. In all of Emilio's recorded complaints about the CAI's editorial process, there is not one complaint about fascist edits.

In the first week of September 1930, Emilio made a pilgrimage to Mazzeni's grave in Valbruna before he attempted the Torre degli Orsi with Orsini. Two seasons before, after the north face of the Riofreddo, he had come here to lay rhododendron flowers on Spinotti's grave. The flowers were an expression of Emilio's mission to follow the example of the fallen climbers and finish their earthly work. They were also an offering in exchange for their spiritual presence and aid.

Emilio and Orsini left at three in the morning the next day and hiked up to the tower in the dark. Orsini kept his thoughts to himself. "Poor Orsini," wrote Emilio, "sad memories assailed him!"[90] Emilio's desire to finish the route for Orsini was tempered by his recollection of the great British alpinist Edward Whymper's admonition that climbers must accept the possibility of a tragic outcome, and Paul Preuss's dictum that a climber must never climb up where they cannot safely climb down.

At the base, the morning sun revealed a crucial traverse around an unclimbable smooth wall high on the climb. Emilio took it as a sign. In little more than an hour, they reached the point where Mazzeni had been killed. Emilio attacked the crux wall, but after 15 metres, the holds ran out. He tapped in a tiny piton and gently hung from it, watching to see if it moved. He lassoed a rock spike above and climbed the rope hand-over-hand to better holds. An exacting free pitch up thin cracks led to the traverse ledge they had seen from below, and after a mere two and a half hours, the climb was over.

They sat down on the summit and wept. "That crying was so good," wrote Emilio. "It relieved us of a great oppression, and at the bottom of my heart the pain was mixed with a kind of joy. We felt that we had done a good thing to go up there, to find [Dario] in his kingdom, where his good and simple soul, free from his earthly remains, wanders… Of all my innumerable alpine climbs, none gave me so much satisfaction and moved me as much as this: and so, I believe for my companion. After our weeping was done, we pulled ourselves back together, although we remained in silent communion with [Dario]."[91] It was not a scene that could be reconciled with the fascist image of heroic, masculine mountaineers.

Emilio's reputation had grown and many climbers now came to watch him, just like they did in Val Rosandra. The climbers below shouted their congratulations as they descended. Emilio stopped in the middle of a rappel to pick flowers for Mazzeni's grave.

Emilio and Orsini renamed the pillar Torre Dario Mazzeni. Torre degli Orsi was Italian for Tower of the Bears, a name chosen by Kugy with ties to local folklore. Bears had long been extirpated from the region. The names of the recent martyrs of alpinism replaced titles rooted in ancient geographies. The fascist government had already taken steps to erase ancient Ladin, Friulan and Slovenian place names and Kugy's folkloric reconstructions and replace them with Italian names. To name a rock tower after an Italian climber who died assaulting it Italianized the landscape in fascist style. Kugy, a Slovenian nationalist who had loved Austria-Hungary, was a classic mountaineer from a bygone golden age, and, like the bears, on the edge of extirpation.

The climb was a visceral response to the spiritual challenge of the presence of a new ghost in Emilio's consciousness. On Torre Dario Mazzeni, Emilio reimagined the heights as liminal space where the climbing living and dead met and strove together. When more came, as they would, he would also hear their voices and feel their presence as he climbed. There have been few more haunted alpinists.

***

The Italian climbing press hailed Emilio and Fabjan's climbs on the Dito di Dio and the Sorella di Mezzo as the greatest triumphs of the season. They said less about the north wall of the Gamsutter Tower in the Julian Alps, first climbed by Rudolf Peters and Adolf Deye, understandably, because the climbers were German and grade VI was grudgingly expected from them. In 1929, however, the press began to pay so much attention to Emilio's climbs that routes of equal or greater difficulty by other climbers were given little or no press.

The 600-metre-high south pillar of the Marmolada di Penia was a dramatic example. The climb was led by Selva di Gardena guide Luigi Micheluzzi, who was accompanied by Roberto Perathoner and Demetrio Christomannos. Micheluzzi used only six pitons (including a few for aid) on the whole route, He might have used fewer had the rock not been icy. Micheluzzi was not renowned for graceful climbing, but he was dogged and brave as befitted the traditional guide he was, in his blazer, broad-brimmed hat and moustache. The climb seemed so unlikely to the Dolomites legend Tita Piaz that he eyewitnessed it in case the ascent was later doubted.

The Micheluzzi Route received little press partly because editors and journalists found it easier to report on Emilio, who courted their attention despite complaining about the results of their work. Guides like Micheluzzi had an aversion to publicity, the press and the grading system that preoccupied top climbers like Emilio and put a sheen of scientific objectivity on less noble impulses. Notions of gentlemanly sportsmanship forbade self-promotion, and a reputation for arrogance might even frighten off timid clients. Traditional guiding clients wanted their climbs to be about themselves, not their guides. Before the Great War, even Preuss and Dülfer could only use adjectives like "very hard" that had no formal definition. Their comparisons between climbs reflected a psycho-geography in which each mountain still existed in the consciousness of climbers as an irreducible totality.

The Micheluzzi Route remained so little-known that in the 1930s, German Walter Stösser thought he had made the first ascent. After the Second World War, British climber Don Whillans and German climbing legend Hermann Buhl both called the Micheluzzi Route one of the greatest climbs of its era.

Politics also played a role in the climb's lack of publicity. Tita Piaz, who witnessed it, had been both an anarchist and irredentist until the fascists came to power, after which time he shifted most of his political allegiances to anarchism. He was imprisoned twice under the fascists for his political views. Although he was the greatest Italian rock climber of the pre-war generation, his memoirs were suppressed under the fascists and only published in 1949.

Emilio became the go-to mountaineering news story in the Italian press. He was skilled, photogenic, ambitious, a committed fascist from Mussolini's stronghold of support in Trieste and, in his own, self-torturing way, craved the attention. From now on, the press, sometimes with some accuracy and sometimes with exaggerations and omissions, identified Emilio as the leading proponent not just of Italian climbing but of mountaineering in the Dolomites in general.

Emilio had craved honours since he had first been denied them. The hunger became chronic when, despite his heroism in the Raspo cave, he was denied a civic medal. Now, the perennially triumphant fascist press identified Emilio as a symbol of his own political ideals. The rewards of this recognition remained, for now, moral, spiritual and unsullied by material entitlements.

Emilio Comici, fourth from right, bottom row, at school in
Trieste, ca. 1909.

The Comicis of six Via Bazzoni.
Standing, left to right: Gastone
Comici; Gastone's wife and
daughter; Emilio Comici; an
uncle; Emilio's father, Antonio.
Seated: Emilio's mother, Renata.

Rifles, ropes and nostalgia for the alpini of the Great War.
Corporal Emilio Comici, on left, serves on an honour guard at a
fascist party function.

Emilio's redoubtable client and
benefactor Anna Escher in the
Sinai, 1937.

Emilio Comici, left, and fellow guide Jova Lipovec in Sierra de Gredos, Spain, 1935.

Selva di Gardena in the South Tyrol, where Emilio Comici was prefectural commisioner in the last half of 1940.

Emilio Comici's body lies in the sanctuary of the Church of Selva di Gardena on October 20, 1940. His head was bandaged to conceal the serious wound that likely killed him after his fall.

The funeral cortege of Emilio Comici, October, 1940, with climbers and guides as pallbearers and the Carabinieri from Bolzano as an honour guard.

Children from the fascist Balilla organization in Selva di Gardena pay respects at the grave of their prefectural commissioner, October 1940.

Emilio Comici, dressed up for town, ca. 1930.

At the interment of Emilio Comici. Front row, left to right: Giorgio Brunner, Alice Marsi, Emmy Hartwich-Brioschi. Second row, left to right: Captain Giuseppe Inaudi, Antonio Comici.

The Caving Group of the XXX Ottobre Society on the Carso with their new ladders and technical equipment and army surplus helmets, the Carso, ca. 1925. Emilio Comici, second from the left.

The instructors of the National School of Alpinism at Val Rosandra, 1933. Left to right, Fausto Stefenelli, Emilio Comici, Ovidio Opiglia, Claudio Prato. Seated, Giulio Benedetti, Albano Barisi.

Julius Kugy, Trieste's most noted 19th- and early 20th-century mountaineer, and a mentor and nemesis to Emilio Comici.

La via aperta dai triestini Emilio Comici e Giordano B. Fabian sulla parete Nord-Ovest della Sorella di Mezzo fra le Tre Sorelle del Sorapiss. Una delle maggiori conquiste del moderno arrampicamento italiano.

The Comici-Fabjan route on the north-west face of the Sorella di Mezzo in the Sorapiss.

Emilio Comici in Val Rosandra.

Emilio Comici's client Antonia Pozzi, who secretly wrote poems about him, and Oliviero Gasperi, 1935.

The alpine contingent of the XXX Ottobre Society from Trieste, Emilio's first climbing club.

Co-educational irredentism in the outdoors: the XXX Ottobre Society, ca. 1925. Emilio Comici, bottom row on the left.

A letter from the powerful fascist commissioner to the Italian Alpine Club, Angelo Manaresi, refusing to intervene in Emilio's feud with the Dimai brothers about who led the crux of the north face of the Cima Grande.

A photograph of the Comici-Dimai route on the north face of the Cima Grande, signed by Emilio Comici.

The letter appointing Emilio Comici to the prefectural commissariat of Selva di Gardena and Santa Cristina.

Emilio Comici's XXX Ottobre Society membership card.

Napoleone Cozzi, father of Trieste climbing, irredentist revolutionary, founder of the Trieste Gymnastics Society.

Mary Varale, one of the best female climbers in the Alps, and Emilio Comici. Varale brought Comici to Lecco to train Riccardo Cassin and climbed the Spigolo Giallo with Comici and Renato Zanutti in 1933.

The Val Rosandra rock school in its informal days in the late 1930s. Emilio Comici in the centre.

The Comici monument on the Cippo Comici with an unknown visitor.

Angelo Manaresi – undersecretary of war, fascist overseer of the Italian Alpine Club and the man with the last word on any issue in that community – was unimpressed by Emilio's sometimes fragile ego.

Guido Buffarini Guidi, who secured Emilio Comici's position as prefectural commissioner in Selva di Gardena after seeing him in a climbing demonstration.

Misurina in the Dolomites, where Emilio Comici lived intermittently through most of the 1930s.

Anna Escher and
Emilio Comici on
Mount Olympus in
Greece, 1934.

Al Podestà di *S. Martino di Badia*

(Provincia di *Bolzano*)

1338 La sottoscritta *Elisabetta Schanung Va Mischi*
di fu *Simone* e di fu *Elisabetta Clara*
nata il *3 marzo 1883* a *Longiarù*
(provincia di *Bolzano*) e residente a *Longiarù*
(provincia di *Bolzano*) in via *Freins*

presa conoscenza degli accordi intervenuti tra il Governo italiano e quello germanico, relati-
vamente al trasferimento nel Reich dei tedeschi dell'Alto Adige, dichiara formalmente ed irre-
vocabilmente, per sè ed i suoi familiari qui appresso indicati, di **voler conservare
la cittadinanza italiana.** *come ladina e non tedesca
e colla volontà di restare ladina —*
Longiarù, li *30-XII.* – 1939-XVIII.

Firma:
Elisabetta Schanung

Familiari:

Moglie: (Cognome di nascita e nome) _____

    Paternità _____

    Nata il _____

Figli minorenni legittimi:

1339 1. Nome *Costantino Mischi*
    fu Francesco
    Maternità _____
    Nato il *24-II.-1925*

2. Nome _____
    Maternità _____
    Nato il _____

3. Nome _____
    Maternità _____
    Nato il _____

4. Nome _____
    Maternità _____
    Nato il _____

5. Nome _____
    Maternità _____
    Nato il _____

6. Nome _____
    Maternità _____
    Nato il _____

All German and Ladin speakers in the South Tyrol were required by the Italian government either to renounce their Italian citizenship and resettle in the Third Reich or to agree, as the signatory of this document did, to become Italianized and give up their language and customs. Emilio Comici's work as prefectural commissioner included enforcing this law.

Emilio Comici in his signature climbing jacket and basketball shoes, Val Rosandra, mid-1930s.

Emilio Comici, right, with climbing impresario, partner, benefactor and correspondent Severino Casara and good friend Emmy Hartwich-Brioschi, Paul Preuss's former lover, at Lake Misurina, 1935.

Emilio Comici as a tough, wind-worn mountain man. The photograph the fascists chose to use on his grave.

Emilio Comici on top of the Cima Grande.

Car breakdowns in the sand were frequent as Emilio Comici and his client Anna Escher drove cross-country to the Red Sea Hills to climb in 1937.

Anche il Centro Alpinistico
epurato dei soci ebrei

Veniamo informati che rapidamente e radicalmente anche la Sezione di Trieste del Centro Alpinistico Italiano ha epurato le proprie file dagli elementi di razza ebraica.

Comunicato stampa riferentesi alla Società Alpina delle Giulie.
Il CAI di Trieste "eliminò" gli ebrei più colorente dei partite.

"The Italian Mountaineering Centre has been purged of its Jewish members. We are informed that the Trieste section of the Italian mountaineering centre has quickly and radically purged its ranks of elements of the Hebrew race." La Piccola, Trieste, November 17, 1938.

The Spigolo Giallo on the Cima Piccola di Lavaredo, first climbed by Emilio Comici, Renato Zanutti and Mary Varale in 1933.

The northwest face of the Civetta. The Solleder-Lettenbauer climbs the wall just left of the prominent snowfield and the Comici-Fabjan climbs the wall farther left.

Prefectural commissioner Emilio Comici in Selva di Gardena, summer 1940.

The rockfall Comici and Brovedani survived on the Pomagnon and which Comici described in his story "The Scythe of Death" was so enormous that people in town had a chance to go home, get their cameras and photograph it.

Emilio Comici on hard moves at a palestra near Vicenza.

Toni Ortelli's drawing of Emilio's plan for the palestra that was quarried out of the cliff face at the army base at Castello Jocteau in Aosta.

Emilio Comici free climbing in Val Rosandra.

Emilio Comici attempting the north face of the Cima Ovest in 1935.

The northwest buttress of the Cima Piccola, first climbed by Emilio Comici and Piero Mazzorana in 1937.

The Trieste Gymnastics Society, which Emilio joined during the Great War, openly encouraged sports and alpinism and secretly supported Italian reunification.

Double-rope aid and free technique at the same time – typical grade VI climbing.

Emilio Comici, mountain guide, Dolomites, 1935.

Corporal Emilio Comici of the Ninth Alpini regiment.

A cartoon by a member of the GARS depicting Giordano Fabjan and Emilio Comici dancing until late the night before a big ascent.

Giordano Bruno Fabjan, one of Emilio's favourite partners and friends.

Emilio Comici in front of the Vallunga cliff where he fell to his death in 1940.

Emilio Comici leading the White Wall at Val Rosandra.

Emilio Comici in the Sinai, 1937.

CHAPTER FOUR

THE WATER DROP

On August 2, 1930, Emilio awoke beneath the warm blankets in the dormitory of the Mussolini hut and felt the cold air of the grey dawn on his face.[92] His partners, Fabjan and Piero Slocovich, a university student from Trieste, still slept.

Emilio didn't mind. He hated early mornings and had a lot to think about. They had come to climb the 500-metre-high west face of the Croda dei Toni, a broad pillar of rock on the complex Croda dei Toni group in the Sexten Dolomites.[93] The Croda dei Toni was easily seen from the hut, but because of an absence of obvious cracks, few had tried to climb it. Slocovich and Fabjan had been so lukewarm when they had seen it for the first time the day before that they stayed at the hut while Emilio hiked up and reconnoitred the wall from the talus. Despite the lack of an obvious place to start, Emilio knew that walls revealed their most important secrets only after he tried to climb them.

"So, what do we do?" Fabjan asked him when he returned.

"We'll try it tomorrow."

When his partners finally got out of bed, Emilio convinced them to hike up the talus with him and at least try the wall. He set off tentatively up the wisp of a crack. Holds appeared, although there were no piton cracks. The impossible-looking wall yielded just enough small holds so that Emilio could pick a strenuous way upwards. As he gave the wall everything he had, he entered into a mental state he called the "wild voluptuousness of climbing."[94]

The wall relented halfway up, where ledges criss-crossed the face. To save time, they roped up to move at the same time without belays, a common technique for experts on rock replete with ledges and holds. The climbers occasionally placed the rope behind a rock spike, but this provided little real protection in the case of a fall. Although the idea was to move briskly, each hold and move had to be considered carefully, because a fall was out of the question.

And yet, Slocovich fell. In the split second in which it was possible to avert the death of the whole party, Emilio, although unanchored, braced himself against the face, threw the rope over his shoulder and caught Slocovich in mid-flight. Emilio recalled that he simply surrendered to instinct and felt no emotion, even when he thought of how they might be pulled to their deaths.

They reached the final overhang an hour before sunset. Emilio was tired and emotionally worn out by the near-miss below, but as the strongest and fastest climber, he took the lead. After an hour of thin face climbing protected by two poor pitons, Emilio had tackled only 15 metres of the wall. The sun was close to the horizon but the summit was still some 20 metres away. Fabjan suggested that they bivouac on the belay ledge and try the wall again the next morning, but Emilio could not find a place for a piton to lower back down to his companions. He climbed on. Near the top, he had to lunge for a hold far above a poor piton. The move would have drawn gasps from onlookers, even in Val Rosandra. At the top of a new route in the Dolomites, with bad protection and darkness setting in, it was a remarkable manoeuvre.

Emilio reached the top as the sun disappeared below the horizon. Slocovich, who was still rattled by his fall lower down, fell again while he seconded. The fall was a luxury Emilio could not have afforded on lead, and despite his patience on the wall, Emilio expected his partners, even if they only seconded, to be efficient and predictable. The climbers remained equivocal about the reliability of the rope. Slocovich had fallen twice that day; once where it might have killed them all, and now, when there was no time to waste before darkness made climbing impossible. Emilio coached Slocovich the rest of the way, but he never climbed with him again.

They rappelled in the dark to a ledge in the Alta della Croda gully that separated the pillar they had climbed from the main peak of the Croda dei Toni. They crawled into Slocovich's three-man Zdarsky-style bivy bag. Emilio stretched his limbs out on the rock. He imagined enjoying a hot cup of tea and thought that the only thing that could have made everything perfect was the company of a girl he merely described as "his brunette."

On the wall, where bourgeois conventions of relations between the sexes had no sway, Emilio proved himself worthy of physical contact with a woman in an atavistic trial by stone, cold, gravity and altitude. The recollection of the woman was followed by a sense of well-being. Emilio fell asleep listening to his companions "speaking of many beautiful things... dreamed a little, and waited out the morning."[95]

The West Face of the Croda dei Toni was graded vi, and it was the last major Dolomites route Emilio would climb in 1930. He spent most of his other weekends in Val Rosandra or the Julian Alps. On average, the rest of his new climbs in 1930 were easier than the Croda dei Toni climb and few were of interest outside of the small circle of Julian Alps specialists.

With Trieste rock school alumnus Mario Cesca, he made the first total traverse of the Cengia degli Dei, a unique four-and-a-half-kilometre circumnavigation of the walls of the Jôf Fuart group. He made a new route on the Bricelik and early-winter ascents of the Grinta di Plezzo and Cridola; it was the itinerary of a climber who felt like he had already done enough that season to prove Italy's ascendancy in alpinism.

Emilio was still employed full-time at the Magazzini Generale. He loved Trieste, the Carso and the Julian Alps, but his love of climbing and the mountains forced him to reassess whether he truly belonged in his hometown.

Political changes Emilio supported in theory inconvenienced or disappointed the young climber in practice. Trieste's militarized ship and aviation industries expanded as Mussolini flexed his muscles in the Mediterranean. Overtime on weekends curbed Emilio's climbing.

Government support for climbing was copious but mostly ideological and propagandistic. The popular sports of cycling and football offered greater opportunities to sway the masses. The government invested in coaches for the Italian national football team, paid the players to train and built stadiums. Mussolini loved bicycle racing so much that his government held the races until it collapsed in 1943. In exchange for their vocal support of the regime, footballer Giuseppe

Meazza and cyclists Alfredo Binda and Learco Guerra were given the freedom to train and compete without the burden of regular work. Many famous cyclists had personal audiences with Mussolini, an honour enjoyed by few mountaineers, and one that would, in 1930, have thrilled Emilio.

Although the government's financial investment in mountaineering was almost negligible, it had no intention of leaving the climbing community to figure out its place in fascism. In September of 1931, CAI political leader Angelo Manaresi held a meeting in Bolzano and summoned 3,000 members to attend. Manaresi's speech to Italian climbers was published both in the newspapers and the *Rivista Mensile*. He exhorted climbers to stop bickering about climbing controversies and work together to build a virile, anti-aristocratic, striving sport rather than a comfortable outdoor pursuit for the middle-class and well-to-do. "We seek the union," said Manaresi, "on a single rope, of blackshirts, mountain guides and amateur climbers."[96] As a reward for their attendance, each CAI member was given a plastic figure of Mussolini, whom Manaresi called "the new Michelangelo in Rome."[97]

In 1931, Manaresi exhorted Italian climbers to catch up with the German Alpine Club with its "240,000 members, 440 sections, 625 huts... a terrible army of German-speaking mountaineers."[98] The solution to this threat, according to Rudatis and many others, was for Italians to redouble their efforts to climb at the highest levels. He explained the spiritual and political importance of the task in a series of instalments called "The Sport of Climbing" in *Fascist Sport* magazine.[99]

The Germans, however, had already lapped the Italians. In 1929, the northwest face of the Civetta was repeated not by Italians but by the German party of Leo Rittler and Willi Reiner. Five more German ascents followed in 1930. That year, Attilio Tissi and Alvise Andrich from Belluno made the first Italian ascent and set a new speed record for the wall, climbing it in a day without a bivouac. Germans had left a note for them in the summit register with the insult: "This [the northwest face of the Civetta] is no food for Italians."[100] The insult echoed the cry of the Austrian troops in the Great War: "Italians, turn back!" and became a rallying call for slighted, ambitious Italian climbers. Tissi said after he read the note that he could have climbed the face without any pitons. Such was his reputation for boldness that no one doubted him.

Invigorated by the German slight, Italian climbing slowly overcame its sense of inferiority. Brothers Angelo and Giuseppe Dimai from Cortina d'Ampezzo in the eastern Dolomites, nephews of the great guide Angelo Dimai, climbed harder every season. Renzo Videsott from Trento was strong on the rock. Ettore Castiglioni and Celso Gilberti accrued a list of grade v and vi first ascents in the eastern Dolomites.

In Lombardy, on the other side of Italy, a crew of talented, hard-working young climbers from Milan honed their skills on the lime-stone rock walls and pinnacles of the Grignetta, as the *Triestino*s had done in Val Rosandra. Alvise Andrich and Attilio Tissi joined this group on occasion, but the leading figures were Riccardo Cassin and Mary Gennaro from Milan. Inevitably, this group would transition to the big walls of the Dolomites.

Emilio's own nationalist ardour was strong. "We do not allow our-selves to be inferior to other climbers across the Alps," he wrote, "otherwise we will continue to be surpassed by them on our most ar-duous walls."[101] The "them" Emilio referred to were Germans.

On July 27, 1932, the mighty Emil Solleder, the greatest German climber of the late 1920s, died when his rappel anchor failed while he was guiding on the Meije in the Dauphiné Alps in France. It is an index of Italian disregard for German climbing, at least at the official level, that the obituary of the man who had brought grade vi to the Dolomites and made first ascents of the northwest face of the Civetta, the north face of the Furchetta and the east face of the Sass Maor war-ranted nothing more than a few lines in the *Rivista Mensile*. Looming in silent mockery over this petty, conspicuous disregard was the northwest face of the Civetta, an enduring monument to Solleder's German skill and bravery. For decades before the Eigerwand, the Walker Spur and even Everest were seen as the ultimate mountaineer-ing challenges, the northwest face of the Civetta was feared and de-sired by alpinists, and no Italians had conquered it by their own route.

A week after Solleder's death, Emilio and his oldest climbing friend,

Giulio Benedetti, went to the Coldai hut to repeat Solleder's climb. Emilio, ever conscious of the presence of the fallen, must have thought about Solleder as he looked at the wall, which soared to a summit that tore the clouds.

Emilio had visited the Coldai hut beneath the northwest face for the first time with Gino Razza in 1927. Razza had pointed out a potential new route to the left of the Solleder-Lettenbauer from the hut. In 1928, he had returned and half-heartedly attempted the Solleder-Lettenbauer, but retreated from low on the wall. "It was an experience," he wrote, "to which my will was unequal."[102]

The Dito di Dio, the Sorella di Mezzo, Riofreddo and dozens of other climbs had made Emilio one of the strongest big wall first ascensionists in Italy. "Although [Benedetti and I] were afraid to repeat the Solleder Route," he wrote, "we wanted to create an even more terrifying one."[103] There is some doubt, however, that Emilio had planned a harder route on the Civetta at all. From the Coldai hut, Razza's line looked more direct than the German climb, but from directly beneath the wall, it looked more diagonal. Emilio's plan to join the Solleder-Lettenbauer two thirds of the way up the wall was a deliberate attempt to ameliorate the severity of his climb with a traverse.

All of these deliberations, compromises and guesses at the best route led Emilio to the discovery of the aesthetic ideal of the *direttissima*, which came to be inseparable from his principles. Traditional route finding involved traversing back and forth on the rock to discover and link together cracks or the best series of handholds. Generations of climbers had prided themselves in avoiding dangerous or excessively difficult parts of the mountain to "find the route" or "unlock the problem" on a given objective. The *direttissima* climber let gravity decide on the line from the bottom of a climb and accepted traverses only as necessary compromises. Pitons, aid climbing and high-standard free climbing had given access to rock that climbers before the Great War considered impossible. The new tools, however, both increased the chances of success and potentially diminished the sense of adventure. By denying modern climbers the option of wandering the mountain for easy rock, the *direttissima* reconfigured the ethic of adventure for 20th-century climbers and elevated route finding from a skill to an ideal.

Like many revolutionaries, Emilio claimed his idea had a historical precedent. He revealed the unlikely source of his idea in a conversation with Benedetti that he later recounted in *Rivista Mensile*:

"You know, dear Giulio," he said, "that the ideal climbing route, the elegant route, follows 'the falling water drop.'"

"Where did you steal this beautiful sentence?" Benedetti asked.

"It's not mine, a famous English mountaineer said it."

"I traced a hypothetical line of a water drop," Emilio wrote, "that came down, down, down [the northwest face of the Civetta] and splashed on the talus. But here Giulio and I disagreed. I said that the water drop had fallen a little to the left, Giulio, more to the right, and he may have been right... But the beautiful line came to us at last, when we agreed where the drop had fallen."[104]

There are a few references to direct lines in British alpine literature prior to 1929, but none use the metaphor of the water drop.[105] In any case, Emilio knew that the quest to follow direct lines on rock walls started in Germany in the 1900s with Hans Dülfer, Otto Herzog and Hans Fiechtl. He was always reluctant, however, to credit Germans for anything.

Emilio could have invoked the plumb line, a strict and mechanical definition of verticality, but a water drop did not follow a plumb line. Water carved the winding caves of the Carso and the sinuous valley of Val Rosandra. Snowmelt streaked the faces of the Dolomites before it fell from the rock and was carried far away by the wind. Emilio and Benedetti argued about where a water drop from the summit of the Civetta would land, given the slope of the talus and the influence of the wind. They both agreed that the vertical line was just a starting point, an ideal, and that not everyone would appreciate their line.

"Someone will object," Emilio said, "'But you took almost three hours to do 150 metres and placed six pitons.' Here is how I make my case: look down. The line falls straight, therefore it is beautiful and elegant."[106]

The aesthetic of the direct line predated both fascism and the futurist aesthetics that pervaded European design between the wars, but the term *direttissima* was borrowed by climbers from the name of the direct Rome–Formia–Naples railway line that opened in 1927. A straight line expressed strength and velocity. The cover illustrators of the *Rivista Mensile* rendered the mountains as world of verticality, unbroken lines and geometric perfection akin to a cityscape of skyscrapers (Emilio measured the Civetta by skyscrapers; five skyscrapers, by his estimate).

The *direttissima* concept was a coeval and ideological cousin of the Germanic fascination with the *Nordwände*, or the great shadowed and ice-lined unclimbed north faces of the Alps. On a *Nordwand*, the worthiness of the race of the climbers was proven in a *Gesamtwerk* of rock and ice where death was as likely as it was on a battlefield. By comparison, Emilio said that direct routes on big walls in the Eastern Alps, which were mostly rock climbs, would not succumb to suffering or heroism alone but to the "most complex means imaginable." German writers described the *Nordwände* as titanic, colossal, forbidding, and even monstrous. Emilio, on the other hand, followed the water drop, and would not climb what he did not consider beautiful. Emilio was no stoic and wept at the news of tragedies in the mountains. Although a patriot and a soldier, Emilio never indulged in the comparisons between war and alpinism popular with German and British climbers.[107]

***

The most dangerous and technically demanding sections on the Comici-Benedetti route on the northwest face of the Civetta combined hard free and aid climbing on bad pitons in poor rock. Emilio described one pitch two-thirds of the way up the wall in detail.

> After having secured a piton in the bottom of the roof, [Benedetti] moves [up] and checks for loose rock at the lip of the roof with hammer blows. He stands up, but not to the point of losing balance, trying to place another piton as high as possible. After many hardships, he succeeds and clips a carabiner into it, and to this, he clips in one of the two ropes. Then he rises up to have that carabiner close to his belt, and is completely suspended from the piton. He then

looks for another crack, he finds it; another piton is placed. He takes the second rope, which is free, and clips it in. The friend below helps him by pulling the rope. And here he hangs from the second piton, with his body almost horizontal, parallel to the roof of the cave. Up and out he goes, placing another piton, he fastens the free rope and binds a stirrup-like cord into it for his foot. This way the body takes up a vertical position.[108]

Benedetti risked a 20-metre fall directly onto the belay, far enough to snap the doubled manila hawser. Even if the rope held, there was no guarantee that Emilio's belay piton would have been strong enough to withstand such a load. At this point, they were more than 300 metres from the ground and did not have enough pitons to rappel. Rescue from above was blocked by 300 metres of overhanging rock. There was no way out but up.

This was the big wall. Emilio and Benedetti had radically broken from the doctrine of never climbing up where you could not climb down. Their commitment to the wall, each other and Benedetti's chain of bad pitons was total. The philosophical ideal of the *sestogradiste* was total immersion into the experience of the wall. The psychological strain it inflicted on the climbers liberated new and unexplored energies. Emilio described a kind of synthesis between mind and body on the Civetta that he compared to the relationship between a driver and a sports car. The harder he pushed his body, the more it revealed its hidden capacities.

Emilio was generally protective of his friends and had a special concern for *Triestino* partners. He was relieved to take the lead on the next pitch and didn't relinquish it to Benedetti until they had climbed several more pitches of steep free climbing protected with poor pitons.

They were some 20 pitches off the talus when they reached the place they had intended to traverse right to the easier final section of the Solleder-Lettenbauer. When Emilio looked more carefully to his right, however, he saw that they had made a serious mistake. The horizontal weakness they had seen from the base was an illusion. Escape to the

Solleder-Lettenbauer was blocked by more than a hundred metres of blank, vertical rock.

They had no choice but to find a path through the overhangs they had originally planned to avoid. It was slow work, made more onerous by the thought that somewhere on the inhospitable wall they would have to find a bivouac site. Bivouacs en route were still mostly extemporaneous affairs to be avoided. Electric headlamps later lengthened the climbing day by many hours, but in the 1930s, climbers had to start at first light and stop climbing when darkness came. Sleeping bags, bivy bags, stoves and food were so heavy that they were rarely carried on hard climbs. On the cold, dark, high-altitude northwest wall of the Civetta, the temperatures fell below zero centigrade every night. Most climbers who spent a night out on the mountain anticipated hunger, cold and sleeplessness rather than rest.

After a few pitches they found a cave in the face formed by overhangs. They pulled their hoods over their heads, tucked their hands in their armpits and settled down for a long night.

The dawn revealed what few weaknesses there were in the serried overhangs of grey, smooth rock. In the night, their caster sugar, their only food, had poured out of its bag onto the wet rope and formed a hard crust that kinked it and made it almost unknottable. As Benedetti played out the frosted rope, Emilio climbed up to the roofs to reconnoitre the route and was so discouraged he retreated to the cave to warm up his hands and calm his nerves.

On Emilio's second attempt, Benedetti eked out the rope as he laboured overhead with outrageous pendulums anchored to pitons that he described as "giving us little [security] beyond being in the rock." It was a masterful piece of rock climbing. Riccardo Cassin described his attempt on the pitch during the second ascent in 1935:

> A long traverse led me to the spot where Comici's notes said "pitons with etriers." The overhang ahead was formidable. After great effort, I managed to clip in to a piton and hook in an etrier, then pull over the bulge using a vertical hold. To get myself over the entire overhang I had to leave an etrier, climb Dülfer style [i.e. with rope tension] and, with

my left hand, reach a small hold; hanging on with my right hand, I tested the hold: it seemed sound. Arching my arms and legs, I flung myself out and up, but suddenly the bloody hold collapsed. Because of my push-off I went into a spin, and because of the sudden somersault, my right hand could not hold me.[109]

Cassin's partner, Mario dell'Oro (nicknamed Boga), bandaged his heavily bleeding wound and they climbed on. Retreat was almost impossible from that point on the wall. It was one of the closest calls with death in Cassin's long and epic career.

After Emilio and Benedetti negotiated these trying pitches unscathed, they were relieved to find good cracks above. A steep chimney, another roof, a pendulum, and then they were at the belay for the last pitch of the Solleder-Lettenbauer.

The transition from the deadly, intricate world of the wall to the sunshine on the summit ridge was as sudden as it was invigorating. In the sunshine, safety and elation of victory, the frozen bivouac and dangerous climbing had all seemed in aid of the aesthetics of their route. They were amused, however, when they looked over the edge and saw that, in Emilio's words, "the water drop landed in the wrong place. We had imagined the water drop falling from the top of the wall, not the true summit, which was invisible from the bottom."[110]

The new route on the Civetta was graded VI by Emilio and Benedetti. Given the pair's experience in the Dolomites and Emilio's reputation, the claim was undisputed. Newspapers called it a heroic victory of national importance. Writers who knew little about climbing speculated that Comici and Benedetti's route was harder and more direct than the Solleder-Lettenbauer. Casara boasted to the CAI that Emilio's line was superior to Solleder's. The notion enraged Emilio.

"Don't say our route on the Civetta is more or less direct than Solleder's route," Emilio said. "This would enter into controversy I absolutely wish to avoid."[111]

This was the first time that Emilio's drive to do new routes led him into controversies, and the publicity frustrated him. He asked Casara, somewhat petulantly, not "to involuntarily drag [me] into alpine affairs which do not interest me, when I have no strength to fight against it and I don't feel like it."[112]

Emilio, however, could not simultaneously avoid controversies and also author spectacular new routes.[113] To Emilio's frustration, the press framed their praise of his routes in ways he thought either irrelevant or incorrect. For example, Solleder had used 15 pitons and free climbed his whole line. Comici and Benedetti had used three times that many pitons, with many for aid, and two pendulums. The Italian climbing press considered Emilio and Benedetti's route to be harder, more modern and sophisticated simply because they used more pitons.

Later writers saw a marked difference between the Civetta and Emilio's more aid-intensive ascents. British mountaineer Doug Scott wrote that the Civetta was a template for a less piton-dependent approach that Emilio forsook later for predominantly aid-climbing ascents.[114] Emilio, however, did not believe that he had used a specific style on the Civetta that differed from his other ascents.

After the ascent, Dino Buzzati pointed out to Emilio numerous unclimbed lines on the Civetta and the neighbouring peaks. Emilio, however, never returned to the Civetta. He gained less satisfaction from new routes on faces that had already been climbed. In the new grade VI idiom, a face could be home to several routes as climbers vied for harder or more direct climbs, but Emilio preferred to be the first on a wall and rarely added a new route, let alone one that partly followed an established line. It was one sure way to avoid the chances of obvious but misinformed comparisons between his climbs and those of others, but it also contributed to his reputation as the conqueror of the unclimbed, which brought with it its own challenges, rewards and scrutiny.

***

On January 6, 1931, after final warnings about the possible disadvantages by Kugy and Fabjan, Emilio left Trieste and followed his dream to become a mountain guide to the Dolomites.[115] What his family thought of the decision is unrecorded, but it must have been an emotional time for his mother, who had come to rely on Emilio emotionally and financially. He promised to continue to visit often and to regularly send money for the expenses at number six Via Bazzoni.

Winter was a good time for an aspiring mountain tourism professional to move to the mountains, since skiing was growing quickly in the Dolomites. Many resorts added their first rope tows in the late 1920s. Most local climbing guides became proficient at the sport to make money teaching Christiania turns and snowplows in the wintertime.

Emilio was a passable if not advanced skier. In 1929, he had his introduction to the sport, not in a resort, where he might have developed good technique, but on ski mountaineering tours, where endurance and safety were more important than elegance. Ski mountaineering in the 1930s involved wet and frozen clothing, avalanche danger, trail breaking in heavy wooden skis prone to breakage, cold leather boots, heavy rucksacks and few downhill thrills. For Emilio's first run at a resort, he threw himself down a steep, rocky hill and spent more time on his backside than his skis. Experienced skiers doubted that he would ever become an instructor.

The demand was high, however, and Emilio easily secured a position as a hotel ski instructor, although he was soon fired, presumably because of his lack of skill. The staff at the Hotel Sass Maor in San Martino di Castrozza were more understanding and gave him a second chance. By the time the snow melted, Emilio could make elegant Christiania and snowplow turns.

When the climbing season arrived and Emilio had to work as a mountain guide for the first time, earning a paycheque became more difficult. Government propaganda, which insinuated itself into climbing publications, encouraged urbanites to move to the mountains because life there was healthy, straightforward and inexpensive. Physical labour in the alpine regions had hardened the bodies and spirits of the *alpini*, who, in the national myth, had saved the nation. Honest labour in the mountains was a spiritual tonic powerful enough to improve the politics of communists.[116] The potential salutary effects of an alpine residency on an already upstanding party member and climbing star like Emilio could be expected to be practically limitless.

Most of this propaganda had been written by urbanite fascists, who knew little about the multilingual, complex, insular, Catholic and decidedly non-fascist native alpine communities. The new Italian fascist would take on the mountains on their own terms. Fascist camps and communities were planned to bring urbanites into nature and re-educate the genetically strong but ideologically weak alpine dwellers in the new Italian reality.

Emilio planned to become a mountain guide, a traditional rural career, developed and maintained by mountain natives whom the regime found suspicious. Before 1931, his experience of guiding was restricted to taking less skilled friends up easy alpine routes and teaching rock climbing in the controlled environment of Val Rosandra. He was the star of a cohesive body of *Triestino* climbers. Among them were many female climbers whose first names fill Emilio's diaries, and not only on climbing days.[117] By the early 1930s, Trieste was home to more women who could lead grade VI than almost anywhere in Europe. Bruna Bernardini, Fernanda Brovedani, Amalia Zuani Bornettini, Edvige Muschi and Germana Ucosich were a few of the women who shared Emilio's passion for rock.[118] Some, like Fernanda Brovedani, who was married to Emilio's friend Osiride Brovedani, were unavailable, but many, like Emilio, were single. The climbers of Trieste of either sex delighted to accompany Emilio on any project he chose on holidays and weekends, regardless of all-night drives, hikes, wet bivouacs and terrifying climbing.

The climbing school was so successful that Manaresi visited Emilio and went on an excursion to Val Rosandra. In April of 1932, Emilio was received, at the Castello di Miramare in Trieste, by Prince Amedeo, the new Duke of Aosta, the highest-ranking Italian official who ever recognized his climbing achievements. These were the honours Emilio had always wanted, but he sensed that the scene in Trieste had plateaued. While he taught locals how to climb 15-metre-high crags, the mountain guides in the Dolomites hosted film starlets, royalty and political celebrities of the first rank. Crucially, they were free to take their days off not to train in Val Rosandra but, Emilio believed, to explore new alpine routes.

Emilio left the Trieste scene for the world ruled by hoary patriarchs with their pipes and moustaches and tough young men in farmer's clothes he had met plodding ahead of their clients. For now, he did not realize that their lives were as far from a day cragging at Val Rosandra followed by an evening in the smart bars of Trieste as alpine goat farming was from working in the Magazzini Generali.

For centuries, intrepid peasants had guided outsiders through the Dolomites for extra income. As mountaineering developed into a sport, guiding became a trade, and therefore, in the old-fashioned mindset of the peasants, a vocation. Occasionally, a guide might cultivate a rich client who would indulge his family with a modicum of upward social mobility. Guiding, however, remained a lower-class pursuit. When the Austrian government sanctioned guiding in 1865, they imagined it as a dangerous service position suited to uneducated men from poor alpine regions.

The client, not the guide, was the "Herr," or "sir." The bourgeois climber Paul Preuss had declined to become a mountain guide, despite his skills and need for employment, because the trade was below his social status. Even the fascist government endorsed a geographical determinism that served the idea that alpine guides came from alpine regions with its claim that mountain-bred Italians were a stronger, heartier, if less intelligent breed than other Italians.[119]

Cortina, Emilio's first home in the mountains, lined both sides of a deep alpine valley. The rock walls of the Tofane, Pomagagnon, Cristallo and dozens of other legendary Dolomite peaks looked down on the town. The valley was divided by Catholic parishes that ministered to a population still mostly employed in ancient forms of alpine farming that kept them exhausted and, in bad years, on the verge of malnutrition. Guiding was a vocation closely related to alpine herding and dating, in one form or another, from the 15th century.

The modern guiding business in Cortina began in 1863, when Austrian Paul Grohmann hired Francesco Lacedelli to guide him on the Tofana di Mezzo. In the last half of the 19th century, new hotels that catered to visitors of all budgets opened their doors. As news of the beauty of the area spread, tourists, sportsmen, intellectuals, chamois hunters, artists, cranks and writers poured into towns like Cortina, Selva di Cadore and Bolzano. Ambitious, hungry young men from the surrounding parishes offered the visitors their services as guides.

Guiding in Cortina, however, was less lucrative than in the Western Alpine towns of Grindelwald, Zermatt, Courmayeur and Chamonix, which tourists associated with famous peaks like the Eiger, the Matterhorn and Mont-Blanc. Although Cortina's Antelao, Pelmo, Pomagagnon and Cristallo were spectacular peaks, climbing them conferred few bragging rights in the salons of London and Leipzig. To further dampen the enthusiasm of potential visitors, climbing in the Dolomites only attracted climbers unfazed by its exotic reputation as the haunt of daredevil rock gymnasts.[120]

Family dynasties of mountain guides protected the limited client resource. The Dimais, Menardis, Constantinis and Ghedinas were large Catholic families. Guide Luigi Rizzi had 12 children; Angelo Dibona had 6. By the 1930s, these families dominated guiding in Cortina. They accrued generations of climbing experience, the benefits of which were handed down in lore. Skills were held to be bred in the bone. Although a few of these men, like Agostino Verzi and Angelo Dibona, became well-known climbers in their own right, to the Cortinesi, no amount of practice at crags like Val Rosandra could replace growing up in the shadows of the Dolomites.

Most guides were ethnic Italians. Cortina had been under Austrian rule until the end of the Great War, but it remained predominantly Italian. The Austrians had ruled Cortina without mercy. In the Great War, 650 men from the valley had been drafted and sent to the Russian Front. Few returned. Cortina changed hands twice during the Great War, and its citizens were forced, on pain of execution, to defend the town against the Italian army.

Despite the evidence to the contrary, fascists suspected that the Cortinesi had collaborated with the Austrians. Thus, Angelo Dibona, one of the best Italian climbers in the first two decades of the 1900s, along with many of the other locals, was routinely excluded from honours and recognition by the fascist government.

Unlike *Triestino* Italians, the Cortinesi had greeted fascist rule from

Rome with indifference. The Cortinesi spoke Ampezzano, an Italian dialect, and the ancient language of Ladin. Their loyalties were to parishes, valleys and their market town, not to a distant nation-state. A guide, like a woodsman, farmer, miller or priest, hewed close to family, land, the rhythms of the alpine seasons and the church. They saw superstition as a lesser vice than modernity. Although Emilio believed in the influence of the dead on his climbs, the manifestations of their presence were mostly psychological. Among the Cortinesi, distinctly unmodern superstitions abounded, from the jewel-studded skeleton of St. Liberalis permanently on view in the basilica, to the fragment of a dead client's bone Luigi Rizzi carried as penance for not insisting that the unfortunate man accept a rope on a steep step.[121]

The guides of the Eastern Alps were, however, in their own way, long-sighted. They competed with each other for business but also depended upon each other in times of scarcity, emergency or tragedy. Ancient and complex rituals, traditions of apprenticeship and intermarriage linked guides across mountain ranges, family lines and generations.

The mountain people had survived their harsh environment for centuries through a combination of controlled competition and cooperation. Guides, likewise, depended on a deliberately forged web of relationships. Jean-Joseph Carrel, of the famous guiding family of Cheneil, mentored Joseph Pellissier of Breil di Valtournenche, as well as his own son, Luigi. Luigi, in turn, mentored Pellissier's son. Oliviero Gasperi was the godfather of Dolomites guide Camillo Giussani. After they had climbed with Emilio, several of his clients reverted to traditional guides like Pellissier and Gasperi. In the eyes of clients, there was much more to *la cosa vera*, the real thing, than being good at climbing.

Climbing credentials alone were insufficient credentials to penetrate alpine guiding cadres. Emilio, however, was an outsider and a fascist who lacked the Catholic convictions and sentimentalism about rural life that might have gained him some acceptance. It annoyed and frustrated him that guides were often uninterested in hard, amateur climbs. Emilio had hoped to do many new routes when he moved to the mountains, but his potential partners viewed his eagerness with suspicion. Most guides attended to religious, domestic, familial or agricultural chores on their days off, rather than chasing after new routes.

Outsiders who had become guides had shown more interest in the local Cortina scene than Emilio. Raffaele "Biri" Carlesso came from Costa di Rovigo, as far from the Dolomites as Trieste. Like Emilio, he was a fine climber. Biri earned his nickname by climbing so quickly that he reminded his partners of the Chiribiri racing car. He was, however, a practising Catholic trained in the ancient wool trade and could converse with Cortina's wool farmers. Like the guides, he valued modesty and rarely published his new routes. He kept no climbing diary.

An episode at the Longeres hut that involved Carlesso illustrates Emilio's insensitivity to guiding's codes of competition and community as well as his naivety about the power of gossip. A former client of Carlesso's complained to Emilio that Carlesso had taken a long time to guide his party up the Cima Piccola. Emilio responded that Carlesso should have hired more guides to help him. To question or insult Carlesso's guiding skills in front of a client was a serious breach of guiding etiquette that might not have occurred if Emilio had been a local steeped in guiding tradition.

Carlesso was furious when he heard the story. Instead of apologizing, Emilio claimed that he had meant no insult. He said that he always spoke well of people, "even when they don't deserve it," and that he thought so well of Carlesso as a guide that he had recommended him to his own clients.[122] Emilio's relationship with Carlesso, however, never fully recovered.

Emilio represented a new kind of threat to the local guides, unmitigated by faith or modesty. He was a fascist and a believer in progress, and he lacked respect for traditions, least of all in climbing. Emilio had taught climbing in Val Rosandra not as an arcane trade but as a recreational skill set, like tennis. The guides feared that he would steal potential clients from the city who knew him through the newspapers. Emilio was, of course, as famous as ever in the mind of the climbing readership of the *Rivista Mensile*, in which he continued to write. His best clients were amateur climbers who were ambitious and rich enough to chase their alpine dreams with celebrity guides. The Cortinesi guides did not realize that this was a small market, but in any case, there was no sign at this point that Emilio would share whatever good fortune came his way.

The guides privately decided not to include Emilio's budding guiding business in their circle. Rumours and innuendoes flourished on both sides of the stand-off. In Emilio's first winter in Cortina, his equipment hut caught fire and he lost much of his skiing and rock climbing equipment. The suspicion of arson said as much about how bad relations were between Emilio and the local guides as it did about the actual cause of the fire.

Despite his differences with the Cortinesi guides, Emilio was wounded when they rejected him. In Trieste, the traditions of hospitality required that strangers be honoured and assisted. In the mountains, he expected the same, and did not understand that the guides saw him as a threat. Vittorio Varale compared Emilio to the character Ivanhoe in Walter Scott's eponymous novel about a medieval nobleman who is dispossessed of what should have been his. Emilio continued to feel like his success as a guide was thwarted by the Cortinesi, success which should have been his by right as a superb climber.[123]

Paradoxically, Emilio's sense of hospitality left him vulnerable to the needs of his competitors when they were in financial trouble. One night at a dance in the Savoie Hotel in Misurina, a friend called Emilio off the dance floor. The police, who were more willing to help out a party loyalist like Emilio than the Cortinesi guides, had apprehended two guides from Sexten who had solicited clients in Emilio's territory. Emilio, however, told the police to release them. Despite his own lack of clients, he had given them permission to guide in his area because they were good men and there was little work in Sexten.

The national reputation that the local guides thought would make Emilio an unbeatable competitor turned out to be a liability. Potential clients respected his reputation as a hard climber but worried about whether they could keep up if they hired him. Would he take them on an overly difficult climb? What if they failed or climbed poorly when roped up with the great Emilio Comici? Would they need to learn new skills when they were used to the guide tying them to the rope and pointing out holds? It annoyed Emilio that more amateurs approached him for an autograph or photo than to hire him as their guide.[124]

Many of Emilio's clients blurred the line between friend and client. Well-off friends like Emmy Hartwich-Brioschi and Severino Casara could afford to pay Emilio, but when Emilio had invited them himself, as he often did, it seemed rude to him to ask them for payment. In photographs of Emilio from this period, he sits shirtless in the sun, entertaining clients with his guitar. The Cortinesi guides rarely allowed their photograph to be taken with clients, and when they did, more often than not, they were standing upright and uphill from the client with an expression that suggested that they were not given to lighter moments under any circumstances. Local guides were not burdened by the awkwardness of charging their friends, or even people from their own villages or regions, for their services. Geographic, cultural and class differences helped to formalize transactions between guides and clients.

Casara had reason to identify himself not as Emilio's client but as his friend and climbing partner. In 1931, the academy of the CAI was ordered by Manaresi to rule on whether Casara had soloed the first ascent of the north face of the Campanile di Val Montanaia.[125] Their ruling, the so-called Lodi di Bolzano, acquitted Casara due to a lack of evidence to the contrary, a decision generally interpreted as a finding of guilt. Casara resigned from the academy of the CAI a month later. His best remaining shred of credibility was his association with Emilio.

Emilio's embarrassment about the commercial nature of the guide-client relationship kept him from asking even his richest client, Europe's top mountaineering aristocrat, King Leopold of Belgium, for his pay. When clients looked for Emilio the day after their climb in order to pay him, he was often nowhere to be found. Emilio's one exception to socializing only with city friends or urbanites who had moved to the mountains almost cost him Leopold's patronage.

The youth leaders of the XXX Ottobre had changed Emilio's life, and he felt obligated to show his gratitude by teaching curious but penniless youngsters how to climb. When Emilio was guiding Leopold III, he learned that a boy whom he had promised to take climbing had taken a rope and headed for the Guglia Edmondo De Amicis, a pinnacle usually accessed by a Tyrolean traverse. Emilio chased after the boy, stopped him before he made it to the pinnacle, climbed a pitch with him and rushed back to his royal client. Leopold must have been surprised by the length of his guide's absence, and likely unconvinced by Emilio's excuse that he had forgotten his camera and gone to retrieve it.[126]

***

In 1932, Emilio lost his patience with the hostile Cortinesi guides and moved 15 kilometres northeast, to Lake Misurina. The massive rock walls of the Sorapiss, reflected in the shallow lake, enticed mountaineers from throughout Italy. The view was also a fine advertisement for Emilio's skills: his routes on the Dito di Dio and the Sorella di Mezzo were visible on any clear day. Other famous objectives, like Monte Cristallo and the Tre Cime di Lavaredo, were close at hand. The Cima del Cadin was a fine peak for short rock climbs, and hiking opportunities were unlimited. In winter, skiers came to fledgling resorts like Col de Varda. Most importantly, in Misurina there were no mountain guides.

The lake's first modern visitors were respiratory disease patients who summered in the sanatoriums, hoping to be cured by the clean air 1754 metres above sea level. By 1930, the area had become popular with alpine tourists. Smaller hotels offered inexpensive lodgings, and the woods around the village provided unlimited potential for campers, but the centrepieces of Lake Misurina were the big, glamorous hotels.

Misurina was off the railway line and main highway, and clients had to travel there from Cortina by car. Emilio's main contacts there were tourists from the city, and a handful of artists, doctors, musicians and lawyers who had moved to the mountains.

Emilio was more comfortable in the ballroom of the Hotel Savoie in Misurina on a Saturday evening than in the humble Cortina bars where his guiding rivals drank beer. Handsome and elegant in his tuxedo, he whirled across the floors with the well-to-do ladies of Venice and Milan, whose jewelry sparkled in the light of the chandeliers.

Through the art-nouveau window frames, he could catch glimpses, mid-waltz, of the moonlit rock walls and glaciers of the Sorapiss.

On Sunday mornings when there were no clients, the weather was bad or the season had ended, Emilio's competitors heard mass in Cortina at the church of Madonna della Difesa (Our Lady of Protection). The church was built in the 15th century to commemorate the Ampezzanos' miraculous defence of Cortina from marauding outsiders, an incident of which the townspeople remained proud 400 years later. While the guiding clans prayed for more clients and the defence of their trade, their families and their lives when they climbed, Emilio took a lounge chair on a hotel patio, drank coffee and read the newspaper – two of the few luxuries he could afford.

Emilio survived partly off money his mother sent him, a gift that embarrassed him but came with the blessing of the most important counsellors in his life. On his own climbing trips, he stayed in the cheapest rooms in huts, and when he could afford to eat in their dining rooms, he ordered plain pasta and slipped in pieces of sausage or cheese from his pockets.

Without climbing, the mountains could not hold Emilio. He did not solo, nor did he enjoy hiking, even to climbs, let alone for its own sake. When there was neither work nor climbing partners, Emilio hopped on his motorcycle and went home to his parents' house in Trieste.

He extended his visits to Trieste for weeks if there were no clients in Misurina. And yet, despite his love of Trieste and the comfort of his parents' home on Via Bazzoni, the city disposed him to depression and lethargy.

In Trieste, he wrote reports on his climbs, fretted about climbing projects and his reputation in the press or met with friends. Often enough, he did not even bring climbing equipment with him, but he would sometimes take work at the rock school in Val Rosandra or, less often, launch out on climbing trips to the Julian Alps.

Emilio was not the only mountaineer whose heart was tied to both the mountains and his seaport home. Kugy, who was well into his 70s, was no longer an active climber, but he was still an active citizen of Trieste. Although Kugy's political embarrassment as a Slavic former

Austrian imperialist forced him to the fringes of the new Italy, he remained Trieste's most eminent living mountaineer.

Despite his differences with Kugy over climbing style, Emilio paid him a visit to ask for help with finding guiding clients. Kugy would not have been surprised that his prediction that Emilio would struggle to make ends meet as a mountain guide had come true. Nonetheless, he was no longer in touch with many climbers in need of a guide, and most of his own partners were either too old to climb or dead. He did, however, arrange a meeting between Emilio and his cousin Anna Escher, a *Triestina*, a climbing fanatic and a woman of means.

Escher was a member of the wealthy Glanzmann clan, but she usually dressed in plain sports clothes and avoided any appearance of wealth. She was suntanned, fit, attractive and had a big smile and a mane of naturally curly blonde hair that she occasionally cropped down to a couple of inches. Unlike the diminutive Emmy Hartwich-Brioschi, she was taller than Emilio.

Anna had grown up a couple of blocks from Emilio in the palatial Villa Bazzoni at the corner of Via Bazzoni and Via dei Navali. The Glanzmanns were a dynasty of self-made merchants from Savoy who had moved to Trieste in the early 19th century. No Glanzmanns worked as labourers in the docks or shipyards. Their children, like Anna, grew up in their world of coffered libraries, tutors and private gardens.

Anna was six years older than Emilio. She had been preceded by three sisters who died infancy, and on the recommendation of a friend, her mother named her after St. Anne, the mother of the Virgin Mary and the patron saint of women in labour. It was an auspicious choice: four healthy siblings followed Anna into the world.

Anna's mother was a patron of the poets, writers and musicians who frequented Via Bazzoni. Anna, however, was indifferent to high culture. Her favourite time of year was the summer vacation in the Swiss Alps, where she had been introduced to climbing by her cousin Julius.[127]

Anna found her future husband in Switzerland. Waldo Charles von Escher was a merchant from Zurich, but his business was based in

Alexandria. Escher was, by training, an engineer, but in the early 30s, he became a consul of the Norwegian government in Alexandria.

Life in Anna and Waldo's house on Rue Ross in the beachfront expat enclave of Saba Pasha was comfortable, but Anna felt restless and isolated. The Eschers belonged to the Royal Automobile Club of Egypt along with stars of desert exploration like Hungarian László Almásy and British major Ralph Bagnold. Anna made a few motor trips to the desert, but she missed the cold and rocky world from which she was exiled. She kept in touch with alpinism through publications like the *Rivista Mensile*, where she read all about Emilio's climbs. The passenger ships of the Lloyd Triestino line took five days to reach Trieste, so trips home were infrequent. After her sons Cyril and Paul were born, however, Anna made protracted summer pilgrimages to the Alps via her family home in Trieste. Usually, Waldo stayed in Alexandria during Anna's vacations, but when her boys were older, she occasionally brought them to the mountains with her.

In the Alps, Anna patronized the best guides and soon learned that there was a whole world of climbing in which her cousin Julius, with his alpenstock and botany kit, had little interest. She was a natural rock climber who was a quick study with the pitons and carabiners her cousin eschewed. In 1925, with guide Angelo Dibona, she made the first ascent of a route that climbed much of the steep north face of Jôf di Montasio in the Julian Alps.

Anna got along well with the traditional guides, but when she met Emilio, she found a *paesano* who needed her emotional and financial patronage as much as the sad poets of the Palazzo Bazzoni relied on her mother's help. Also, Emilio was a handsome young man whose melancholy face in the newspapers contrasted with his enthusiasm for climbing, balletic technique and victories over the hardest climbs in the Alps. Emilio was an unconventional guide who was willing to make friends with his clients. Anna's isolation was geographic and literal, Emilio's was internal and spiritual, but they turned out to be complementary.

From the start, Anna's relationship with Emilio was proprietorial. When Anna was ready to climb or ski, whether it was in the Middle East, Spain or anywhere in the Alps, Emilio simply understood that he would show up, even if he had to cancel other plans. Without complaint, he catered to the needs of whomever else she brought along from her impressive circle of climbing friends and relatives. The arrangement worked well for patron and guide alike.

Anna and Emilio made their first trip together in spring of 1933. Their destination was the rock pinnacles and walls of the Grignetta, near Lecco, above the shores of Lake Como on the opposite side of northern Italy from Trieste. The climbs of the Grignetta were up to 150 metres high – much smaller than the Dolomites, but three times as long as most routes in Val Rosandra.

Emilio had been invited to the area by Mary Varale, who now climbed with a talented and ambitious crew of working-class climbers from the Milan area. Trieste had a population of about 200,000, but the population of Milan, the second-biggest city in Italy, was more than a million. The Grignetta was close enough to Milan that in some places, the city lights were visible at night.

Climbing standards in the Grignetta, however, lagged behind Val Rosandra. When Emilio was not guiding Anna, he demonstrated his advanced piton and aid techniques to a group of strong but unknown young climbers that included Riccardo Cassin, Giulio and Nino Bartesaghi, Mario Spreafico, Vittorio Ratti, Gigino Amati, Antonio Piloni, and Mario "Boga" dell'Oro.

Cassin, Mary Varale and a half dozen others in patched factory workwear and gymnastics gear watched as Emilio Comici tied the rope around the waist of his clean and fashionable climbing shirt. He looked just like he did in the newspapers. Above him rose the smooth, 80-metre-high, ledgeless unclimbed north wall of the Corno del Nibbio, one of the last unclimbed problems of the Grignetta. The only possible line was an overhanging thin crack.

Twenty-four-year-old Cassin was a blacksmith and a boxer and looked it, with his bull head, thin hair and crooked nose. Stripped down to his undershirt in the hot sun, he squinted and made mental notes about how Emilio organized his pitons and carabiners.

Emilio stepped off the ground and climbed some free moves with the elegance of a spider before he pounded in his first piton with the hammer in one hand. With double rope tension, Emilio gracefully proceeded up a problem that Cassin and his friends had not even known how to attempt.

On the same trip, Emilio climbed with Varale for the first time. She was a short, powerful climber with the prominent facial features of an opera diva. Her skill and determination were as well known as her self-confidence. Varale was proud of being a strong woman climber and wore a scarlet climbing jacket so that she would be visible high on a rock wall. Cassin described her as "an exceptional companion, alert, ready and utterly trustworthy."[128] Cassin also recalled that she kissed her male climbing partners after a climb.

With Emilio, Varale and Grignetta locals Spreafico and dell'Oro, Cassin led the first ascent of the west face of the Zuccone di Campelli, one of the biggest faces in the Grignetta. Emilio, however, only felt that he could claim a first ascent when he led the crux pitches. Before he left the Grignetta, he tried to make the first ascent of the so-called Lictor Route on the Torre Costanza. The climb drew its name from the statue of a fascist *lictor*, a stylized bundle of sticks lashed to an axe, that zealous fascists had erected on the tower's summit. Varale belayed and shared her knowledge of the proposed route. Augusto Corti came third. On the crux thin crack, Emilio tore out a piton and fell five metres. It was not a long fall, but he injured his arm badly enough so that he had to abandon the attempt.

After a few days in Misurina, it was obvious that Emilio's injury needed longer to heal before he resumed serious climbing. He withdrew to Trieste, his mother and the family home to rest and nurse his arm.

"I will stay about ten days in Trieste," he wrote Casara, "and I hope to cure myself while doing nothing. But it will be difficult..."[129]

In Trieste, Emilio was struck by the ailment he simply described as "something worse," likely the depression that hounded him throughout his life.[130] The physiological sources of depression had not yet been discovered, and the disease was still stigmatized as a sign of unmanly mental weakness. Sometimes Emilio could block out the feelings of depression, if not the condition itself, with a demanding first ascent. When he could not climb, the symptoms of social withdrawal and sadness became worse. He vacillated between blaming the climbing weather, the press and the guiding business for his malaise. If anything, his occasional attempts to distract himself by writing for climbing journals or going out with young women from the GARS increased his frustration.

A month after he left Misurina, Emilio remained in Trieste. A combination of rest, the spring sunshine and news in the alpine papers, however, stirred his desire to return to the Dolomites. The crew in the Grignetta had already put what they had learned from Emilio last season to good use. Cassin had completed a new route on the north face of the Corno del Nibbio that was harder than Emilio's and then climbed the route on the Torre Costanza that had taken Emilio out of commission and added another, even harder climb beside it.[131]

Emilio admired other Italian climbers' skills, whether they were from Milan or Trieste, and had no projects on the relatively short climbs of the Grignetta. He was, however, aware that the revolution in Italian climbing in which he had played a pivotal role had begun to catch on elsewhere. In addition to his Trieste group and the Milanese, there was the guide Bruno Detassis, expert amateur Ettore Castiglioni, Gino Soldà, Raffaele Carlesso, Gian Battista "Hans" Vinatzer and a dozen other Italian climbers who would inevitably turn their attention to the remaining great challenges of the Dolomites. The thought vexed Emilio, because as the glory of Emilio's greatest climbs wore off, he came to believe that there were a finite number of truly great Dolomite routes left unclimbed, and he intended to continue to add to his legacy.

In Trieste, in the spring of 1933, he made plans to take on a climbing goal that was bigger than the Civetta, something that would renew his enthusiasm. As Emilio well knew, there was one wall in particular in the Italian mountains that towered above all the others in prestige, height and difficulty: the north face of the Cima Grande, the tallest face of the gigantic stone pillars of the Tre Cime di Lavaredo.

CHAPTER FIVE

NEMESIS

The Tre Cime di Lavaredo are a trio of massive adjacent peaks near Misurina. Their summits can only be reached by technical climbing, and all of the peaks have steep north faces. The first ascent of the highest, central peak, the Cima Grande, on August 21, 1869, by Paul Grohmann, founder of the Austrian Alpine Club, and guides Franz Innerkofler and Peter Salcher, marked the beginning of the age of technical Dolomites climbing. The lower two peaks, the Cima Piccola (also known as the Anticima) and the Cima Ovest, first climbed in 1879 and 1881 respectively, were major climbing objectives in their own right. The first route up the complex topography of the north face of the Cima Piccola was climbed in 1890 by Sepp Innerkofler. Preuss had climbed the Preuss Chimney on the Cima Piccolissima, a pinnacle in the Cima Piccola massif in 1911; Dülfer had climbed the Dülfer Chimney on the west face of the Cima Grande in 1913. Both routes were V+ and among the hardest of their day, but by the early 1930s, the north faces of the Cima Grande and Cima Ovest remained unclimbed.

There was nothing anywhere in the Dolomites to compare in beauty and verticality to the 550-metre-high north wall of the Cima Grande di Lavaredo. Even the more overhanging but slightly lower 500-metre-high north face of the Cima Ovest looked less impressive than its neighbour.

The permanently shadowed north wall of the Cima Grande began with a broad yellow-and-white bald spot in the lower part of the wall, which was so steep that water never touched it. The vertical, black-streaked upper reaches of the face were broken by a single ledge big enough for two climbers to bivouac. In all, the face overhung 30 metres from base to summit.

The redoubtable mountaineering writer Dino Buzzati was agog at the sight of what he called "the most audacious wall in the Dolomites, with a sharp overhang at its base, then it straightens up, like fir trees are bent at the base, then upright as candles. It overhangs for hundreds and hundreds of metres."[132]

On the lower half, it appeared uncertain that there would even be sufficient piton cracks to make any progress on the steepest sections. It was the biggest, hardest, most intimidating pure rock route to a summit in the Alps that was within the comprehension of the climbers of the 1930s, the ultimate test of rock climbing prowess and commitment on Italian limestone, potentially the greatest rock climb ever made, a breathtaking prize for whoever claimed it.

It was also the only Italian wall on the roster of great unclimbed north faces of the Alps that then preoccupied the climbers of Europe.

***

The golden age of alpinism, when mountaineers vied for the first ascents of Europe's highest peaks, started in 1854 with the first ascent of Switzerland's Wetterhorn, and ended in 1865, when the Matterhorn was finally climbed. The silver age followed, in which less well known, harder and sometimes unnamed peaks were climbed. The silver age ended with W.W. Graham's ascent of the Dent du Géant in 1882. After 1882, many British climbers considered the Alps climbed out and turned their attention to expeditions in the far ranges of North and South America and Asia. Expeditionary climbing was born.

Another age of climbing, largely ignored or derided by British climbers, started in the Eastern Alps, where many of the most impressive peaks remained unclimbed because they were lower and much steeper than the mountains of the Western Alps.

The introduction of the carabiner and the Fiechtl eyelet piton to accommodate it, and fierce disputes about climbing style, fuelled the next period of rock climbing. The first ascents of the Campanile Basso (1899), the Campanile di Val Montanaia (1902), Torre Venezia (1909), Torre Trieste (1910) and Aiguille Dibona (1913) were tours de force in an era of steep, hard, dangerous and gymnastic climbs. Climbing activity in the Alps was sporadic during the Great War. When Emilio began to climb in the 1920s, a creative new generation of climbers were eager to prove themselves on the highest, most challenging and most beautiful unclimbed walls of the Alps. The symbol of their aspirations became the list of the so-called seven great north faces, the *Nordwände*, of the Cima Grande in the Dolomites, the Petit Dru and Grandes Jorasses in France's Mont-Blanc range, and in Switzerland, the Piz Badile in the Bregaglia range, the Eiger in the Bernese Alps and the Matterhorn in the Pennine Alps.

In August 1931, Munich brothers Franz and Toni Schmid made the first successful ascent of the dark and cold north face of the Matterhorn. The brothers had spent much of their youths at the Munich *Klettergarten* of Buchenhain and were more technical wizards than seasoned alpinists. But after cycling to Zermatt, they climbed the route on their first try even though they made the summit in a storm. The ascent confirmed the suspicion of many: technical mastery, elan and a few pitons and carabiners trumped everything else.

The ascent was reported around the world. After Toni fell to his death from the Grosses Wiesbachhorn in Austria in 1932, Franz accepted a gold medal for the Matterhorn climb at the 1932 Los Angeles Olympics on behalf of himself and his fallen brother. He later played himself in a film about the first ascent of the first great north wall.

Some climbers took the Matterhorn *Nordwand* affair as a warning against extreme climbing to come. British critics tended to exaggerate the role of hardware on hard continental climbs and lamented that the Continental pursuit of the walls would lead to the technologization of climbing. In the golden age of alpinism, when British climbers dominated the alpine scene, such techniques were unknown. To British writer Frank Smythe, the technologization of climbing through the use of "an assortment of pitons and carabiner [*sic*]" was not associated with an excess of safety but with a philosophy of "'live dangerously,' and 'my life for a climb.'"[133] Some British and American climbers even associated the use of pitons with the rise of fascism, although their use in numbers started before the Great War. The objection to hard climbing in the Eastern Alps, from which British and American climbers were more or less absent, is summarized in the review of Rudatis's *Das letzte im Fels* in the *American Alpine Journal*:

There have always been those who, for good or bad reasons, wished to grade climbs according to their difficulty. And, although the scale has undergone considerable alteration in the past ten years, peaks are usually divided into six groups, in which the first is the only one not requiring Kletterschuhe, and the last, in its conclusion, is best represented by a one-way ticket to the cemetery. According to the author, in the third grade "the best climbers may go without assistance, but it is better not to. Almost all descents by roping-off. Nailed boots practically excluded. This grade, fifty years ago represented the limit of possibility as, for example, in the Schmitt chimney of the Fünffingerspitze." More than half of the book is then taken up by examples of sixth-grade acrobatics in the Civetta Group. While such a method of gradation is doubtless an attempt to establish a standard, it will, in the opinion of this reviewer, always fail, since the many variable factors remain uncontrolled. Second grade may become sixth grade when a storm breaks, or seem so merely as the result of dietary indiscretion. And what will the author think of sixth grade, one day when a tractor with suctiongrips, loaded with first-grade climbers, comes steaming past him, as he blacksmiths his way up walls that once were best left alone?[134]

On the Continent, a few writers pointed to the ideal of Paul Preuss, who encouraged climbers to rely on themselves, not their equipment. Others pined for the simplicity of the late 19th century. Kugy and the aging veterans of the days of Victorian clubmen unaverse to the occasional day spent forsaking the rocks for botanizing warned that the dangerous rush to harder and harder routes distracted mountaineers from climbing's simple joys.

On both sides of the Channel, a few writers dared to object that the *Nordwand* propaganda would lead youthful climbers to their destruction in pursuit of fame. Emilio and other sixth-grade climbers were unconcerned. They had redefined climbing precisely as the pursuit of difficulty and were willing, if necessary, to pay for their conquests with their lives.

By 1933, only two out of seven of the great north walls had even been attempted. Besides the Matterhorn, the north face of the Walker Spur on the Grandes Jorasses, a remote, high-altitude granite wall, had been attempted in 1929 by a French party led by the famous Chamonix guide Armand Charlet. In 1931, three German parties – the Schmid brothers; Anderl Heckmair and Gustl Kroner; and finally, Leo Rittler and Hans Brehm tried the face. Rittler and Brehm lost their lives in their attempt.

The north face of the Cima Grande lacked the ice, glaciers and snow of the other great north walls. On the northwest face of the Civetta, escape to another route had been contemplated. On the other north faces there were lower-angle sections of climbing. The Cima Grande's unbroken verticality and lack of crack systems gave no respite from the exposure.

The first reconnaissance on the north face of the Cima Grande was made by German guide Hans Steger and his girlfriend, Paula Wiesinger, the first woman to climb grade VI in the Dolomites. They rappelled after a mere 60 metres.

Climbers rejected the idea that the Cima Grande's north wall was impossible, and the face saw more attempts than any of the other north faces. Attilio Tissi of Cassin's circle, Cortina guide Angelo Dimai, Raffaele Carlesso and Austrian rock ace Sepp Schintermeister all tried to push the route beyond Steger's high-point, but only managed a few more metres of the wall.

The Tre Cime were close to Misurina, and Emilio knew all of the existing routes and possible new lines. From the first time he saw the north Face of the Cima Grande, in 1925, he had dreamed of climbing it.[135] By 1932, the wall was so famous that climbers attempted it just for the temporary fame of being the party that had raised the high-point by a few metres. Five attempts had been made before Emilio tried the wall in 1932 with *Triestino* Renato Zanutti, an experienced but cautious climber.

Their new pitch ended 30 metres beyond the previous high-point. It included a ten-metre traverse that was, in Emilio's words, "difficult and without protection, [followed by] a crack… too wide for pitons, too narrow for chimneying, that had to be free climbed."[136] Emilio tied a red handkerchief to a piton to mark his high-point and they retreated. Bad weather and Zanutti's lack of time brought an end to further attempts in 1932, and they both returned to Trieste.

The comparisons between Emilio's route and Solleder's climb on the Civetta had frustrated Emilio, as had discussions about how his grade vi's compared to those of other climbers' routes of the same grade. To avoid this, Emilio usually stayed away from a route once another climber had made it their project. With no partner and several other teams interested in the Cima Grande, however, Emilio decided to suspend his usual objections. His decision necessitated an agreement, if not an alliance, with the most active climbers on the wall in 1933, Emilio's Cortinesi guiding competitors, the brothers Giuseppe and Angelo "Deo" Dimai.

The Dimai brothers were skilled free climbers. In 1927, they had made the first ascent of the Via Miriam on the Torre Grande in the Cinque Torri above Cortina, a 200-metre vi.[137] Angelo later soloed the route. In 1932, Giuseppe led the first ascent of the Diretta Dimai on the same tower, at a solid grade vi. He was seconded by Antonio Verzi, Giuseppe Ghedina and Oliviero Gasperi, who were also mountain guides. The Dimais, like Emilio, preferred to climb with their *compaesani.*

On the Cima Grande, the Dimais stood to become the best climbers in Italy, secure the honour of their village and their profession in the face of emerging amateur alpine expertise and garner publicity for their business that they could never hope to buy. Emilio was more reticent about the benefits of fame, at least for mountain guides, but the climb was the next natural progression in his climbing. He was conscious of potential bad press and political problems in the local guiding scene if he nabbed an ascent without any local climbers on his rope. And yet, he could not bring himself to approach the Dimais.

On almost every attempt on the north face of the Cima Grande, and on most attempts on the other unclimbed north walls, the most successful parties were members of primary groups, often families or small communities. The Dimais and Schmids were brothers, the successful party on the north face of the Grandes Jorasses was mostly from the Grignetta, the Dimais and Ghedina came from Cortina, Steger and Wiesinger were spouses.

Emilio had lost many of his closest relationships since he moved to Misurina. Death, which often rearranged the talent roster in inter-war alpinism, also played a part. Celso Gilberti, a good candidate for a partner on the Cima Grande, had survived the north face of the Riofreddo, unlike his partner Spinotti, as well as 46 other first ascents, only to fall to his death on the Paganella on July 11, 1933.

Emilio was devastated by Gilberti's death. In a letter to Casara, he revealed both his preoccupation with unwanted attention on the Cima Grande and his grief at the loss of Gilberti, "a true knight of the mountain who never said whether what he climbed was grade v or vi. It really hurts when a pure one like him falls… His routes were never in the newspapers but remain to one day be discovered."[138]

In anticipation of the climb, Emilio asked Casara for more equipment. "If [the ropemaker in Vicenza] makes those silk cords in sections, I'll definitely take 30 metres."[139] By late July, Emilio had a new rope and enough pitons, but still no partner for the wall.

***

Emilio hated approaches, but he could not resist the hike up to the Cima Grande when heard that a party from Cortina was making a serious attempt on the north wall. The yellow rock was streaked with jet-black water marks. Ravens floated in the breezes that scoured blank and bulging rock that seemed to go on forever. Everywhere else, it was a warm sunny August day perfect for climbing, but this wall lay in eternal shadow. The climbers looked like ants on a wall.

Through the wind he heard the blows of Giuseppe Dimai's hammer. Giuseppe was halfway up a crack on a pitch above the handkerchief Emilio had left behind the year before. At the belay where Emilio and Zanutti had retreated, Ignazio Dibona, the son of Angelo Dibona, and Giuseppe Ghedina hung patiently with the bulging rucksacks for their spare pitons and bivouac gear. This was a serious, well-planned foray.

Emilio was ashamed of his jealousy, but he couldn't help himself. It was like seeing a rival with a woman he loved. He wished it was him up there on the lead, not Giuseppe. Emilio always tried to think the best of other climbers' efforts and not to compare himself. But here, professional rivals, who he held responsible for his self-imposed exile from Cortina, were using his route-finding efforts to snatch the greatest prize in Italian climbing and, more importantly, the present object of his desire. Emilio could not linger and stew in his sadness and annoyance. A client waited for him at the Principe Umberto hut.[140]

The next morning, he was drinking coffee in the sun on the terrace outside the hut when he was surprised by Giuseppe Dimai. Emilio said he had seen him on the wall the day before and asked what had happened. Giuseppe explained that they had rappelled a pitch after Emilio's handkerchief before Ignazio and Giuseppe made an excuse to go down. The Dimais needed stronger companions. He offered Emilio a place on their rope on the next attempt.

It was a startling and unexpected offer, but Emilio jumped at it. He had a couple more clients to deal with, but they agreed to go up together in three days.

Emilio honoured the agreement even when Renato Zanutti came to Misurina the next day to ask him to try the wall a second time. Raffaele Carlesso, who was guiding in the eastern Dolomites that summer, forgave Emilio's insult to his guiding and asked him to attempt the wall the day after. Carlesso was surprised to hear that Emilio had teamed up with the Dimais and more surprised that he had no intention of breaking off the arrangement.

The same day, Emilio was at the Principe Umberto hut when another guide came looking for him. He breathlessly described how he had seen the Dimais, Ignazio Dibona and Giuseppe Ghedina on the north face with rucksacks and equipment for a serious attempt. Emilio could hardly believe it, but he had to guide that day, so he could only brood over the possible betrayal without verifying it himself.

That night, at the Principe Umberto hut, Emilio had another unexpected encounter with Giuseppe Dimai, who looked displeased to see him. This time, he was accompanied by his brother Angelo. Emilio told Giuseppe he had heard that he and his brother had broken the agreement to team up. Giuseppe dismissed the attempt as a reconnaissance. Angelo, however, was surprised that his brother had made an agreement with Emilio. It was the first he had heard about it.

It was more likely that it had been a legitimate attempt than a reconnaissance, given the amount of equipment they had brought. The most likely reason they had failed was that the Dimais' partners had once again decided to turn back. The Dimais, after all, were the best climbers amongst the local guides and were in a unique position amongst the guides to take on a route like the north face of the Cima Grande. Emilio suspected that he had been tricked, either to prevent him from trying it with someone else before the Cortinesi, or because they wanted to keep him in reserve in case the attempt with local talent failed and they needed to try again.

He made the Dimais promise to try the route again the next day. They agreed, with the condition that they bring Angelo Verzi and Ignazio Dibona. The Dimais knew that Emilio lacked sympathy for their obligation to bring less qualified climbers from other guiding families on important new routes in order to share the honour. Their obligation to look out for their neighbours, however, outweighed their word to Emilio. Although Emilio preferred to climb with *Triestinos* for hard climbs, he chose carefully from the strongest members of the GARS and, so far, had brought no one with him whose presence decreased the chances of success. At this point, however, Emilio realized that any objection would make his place on the Dimais' next attempt even more tenuous, so he agreed to join the proposed team.

That night, they prepared their equipment: rucksacks; food; water; 40 steel carabiners that weighed, in total, approximately six kilograms; 80 pitons (more than four times as many as Ignazio's famous father, Angelo, placed in a lifetime of hard, long new routes) that weighed some eight kilograms; an assortment of double climbing ropes and tag lines, adding up to 140 metres; hammers; *staffe*.

A single variation between Emilio's and the Cortinesi's kits distilled their differences. On the face, Emilio would wear American-designed, mass-produced basketball shoes. They were light, inexpensive, stickier than espadrille or rope-soled shoes, and thin enough to feel the rock through the soles. Basketball shoes were practically a symbol of the GARS. To the Dimais, Dibona and Verzi, who came from one of the traditional shoemaking regions of Italy, factory-produced footwear was an unnecessary extravagance. They packed suede *scarpette* made by a local cobbler with the same espadrille soles used by shepherds for thousands of years.

Something else was taken along that was hardly ever discussed in subsequent accounts by the climbers: a chisel to drill a hole in rock and at least one piton with a circular blade designed to fill the hole.

In 1933, protection placed in drilled holes was rare, but not unknown. Ring pitons hammered into drilled holes were the only artificial form of protection used on the Elbsandsteingebirge, the sandstone towers along the Elbe River in eastern Germany, but the area was still seen by alpinists as a backward outlier. A chisel had reportedly been carried, but not used, by Hans Dülfer on the first ascent of the east face of the Fleischbank in 1913. Overall, however, the climbers of the Alps had been slower than those of the Elbsandsteingebirge to adopt the concept of protection placed in drilled holds.

Although drills and chisels had been used by guides on popular routes in the past, the first recorded use of a bolt in the Alps was in 1927, on the first ascent of Père Eternel, a 60-metre granite spike on the Brenva Ridge on Mont-Blanc. The climbers, Laurent Grivel, Arturo and Osvaldo Ottoz and Albino Pennard, also used a weathercock on a pole jammed in a crack. Grivel came from a family of guides and would produce one of the first commercially available drill-and-bolt kits for climbers.

Paul Preuss had once made the dry joke that he had never mastered the technique of climbing blank walls because, despite some climbers' hyperbole, a truly blank wall could never be climbed. Bolting equipment had only one use, which was to remove blank rock from the catalogue of unclimbable obstacles. In the case of the north face of the Cima Grande, there were two main reasons to take the kit. The most benign was the fear of being stranded by blank rock, high on the wall, where rescue or rappelling were impossible. The most problematic was the will to conquer the wall at all costs and by any means.

In the alluring shadows of the unclimbed north wall of the Cima Grande, Emilio simply could not turn back. He could not choose a life in which he did not climb the wall, even if it meant his death, or the transformation or transgression of his ideals.

***

It rained the night before Emilio and the Cortinesi made their first attempt. A pitch above his previous high-point, Emilio reached into an overhanging crack that ran with water. A frigid trickle ran down his sleeve to his armpit. The crack was too wide for pitons, and his last protection was five metres below him. He leaned back and looked up at the grey sky. Rain fell at a raking angle against the wall. The manila rope was heavy, dark, soft to the touch and, as he knew, weaker when wet.

He cursed. If he took too much time off his guiding schedule, he would lose his much-needed fees. Even on this wild rock wall, he fretted that he was already living off money from his mother to get through August. He climbed down a few metres to a small ledge to rest.

"Let one of us try," said Giuseppe.

Emilio looked 20 metres down to the belay ledge. The Dimais, Verzi and Dibona all watched without offering encouragement. The crack above was too wide for pitons and even if it had been dry, it would have been at the upper end of his free climbing abilities. He doubted that anyone else on his team could fare any better on it in its present condition, but he climbed back to the belay.

Angelo tied in next, but the wet crack turned him back before Emilio's high-point. For Verzi and Dibona, there was no point in another attempt. It was the end of their time on the wall because they both had clients the next day. After hours of lurching rappels on wet ropes, they reached the ground. Emilio and the Dimais agreed to give the route one more try if the weather was good the next day.

Emilio woke late the next morning. On the other side of the dormitory, the Dimais were packing their rucksacks. Emilio threw off his blanket and got out of bed with uncharacteristic haste. The climb was back on.

A few hours later, they reached the crack that had turned them back the day before. It was damp, but no longer running with water. Emilio led and resorted to a couple of wobbly aid pitons where it narrowed higher up. The crack ended at a traversing seam in the rock that led to a good ledge. The ropes were still heavy with water, and friction on the lip of the overhang below dragged hard against Emilio's waist. He decided to stop and belay.

Unburdened by rope drag, Giuseppe quickly led the traverse and the rock above, which brought them to a series of easier pitches that ended at the only good ledge on the wall, soon to be known as the Italian Bivouac.

They were exultant. For ten years, the lower wall had defeated all comers, including the best climbers in Europe. On ten exacting pitches, they had utilized every known technique and some 75 pitons. The 250 overhanging metres they had climbed comprised some of the hardest rock climbing yet done in the Alps. Above them rose a line of chimneys and cracks that promised challenging free climbing but led right to the summit. They knew how to assess Dolomites rock, and that the upper wall, on its own, would be a harder and longer version of the V+ Dülfer Chimney on the west face of the Cima Grande, but it was a minor obstacle compared to what they had already climbed.

They sat on their rucksacks and settled in for a long, cold night under the stars. In the morning, they left the unused drill and the bolts on the ledge to lighten their packs. Clearly, although they left the bolting gear out of their reports on the climb, they were indifferent as to whether anyone found out about it. As expected, the upper wall went free with only occasional aid pitons. They exchanged leads, and since all three were superb free climbers, they moved quickly. At 10:30 a.m. they reached the summit. They signed the summit register and descended the Via Normale, where they surprised guided parties and amateurs on the way to the top.

In the log of the Principe Umberto hut, Emilio entered a complete description of the route and the following dedication: "By the same light that illuminates the value and tenacity of the Italians of Mussolini," he wrote, "we have opened the path to the north face of the Tre Cime di Lavaredo."[141]

The newspapers appreciated Emilio's fascist spirit and added their own superlatives, with their usual half-truths and illogicalities. The sensationalist weekly *La Domenica del Corriere* ran a few hundred words by Dino Buzzati. The face, wrote Buzzati, "was considered by alpinists around the world to be impossible," which might have left informed readers wondering why it had been attempted so many times. In words that must have been bitter for Emilio to read, after all of his problems with the Dimais, Buzzati called the first ascent team "an alpine Utopia."[142]

Climbing Italy's *Nordwand*, the greatest Italian climb in history, won the trio no official accolades or material rewards. Emilio and the Dimais went back to guiding work right away. Every fine-weather day spent on the Cima Grande, they had lost potential guide's wages. The Dimais never made another first ascent of comparable scope again. A week after the ascent, Emilio was the most famous climber in Italy, but he still struggled to find clients, or even climbing friends with time to visit him in Misurina. Emilio was isolated, underemployed and short of money, and yet he planned another new route right away.

The Cima Piccola di Lavaredo, unlike the more monolithic Cima Grande and Cima Ovest, comprised several independent features, including Punta Frida, the Cima Piccolissima and the striking pillar of the southeast buttress, with its unclimbed 330-metre vertical prow, dubbed by climbers the Spigolo Giallo (Yellow Edge). After the first ascent of the north face of its neighbour, the Cima Grande, it was a prize second only to the bulging, overhanging north face of the Cima Ovest, which had only begun to seem possible after the Cima Grande was climbed. The Spigolo Giallo itself had been declared impossible by no less an authority than Antonio Berti.[143]

Emilio, however, was smitten by the Spigolo Giallo. "It looks like the cut-off of a fantastic ocean liner stranded on the talus or the prow of a Cyclopean ship," he wrote, "or the edge of a 330-metre-long red-hot sword thrust forward out of the huge yellow cliffs."[144]

"I do not know if anyone has thought of trying to climb up that ridge," Emilio said, "but for me, it was the most aesthetically logical way, even if it was also the most far-fetched. I already knew, however, that among us mountaineers, the feeling of art is superior to any consideration of practicality… So [the Spigolo Giallo] was an ideal way and I was willing to pay for it."[145]

On the Cima Grande, circumstances had led Emilio to settle for a partnership of convenience. For the Spigolo Giallo, he chose Mary Varale, an ally and one of the best female rock climbers in the Alps, and Renato Zanutti, who had lost a chance with Emilio on the Cima Grande. Emilio considered the two-day grade VI climb, with its loose rock, tricky unprotected traverses and vertical face climbing, his most elegant and exposed route. He attributed his success on the Spigolo Giallo to his partnership with Zanutti and Varale.

"All those who want to experience the satisfaction of the great climbs should take great care in the choice of the companions," Emilio said. "These must possess the highest possible athletic and moral qualities. The companion must always have ready a word of encouragement to refresh the team locked in tremendous efforts and they must be ready in any situation to make any sacrifice. Only such sacrifices can bond two or three individuals, tied to the same rope, and make them stronger than the gates of death which await them at every step. It is only in this way that goodness and brotherhood flower among all those rough and wild cliffs, in the severe solitude of the mountain."[146]

Casara, never one to restrain his operatic impulses, locked himself in his study to weep at the beauty of the new climb. The editors of the *Rivista Mensile* and the alpine journalists of the newspapers hailed it as one of the most beautiful rock climbs yet done in the Dolomites.

1933 had been a glorious season.

***

In 1933, Kugy turned 75 years old. He no longer climbed, but he maintained his contacts with the CAI and the Austrian Alpine Club and continued to write about the mountains. Throughout their friendship, Kugy had ignored Emilio's fascism and Emilio had ignored Kugy's Slavic and Austrian sympathies. Kugy had used his class status to help Emilio, against his own advice, become a guide. Emilio had paid his respects to Kugy.

Kugy's appraisal of Emilio and Fabjan's climb on the north face of the Riofreddo had been the single, ambiguous word "colossal." Kugy's comment on the first ascent of the north face of the Cima Grande, and the means by which it was made, left no room for interpretation. "The north face of the Cima Grande di Lavaredo," Kugy wrote, "remains unclimbed."[147] The greatest ascent of Emilio's career, was, in

Kugy's mind, invalidated to the point of erasure by the pitons, rope manoeuvres and modern techniques. Kugy could be generous, but the statement showed an indifference to the effect of his words, and despite his subsequent attempt to present them as a casual comment not meant to wound Emilio, their friendship never recovered.

There were other critics. Artificial climbing had been pioneered by German and Austrian climbers on the Kaisergebirge, and yet, the vast and influential German Alpine Club censured the north face of the Cima Grande in the pages of its vaunted journal. "The alpine world has gained a great attraction," wrote its editors; "the mountains have lost a sanctuary."[148]

The British *Alpine Journal* decided that the safest course was to continue to ignore Italian big wall climbing altogether.

Many pre–Great War climbers like Emil Zsigmondy and Paul Preuss climbed with British mountaineers and might have been affected by their criticism. Although Emilio claimed to have cribbed his comment about the water drop from an English mountaineer, he did not speak English and never shared a rope with a British climber. Emilio's anti-German fascism followed the views of Italo Balbo and others who hoped that Mussolini would make an alliance with Britain, Italy's ally in the Great War, rather than Germany. In all likelihood, Emilio would have been surprised to find out that the Cima Grande had earned him a place of notoriety in British climbing mythology.

***

In the rush to meet deadlines for the Cima Grande story, Buzzati, like many other writers, had no time to interview the climbers. He focussed on Emilio, a familiar figure in the press, whom he called "a guide also known for many other wondrous deeds," and only mentioned the Dimais in a subordinate role.[149]

"I do not think I deserve so much [praise]," Emilio wrote, "I do not think I have done so much, and the merit is not all mine. Naturally, after the joy of victory, the petty vanity of men wanted to disturb my quiet satisfaction… my intimate satisfaction is enough for me, what others think does not matter."[150]

Emilio's misgivings about the press were soon validated. The Dimais were understandably upset that they had been all but left out of the story. If Emilio's *Triestino* partners were happy to accept second billing on new routes they climbed with their hero, that was their affair. The Dimais wanted and deserved equal credit. Giuseppe told the alpine press that he had taken over the lead from Emilio after the crux overhang because he, unlike Emilio (who actually only stopped because of rope drag), was strong enough to go on.

Giuseppe's story was not widely discussed in the press and had no effect on those who already believed that Emilio would be the superior climber in any situation. Emilio, however, sunk back into the depression he had temporarily escaped in the Tre Cime di Lavaredo. Emilio made few friends and few enemies, and neither of them wisely, so he hardly knew who to turn to and how to react to the slight.

Manaresi knew that the Cima Grande was comparable to Alfredo Binda's victory at the Giro d'Italia that year, and he told the press to make Emilio the hero of the climb. After all, he was the only fascist on the team. The Dimais' complaints were no match for the clamorous praise Emilio had received, but Emilio pompously asked Manaresi to force Berti to print a retraction of the offending piece.

"I won't involve myself in demanding a retraction of a personal, polemic nature," Manaresi wrote back, after he had ignored Emilio's letter long enough to emphasize its unimportance, "but I welcome your writing on the subject of the past and future magnificent deeds in which you remain the protagonist. End of letter."[151]

The fascist party kept dossiers on the political views, embarrassments and peccadilloes of most Italian citizens. This instance of Emilio's ingratitude to his leaders and those who had praised him could not have gone unrecorded. When the party and the CAI apparatus in Rome finally produced the heroic literary paean to Emilio Comici, the fascist mountaineering hero, they left out the climb Emilio and every other climber of his day considered his greatest, the north face of the Cima Grande.

Emilio was not invited to join the Italian Andean expedition of 1934, the only major Italian mountaineering expedition of the 1930s.[152] Before the team set sail for Chile, there was a photo shoot with Mussolini himself. The leader, ardent fascist mountaineer Count Aldo Bonacossa, star climber Giusto Gervasutti, and almost all the other climbers wore their *squadrista* blackshirts. Emilio's climbing friend and fellow GARS member Giorgio Brunner was the only exception.[153]

Mussolini saw the right-wing movements and sympathetic governments of South America as a potential field of Italian influence.[154] The Chilean diplomatic corps was as entranced by uniforms and titles as Il Duce himself, and Mussolini's charm squad of neatly uniformed alpinists in jackboots led by an aristocrat were treated as foreign dignitaries.

The expedition enjoyed less success in the Andes than on the diplomatic front. Climbers joked about the expedition's lack of success and nicknamed it "The Cruise to the Andes" because they achieved so little, partly because of a lack of hard climbers. Gervasutti and Luigi Binaghi, the team's most accomplished alpinists, were so frustrated by the team's failures that they stayed on to do more climbing after the others shipped for Italy. The expedition could have used Emilio, but he was not even invited when Bonacossa launched a second, even less successful expedition in 1937.[155]

The most probable reason Emilio was left off the team was that Bonacossa – a traditional climber who had climbed with Paul Preuss, and a trusted fascist – knew he was a prima donna. Manaresi could have intervened, but after Emilio's request that he publicly set the record straight about his performance on the Cima Grande, Manaresi had told Emilio to make his own way in climbing without his help. Emilio's own silence on the matter suggests that he knew that there could be no more letters of protest to his superiors.

***

After the north face of the Cima Grande, Italian climbing clubs asked Emilio to speak about his ascent and show lantern slides. From 1933 to 1939, Emilio made about a hundred presentations; not enough to make a serious living, but between preparation and travel, enough to occupy much of his time in the off-season.[156]

The government did not sponsor Emilio's lectures. They did not have to. Emilio voluntarily acknowledged the country's debt to Mussolini in his talks, which he continued to give even after he realized that he rarely turned much of a profit after paying for his train ticket, hotel expenses and lantern slides.[157]

Public speaking isolated Emilio from both Trieste and the mountains. Day-long train trips to unfamiliar cities, wearing a suit and tie, trudging from the train station to the local Alpine Club section hall in uncomfortable shoes with his suitcase of slides, was an alienating ritual. After announcements, the middle-class amateur climbers in their suits and spectacles would stand and they would all sing the fascist anthem, the "Giovinezza": "Youth, Youth / Spring of beauty / In the hardship of life / Your song rings and goes out! / And for Benito Mussolini / Hip, hip hooray..."

"I am proud of modern climbing technique," Emilio would finally begin, "but I would not separate it from the spiritual goals of climbing. Spirituality is the thing that draws us towards the mountains in the first place and technique only improves by that high goal."[158]

CHAPTER SIX

THE PLAIN OF MUSES

"Each pinnacle is a little God and the summit, Jupiter," Emilio remarked when he first saw the vertical 200-metre faces of Olympus's peaks, Agios Antonios (the highest mountain in Greece, at 2815 metres), Mytikas and Skolio. His client, Anna Escher, must have been amused to see Greece bring out a rarely seen scholarly side of Emilio. When it rained he blamed the god Fluvius. "Thank Phoebe, the goddess of light," he said on the summit of Olympus, "there is enough time to get down."[159]

Their guide and bodyguard was long-haired, wild-eyed Christos Kakkalos from the nearby village of Litochoro. Kakkalos carried a rifle, which doubled as an ice axe. When wild dogs closed in on the approach to their campsite on the Plain of Muses, Kakkalos chased them away with a fist and a feral growl. On the hike in, when a mule bucked off its load and ran away, Kakkalos had piled its load on his already heavy pack.

The ancient Greeks had built a small shrine on the summit of Agios Antonios. In the modern period, the sport had been slow to catch up with western Europe. In 1921, Kakkalos had guided Swiss explorers Marcel Kurz and Fritz Kuhn on the first ascent of Stefani. The steeper walls of the mountain had not even been considered.

Emilio and Escher, however, made quick work of the first ascents of the northeast ridge and northwest face of Stefani and the northwest ridge of Mytikas while Kakkalos and Escher's friend, Dr. Gizman, watched Emilio and Escher with a telescope. After the climb, Emilio showed Kakkalos how running belays worked, with a tent pole as an anchor point.

Most of Emilio's account of his Greek trip, however, concerns not the technical climbing on Olympus but the approach to Smólikas (2637 metres), in the Pindus range, with Escher and Gizman. Smólikas, the second-highest mountain in Greece, was in the Ioannina area, close to the Albanian border, and no one knew how to get there from Athens. A travel agent told Emilio to take a one-day bus ride to Grevena, but there was no bus, and the taxi ride took them two days. In Grevena, they hired taxis for the long drive on bad roads to Kastoria.

In Kastoria, the best hotel in town was so infested with bedbugs that they slept in their sleeping bags with the drawstrings cinched around their faces. In the morning, they paid a local with a car to drive them, partly cross-country, 70 kilometres to Samarina, a hamlet that Emilio said "in the winter would be difficult to reach, as it then lay buried under high drifts of snow, far from the inhabited cities, the haunt of wolves, in a land that knows no skiing."[160]

The innkeeper of Samarina knew a little about Italy from the Italian soldiers who had crossed the mountains from Albania in the Great War to pasture their horses. Along with the local gendarme, he entreated the climbers to hire armed escorts if they travelled further, in case of brigands. Emilio declined.

Climbing Smólikas was easier than getting to Samarina. "Some of my good friends will think," Emilio wrote, "what a delusion for Comici, after having travelled so far to reach it, he finds a climb that is not even in the first degree of difficulty!... both me and my two companions were equally amused. Even if Smólikas did not let us feel the thrill of a virgin summit, it introduced us to a unique country, barren, sad, monotonous, burnt by the sun... and yet a memory remains in my heart. A nostalgia, even. We had met strange inhabitants, renowned for their warrior and brigand spirit; we had climbed a distant mountain, without any difficulty, but with a mountaineering purpose. We did not regret the trip as lost time. And we returned, intimately pleased, bringing with us the dear memory of so many new things seen and lived."[161]

***

Although Emilio had enjoyed the vacation from the Italian climbing scene, as soon as he returned from Greece, he fretted over his project to make a newsreel movie about basic climbing techniques.

Emilio's diary has many entries for trips to the cinema where he would have noticed that German climbers dominated the screens, as they had once dominated the Dolomites. In *Struggle for the Matterhorn* (1928), Tyrolean climber Luis Trenker had starred as the Italian guide Jean-Antoine Carrel. Leni Riefenstahl had played a climber in half a dozen films. German climber Franz Schmid, like Emilio, had made the first ascent of the one of the great north faces, but Schmid, unlike Emilio, reprised his great climb in a movie. *Gipfelstürmer* (released in English as *The Mountain Conqueror*), was a fictionalized retelling of the story of Schmid and his brother Toni's 1931 first ascent of the Matterhorn *Nordwand*. Toni, however, had died in a climbing accident on the Grosses Wiesbachhorn and was replaced by an actor whose character, out of respect, was given the name Bertl.[162]

Emilio might have been disappointed to note that Italian mountain filmmakers preferred war stories to alpinism. By 1934, the only Italian feature film with a climbing theme, *Il gigante delle Dolomiti* (Giant of the Dolomites) was seven years old.[163] It was set in the Dolomites, where the heroic Italian character, Maciste (Strongman), a fixture in films with a variety of settings but similar plots, takes the part of a mountain guide and exposes an ethnically German guide named Schultz and his client-accomplice as spies.[164] The film also portrayed alpinism to the public as the proper activity of strong, simple, but morally upright Catholic guides, rather than urban sports enthusiasts, a model for the guiding profession that worked against Emilio's vision and interests.

Mussolini thought it was essential for the Italian film industry to catch up with other European nations and founded the Direzione Generale per la Cinematografia (General Directorate for Cinematography) to loan expertise and fund film projects of all sizes. Emilio, however, was skeptical about experts in Rome and believed that things worked out best when he kept them to himself and his friends. He decided to become his own scriptwriter, producer and director.

When he needed a film crew, Emilio turned to the army, an institution for which he had always nurtured a childlike trust. It was in the army, after all, and not film school, that Emilio's idea for the film had been born.

In the early 1930s, a mountain warfare school had been founded at Castello Jocteau, near Aosta, on the Italian side of Mont-Blanc. Castello Jocteau became the headquarters of Emilio's reserve regiment, the Ninth Alpini. The original concept of the school was that its candidates would be selected by doctors on the basis of their physical and racial suitability for high-altitude warfare. They would be armed with modern weapons, should such become available to the Italian army, and trained in both the latest mountain warfare skills and alpinism. A certain Colonel Luigi Masini knew that Emilio was a mountain guide and made him an instructor without a promotion from his present rank of corporal.

Prompted by Captain Giuseppe Inaudi, an enthusiastic climber, Colonel Masini urged Emilio to make detailed plans and a model for an artificial climbing wall to be quarried out of the granite hilltop in the park adjacent to Castello Jocteau. Emilio, with the assistance of the climber and musician Toni Ortelli, proposed a 60-metre-wide outcrop roughly the shape of the Montasio, Emilio's favourite teaching crag in Val Rosandra. The wall would have cracks, chimneys, artificial climbing, routes of all grades, and a ledge to teach multi-pitch climbing belays. It was the first plan for a purpose-built artificial rock climbing wall intended to teach modern skills.

During the Great War, the army had developed extensive expertise blowing up rocks and excavating tunnels and fortifications, but this might have been the first instance when they used their skills to create a climbing area. Explosives and drills turned out to be inexact translators of Ortelli's sketch based on Emilio's ideas, but the engineers rendered something recognizably similar to Emilio's plan and added a small amphitheatre in front so that troops could watch demonstrations.[165] The instructors referred to the facility as the Rocciadromo.

The officers who had watched Emilio climbing from the comfort of the amphitheatre could imagine how his idea of making a film might be useful, popular, and even bring some attention to the regiment. After several delays and cancellations, an army cameraman finally arrived in Trieste and announced that he would be the sole crew member and that he did not climb, so he would be filming from the ground. The cameraman, Emilio and local Giorgio Pirovano headed out to Val Rosandra on two motorcycles with all of their climbing and camera equipment in rucksacks.

For the first scene, Emilio attacked an overhang on the Montasio outcrop. Less than five metres up, he dropped a piton, lost his balance as he grabbed for it and fell. The rope caught him, but the film project he had waited weeks to start was paused no sooner than it had begun. He needed the piton to complete the climb and was impatient to start filming again, so a desperate search of the unstable talus ensued.

Pirovano accidentally rolled a boulder downhill towards Emilio. There was no time to move out of harm's way. The rock would have broken Emilio's neck if it had not burst into pieces when it struck a boulder close to him with so much force a splinter lodged in Emilio's leg. Emilio could tell he needed a doctor. Despite the pain, he hopped back on his motorcycle and drove straight to the hospital.

The star climber and director was out of commission, and the time waiting for the cameraman, who returned to his regiment, was wasted. Emilio convalesced in his parents' house, where he washed the wound every day and dampened the pain with aspirin. Penicillin was not yet available for medical use, and recurrent infections kept the wound from closing.

After a few weeks, Emilio felt strong enough to do some easy climbs. The cameraman returned. Instead of documenting the latest hard rock techniques, for which Emilio's leg remained in too much pain, they made a semi-comical piece contrasting Emilio's efficient climbing with Pirovano's, who hammed it up and pretended to be a terrible climber. Although they did not realize it at the time, it was the first short documentary climbing film.

***

Climbers like Riccardo Cassin in the Grignetta dressed in a sloppy mix of factory, alpine and gymnastics garb that reflected their view of the cliff as a place where normal social conventions could be ignored. Emilio and the GARS wore proper climbing trousers and a jacket or sweater vest. They dressed well to climb well, and Emilio's climbing style, which had been compared to the flight of an angel, was much observed and emulated.[166] Climbers from neighbouring routes gathered to watch Emilio climb. He showed off to the crowds by climbing problems with one hand and, on one occasion, feet-first, always while smiling and clowning, always perfectly dressed.

Young women were plentiful in the Val Rosandra scene, and Emilio's personal style and reputation attracted their attention. Emilio preferred the women of his hometown, but he related best to the female members of the GARS.[167] In the early 1930s, the strongest of them all was 18-year-old Brunetta Bernardini (nicknamed "Bruna"). Unlike Paula Wiesinger, Mary Varale and many other women who climbed grade VI, Bruna mostly lead climbed, and only rarely seconded. Her first ascent of the grade V pitch Bavarese del Fiume had caught the attention of the instructors at the climbing school. Although, due to sexism, her name was not listed in the school's roster, she was nonetheless an instructor.[168]

Emilio joined up with Bruna to make the first ascent of a grade VI dihedral at the Crinale cliff. Bruna led the more strenuous second pitch. The next day, Emilio went to the cinema with her in Trieste. Usually, Emilio recorded the initials of his dates in his diary. Bruna is the first woman to warrant a surname alongside the dates of their encounters in the city.[169]

Bruna was more than ten years younger than Emilio, but aggressive on the rock, fit, immersed in the world of climbing and the only woman he had ever climbed with who could lead grade VI. Emilio's relative maturity (which older women might have questioned, since he still lived with his mother), stature in climbing, good looks and his motorcycle overcame any misgivings Bruna might have had about his age. They began a romantic but, as yet, uncommitted relationship that seemed nonetheless full of promise.

A couple of months after their first ascent, Emilio went alone to the Pellarini hut in the Jôf Fuart group to await a partner. The December rain soaked him to the skin as he hiked through the dark firs. The mountains above were hidden by the clouds. The hut was abandoned and the air so damp that the fire would not light. He crawled under the wool blankets and lay awake for hours before he drifted into sleep.

A woman's scream awoke him, but he was unsure whether he had just had a nightmare or actually heard something. He went out into the drizzle in his wet boots. The black forest was silent. Fog hid the mountain walls that were just a hundred metres away. He waited for a few minutes before he went back inside. He lit a candle, then heard two knocks at the door. He opened it, but once again, no one was there. He held his hand over the candle flame and pulled it away when he felt his palm burn. It wasn't just a bad dream.

He looked outside again. The mist had cleared, and in the pre-dawn gloom he saw a woman climbing the rock wall above the hut. He grabbed his pack and soloed after her in his nailed boots. Her route became steeper and harder the higher she climbed. She climbed quickly and when she reached the top kept climbing into the sky until she became smaller and smaller, then disappeared.

With this, Emilio realized that he had chased after a mirage. He stopped to collect himself and decided to climb down to the talus. When he looked down, however, he saw the woman waiting for him. He climbed down carefully, more unsure than ever of whether he was in his right mind. When he reached the bottom, she was gone.[170]

The next day, in Trieste, Emilio learned that when he had been at the Pellarini hut, Bruna had slipped on the second pitch of their Diedro route. Her fall strained the manila rope beyond its breaking point. The rope snapped and she fell 40 metres to her death.

Emilio's diary entry for December 8, 1932, reads: "Death of Brunetta on the dihedral. Sore throat."[171] It would be a couple of years before Emilio ever recorded any emotions in his diary that did not relate to climbing disappointments, but he did not comment on his sore throat to diminish the importance of Bruna's death. His reticence was a symptom of a physical and psychological crisis. Emilio's heart broke. He was treated for heart pain and congestion likely caused by inflammation due to stress exacerbated by depression. Bruna was the first woman Emilio had loved, but like his sister, Lucia, she had been stolen from him by death.

Sestogradisti were temporary, and losing rope partners was hard for Emilio. Losing a climbing partner who was also a romantic interest shattered Emilio. Whether Emilio composed the story of Bruna's ghost retroactively to come to terms with her death, or believed that he had a supernatural experience at the Pellarini hut, her death on a climb he had created affected him in at least one way. From now on,

Emilio only dated women for whom climbing was a pastime rather than an obsession. Even fighting with women about his lack of serious employment and how he preferred climbing to all else was easier than climbing with the ghost of a lover.

Sometime in 1934, either at Val Rosandra or at one of the GARS after-climbing meals with drinks at the Hotel Moccò, Emilio met Alice Marsi. Alice was a working-class *Triestina*. In his diary, he referred to her either as "A." or "A.M.," although sometimes he used the nickname *la bionda*, the blonde. She had strong facial features, high cheekbones, fashionably permanent-waved hair and wore trendy blouses, even when she climbed. Alice became a common sight on the pillion seat of Emilio's motorcycle or beside him in the Hotel Moccò, where Emilio held court over the GARS in his own, self-contained manner.

Emilio and Bruna had mostly kept their relationship to themselves. Alice was the first woman whom friends described as Emilio's serious girlfriend. Emilio nonetheless only lingered in Trieste long enough for his leg to be barely useable. In late August, as soon as he was able, he parted from Alice to resume guiding in Misurina.

Emilio's friend Fausto Stefenelli was not surprised. He considered Alice very beautiful and assumed that this was the attraction for Emilio. But Alice wasn't simply a *Triestina* of the season. Alice attracted Emilio for the same reasons she frustrated him. She was a mature woman who challenged him to be an adult.

One of many expressions of the fascist party's fascination with male immaturity was its aesthetic praise for the lifestyle of the wanderer: "It was my wander-life," wrote Mussolini, "now full of difficulties, toil, hardship and restlessness, that developed something in me. It was the milestone which marked my maturity."[172] The fascist measure of maturity was not the ability to build a home and a stable life but the desire to live intensely and seek out extreme experiences. It was a credo that fit the lifestyle of many semi-employed mountaineers.

Alice, however, wanted stability. And as a working-class woman who wanted to establish her own home, she needed a reliable boyfriend, worker and partner. Emilio lacked the funds and the natural inclination to settle down but thought he could overcome her resistance to his lifestyle with a dogged attempt to prove that he was, in fact, gainfully employed as a climbing guide. But when he returned to Misurina in August of 1934, clients, as always, were hard to come by. He unsuccessfully tried to get friends who sometimes doubled as clients to come to Misurina.

"I do not hide that I was a bit annoyed and even, on certain days from Aug 20–26 angry with you," he wrote Casara, "and other people who did not come [to Misurina]. I was hurt by their absence during so many wasted days of good weather, used for nothing... you and Emmy [Hartwich-Brioschi] do nothing but chat and chat..."[173]

After a few days, Emilio took a break from this half-hearted attempt to find work and climbed a new grade vi on the east face of Punta Frida with Fabjan, Vittorio Cottafavi and Gianfranco Pompei.

Casara admitted, after cancelling many plans, that he was, at present, too busy with his law practice for climbing. Anna Escher had returned to her husband and children in Alexandria. Emmy's latest husband, Otto Brioschi, was tall and athletic, but not much of a climber.

That summer, Emmy and Otto had forsaken the Alps to celebrate Shavuot in Palestine. Political unrest at home in Vienna undoubtedly played a part in Emmy and Otto's decision to take an extended vacation. In February 1934, the Austrian government had brought in a new constitution along the lines of Mussolini's fascist constitution. Fighting broke out in the streets, but the government crushed any opposition. The violent anti-Semitism common throughout Germany had become part of daily life in Vienna.

Emilio, however, continued to believe that Mussolini would not introduce anti-Semitic laws in Italy. He also ignored the rising anti-Semitism in the cai, where some sections banned Jews from their huts. Emmy must have told him that her friend, and Preuss's former climbing partner, Count Ugo di Ottolenghi di Vallepiana was banned from the alpine club because he was a Jew. Like so many less radical fascists between the world wars, until anti-Semitism affected his immediate circle, Emilio treated news of the party's acts of violence and repression as anomalies or rumours.

On a rare visit to Misurina, Otto took a photograph of Casara, Emilio and Emmy together by a jetty afloat in the silver lake. Emilio wears climbing clothes and his guide's badge; his smile looks a little strained. Casara also wears climbing clothes, but unlike Emilio, manages to look like a golfer. Emmy is in a fashionable cap, her face made up and her dress too close-fitting for climbing. She leans on a cane.[174] Emmy, a deeply intelligent woman who spent her life brooding on the significance of the death of her famous lover, found in Emilio a man as unlikely to deny himself to the mountains as Preuss. On the altar of the mountains, men of any creed might be accepted for sacrifice, but Emilio's mastery of the pitons that Preuss had rejected made his sacrifice seem, for now, less likely to be fatal.

***

Although Emilio blamed his lack of new routes in 1935 on the rainy weather, his output would have been limited under any conditions by his leg wound. In the year since the injury, the infection had spread to much of his calf.

In 1935, he continued to try to show Alice that climbing was a real career by taking as many guiding jobs as he could get in Misurina and combining his visits to her in Trieste with instructing in Val Rosandra. Unfortunately, his frequent commutes from the mountains to the city exposed his calf to the heat from his motorcycle's red-hot exhaust pipe. Instead of the heavy leather boots preferred by most motorcyclists, alpinists wore only their knickers and long climbing socks. By midsummer, Emilio had added a serious burn to his wounded calf.

When Emilio's wound became so painful that he had to favour his other leg when he climbed, he dubbed it "The Evil." Guiding clients were impressed by his stoicism, but doctors warned him that any vigorous exercise would reopen the wound and renew the infection.

The warning came at an inopportune time for Emilio. The race to be the first to climb the overhanging 500-metre-high north face of the Cima Ovest, the last unclimbed north face of the Tre Cime, had begun. The face was steeper and more devoid of obvious cracks than the north face of the Cima Grande, but that face had opened up the eyes of climbers to the possibilities of using modern extreme piton technique on apparently blank faces. Before 1934, a few local guides had discussed the line, but unlike the Cima Grande, the wall was so overhanging that retreat was complicated enough to keep off any half-hearted parties, and no one had even tried it. In 1934, Angelo Dimai, Antonio Verzi and Selva di Gardena guide Toni Demetz tried the face, as did Carlesso, but neither attempt had gotten more than a couple of pitches up. A successful ascent would have been a master stroke by any party.

Despite his injured leg, Emilio was incapable of staying out of the contest. His first ascents on the Cima Piccola and Cima Grande gave him an almost proprietorial sense of his right to the last north face of the group, despite his usual habit of renouncing contested projects. He had procrastinated before attempting the wall in the belief that the obvious difficulties would keep off most competitors. An aggressive, younger generation of climbers was about to show him that he had miscalculated.

On August 12, Hans Hintermeier and Josef "Sepp" Meindl cycled 300 kilometres from Munich to the Dolomites, loaded down with all of their camping and climbing equipment. With no money to stay in huts, they set up their tent against the base of the Cima Ovest.

In their first week on the wall, the Germans managed to climb only a few pitches before they retreated, leaving two fixed ropes on the most overhanging pitches. Another attempt ended with a frightening bivouac hanging in slings during an electrical storm. They rappelled to their tent in the morning to recover and wait for better weather.

News of German youngsters on the last great problem of the Tre Cime travelled quickly through the network of guides, amateurs and hut custodians to Misurina. Emilio could not nurse his leg and play the part of Alice's responsible working man for another moment, as German interlopers tried to snatch the last great prize in the Tre Cime away from Italian climbers and, of course, Emilio himself. He convinced his Spigolo Giallo comrades of 1933, Mary Varale and Renato Zanutti, to make an attempt with him.

Varale told Cassin and her Grignetta comrades about the German attempt on the Cima Ovest before she left to join Emilio in Misurina. A few days later, she and Emilio and Zanutti threw themselves at the wall with as much vigour as they could muster, given that they had rushed into action behind an injured leader. After a few pitches, the trio reached a point where the route struck leftwards on 150 metres of rock that consistently exceeded the vertical. From here, each pitch pushed Emilio to the limit of his ability. When aid climbing, the second did not climb the rope with the as-yet-uninvented mechanical ascenders or even the prusik slings that were reserved for emergencies. The second climbed on the same pitons as the leader and hammered out most of the pitons. Often, on traverses, second climbers took even greater risks than the leader, and on the Cima Ovest, there were several.

Varale wasn't as versed in aid climbing as Emilio and Zanutti and began to struggle with fatigue. Emilio realized that climbing with the Dimais had been tense and competitive but more efficient than climbing with amateurs. Rain and mist enveloped the face before they reached the 17-metre overhang that appeared from below to be the crux of the whole route. If Emilio and Zanutti had been alone, they might have continued. The overhanging aid climbing offered some shelter from precipitation. If they went higher, however, retreat would have become increasingly challenging. They turned back, and Emilio never roped up with Varale again.

Desperate to make another attempt, Emilio forsook his dignity and telephoned the Dimais in Cortina to ask them to overcome past resentments and help him stop the Germans from snatching the north wall of the Cima Ovest. The Cortinesi, however, had considered the Cima Ovest already and decided it was not worth the effort. Whether Germans or an outsider like Emilio climbed it, it simply wasn't their affair. They stuck to their own climbs and guiding appointments.

After the Dimais turned him down, Emilio asked Renato Zanutti, who had returned to Trieste, to make another attempt with him. Zanutti knew that a tough and ambitious German party was on the wall already and that Emilio was injured and not climbing well. He also knew that the climb was the hardest long rock climb yet attempted, anywhere in the world. He agreed, nonetheless, to drop everything and rush back to Misurina, although this time he brought with him a third climber, Marcello Del Pianto. Although Emilio remained the director of the Val Rosandra rock school, he only taught courses occasionally and no longer knew the abilities or even the names of the young climbers in Val Rosandra. Del Pianto was inexperienced on long routes and a poor choice for such a serious climb, but it turned out not to matter. The three made their attempt in weather so atrocious that the Germans stayed in their tent. The pain in Emilio's leg was too much for him, and they retreated after climbing just 12 metres past his previous high-point.

Determined and patient rivals, bad weather, injury and the need to make money took Emilio out of the running for the last great challenge of the Tre Cime. He followed the rest of the summer's events on the Cima Ovest with increasing bitterness, not against the other climbers but at his own loss.

In the third week of August, the weather broke long enough for the Germans to try again, but they only pushed the route a few more metres before another cycle of rappelling and waiting.

The patience of Hintermeier and Meindl was soon to be challenged by the impetuosity of Riccardo Cassin and Vittorio Ratti from the Grignetta, whom Emilio had taught his advanced aid techniques. They had heard that Germans were camping out below the north face of the Cima Ovest with the intention of stealing the route from Italian climbers.[175] With Mino Rossi, who would help carry their gear to the mountain, Cassin and Ratti took the train to Cortina and arrived at the Lavaredo hut on August 27. On the morning of August 28, the mountains were hidden by clouds and rain. They made their way to the face unseen through the fog, deliberately avoided the Croda hut and whispered on the final stretch to the wall, so as not to alert the Germans. Emilio's attempts had come to an end and the weather remained poor, so the Germans expected no more competitors and had taken the day to rest in their tent.

As Cassin and Ratti neared the top of the first pitch, the mist thinned enough to reveal the Germans peering out of their tent, trying to figure out where the noises outside were coming from. They decided that no one could be climbing on such a wet day and went back inside their tent. Cassin and Ratti rappelled the first pitch, left a rope in place, stowed their equipment and returned to the Lavaredo hut for the night. The next morning, the weather was just as bad, but Cassin and Ratti climbed four pitches, thanks partly to the pitons left behind by Emilio and the Germans, before their competitors figured out that they had been outmanoeuvred. The Germans attempted to pass them by a new variation, but they realized it was futile and rappelled.

Cassin later claimed that "the difficulties up to Comici's high-point were nothing compared to those above."[176] The 40-metre pitch after Emilio's high-point took Cassin seven hours and three falls to complete. The cracks were so poor that it took Cassin four hours to figure out how to place a piton on the hardest section of the pitch.

After two more bivouacs in the rain, Cassin and Ratti made the summit. Rossi befriended the Germans, and all three climbed the Innerkofler Route to congratulate the winners of the race for the north face of the Cima Ovest. Emilio stayed home in Misurina, undoubtedly disappointed by his loss. Back in Lecco, Cassin, Ratti and Rossi were greeted with fascist honours and a military parade, in which they participated with enthusiasm if not much ideological conviction. The honours Emilio craved once more went to others, who in this case were more indifferent to such attention than Emilio himself.

***

In mid-September 1935, Emilio was guiding Anna and her son Cyril on Triglav in Yugoslavia when he heard rockfall directly overhead. He looked up to see a boulder flying towards Cyril and threw himself between the boy and the rock before it smashed into his ribs and his hip. If it had hit the boy straight-on, Emilio recalled, "he would have been crushed like a peanut."[177]

Emilio finished the climb with the Eschers, but Anna feared that he had suffered internal damage and insisted that he check in to the hospital in Ljubljana. Although the only damage from the rock was a minor bowel and kidney displacement that would correct itself with time, the doctor told Emilio that his infected leg required an immediate operation or he might eventually lose it altogether.

Emilio agreed to the operation. Afterwards, he took the doctor's advice and rested his leg until he had to report to the army mountain school in Castello Jocteau for his longest period of active duty since his compulsory service in 1925.

By 1935, the plan to modernize the *alpini* had faltered on the old-fashioned traditions and regionalism of the Italian army. Mussolini later bragged about the warplanes and tanks he sent to the

Spanish Nationalists, but for the Italian army at home, weapons and equipment were old and even boots were in short supply.

Conscripted urban proletarians and alpine peasants made up the ranks of the Ninth Alpini. The officer class was not a classless hierarchy based on fascist values of merit and strength alone, but a club for poorly trained, conservative, Catholic, Piedmontese aristocrats. The officers' impression of Emilio illustrates the sophisticated but unmartial atmosphere among the regimental elite. Captain Giuseppe Inaudi reported that Emilio's "didactic sense, culture and sensitivity made him welcome among the officers."[178] Presumably, Emilio's lowly upbringing and lack of education were obstacles to his promotion by the same officers who found him so sensitive. He remained as he had begun ten years before, a reserve corporal.

The regiment treated Emilio more like a visiting sports star than a recruit. Colonel Masini, for whom Emilio had designed the *palestra*, indulged his need to take days off from his military training to climb. Despite Emilio's humble rank, a young Lieutenant Gracco had Emilio removed from his normal duties as a junior non-commissioned officer in a foot platoon and made him a climbing and mountain travel instructor.

At first, Emilio planned to address the deficiencies in the army's alpine skills. He gave the troops courses in rock climbing and other skills, much like those the *Triestino* civilians had enjoyed at Val Rosandra. Army photographers captured Emilio, bare-chested and grinning, posing with a climbing rope while the other soldiers (all fully dressed) stood at ease. When photographed in uniform, or with a rifle, Emilio was joking with his comrades or taking a siesta on a march. In these images, life in the *alpini* looked more like a mountain holiday than boot camp. Whether or not this was a cynical propaganda scheme to attract recruits, the officers, at least, genuinely enjoyed the training in alpinism afforded by their regiment.

Emilio's commanders decided that Emilio's skills were too good to waste on the recruits, and Emilio's role shifted to that of a mountain guide paid in corporal's wages for officers who booked him for "courses" that were little more than guided climbing holidays.

***

In mid-October of 1935, Emilio was invited to join the retinue of fascists from Trieste and attend the October 27 anniversary of the March on Rome. His officers had no choice but to generously issue him the required furlough with fulsome expressions of enthusiasm. In any case, it was too cold for Emilio to take them climbing, and ski season had not yet begun.

The anniversary festivities included a parade in which Emilio marched with other Italian athletes. The parade ended in the Piazza Venezia, beside the massive Altare della Patria and tomb of the unknown soldier. Every year, Mussolini himself gave a speech to the crowd from a balcony overlooking the square. "The whole crowd seems to vibrate with one soul to express with one outburst of passion its faith, its devotion, its admiration for Mussolini," reported the newspaper *Il Popolo d'Italia*. When Mussolini appeared, the crowd expressed "its truest and most ardent sentiments of enthusiasm of the most incomparable force... Mussolini began his speech with the proclamation 'I am your leader!'"[179]

Among the throng's thousands of young men in blackshirt, breeches and boots was Emilio, who, since he had been a boy, had wandered off to lonely places and avoided crowds. A predictable response to seeing his leader would have been a redoubling of the fascist rhetoric in his writing and climbing dedications, enthusiastic accounts of the event and renewed expressions of political fervour in his correspondence. Instead, after seeing Il Duce in person and hearing him speak, Emilio never mentioned the event in his letters and never dedicated another climb to Mussolini again.

CHAPTER SEVEN

THE INEBRIATION OF EMPTINESS

In spring of 1936, Emilio's officers dispatched him to the Pedrotti hut in the Brenta Dolomites to guide a group of officers who wanted to climb the Campanile Basso. As was usual in the army, they were late, and Emilio was ordered to wait at the hut at their pleasure. Emilio hated forced indolence as much as he hated doing anything before he felt like it, and watching the summer sun shine on the legendary climbs of the Vajolet Towers, the Catinaccio group and the steep-sided plinth of the Campanile Basso without being able to climb excruciated him.

Four years earlier, he had made a brief visit to the area. When the climbing legend Tita Piaz called for climbers from the full-to-capacity Vajolet hut to assist in a rescue, only Emilio and two other climbers had volunteered. Roping up with Piaz must have been thrilling for Emilio. Piaz was a hero of Dolomites climbing, but he was also a living connection to Paul Preuss. Piaz, a soloist of some note himself, admired Preuss's boldness but had also warned Preuss, without much effect, about the dangers of his uncompromising ethics and penchant for climbing solo.

When Preuss died in 1913, the Alps lost its most rigid practitioner of pure climbing, but the dream of perfect style survived him. Alone in the hut where he had met Piaz and with so many of Preuss's great climbs within view, Emilio brooded on the great Austrian's achievements. Superficially, it seemed that they were opposites, one opposing pitons and the other embracing all of the possibilities they presented, but both were pioneers and superb free climbers, and Emilio praised Preuss as the purest alpinist in the history of climbing and the ultimate soloist, and Dülfer for showing the way with roped ascents.[180] For Emilio, soloing and roped climbing were two expressions of the same tradition, branches on the same tree of alpinism, and Emilio was more obsessed by that tradition than almost any climber who had ever lived.

Emilio's engagement with the traditions went beyond ethics and philosophies. It engaged him viscerally, spiritually and at a cost that only a few climbers would ever deliberately incur. Emilio knew that Preuss's achievements had survived his fall from the Mandlkogel. People of a more ordinary, unharried habit of mind than Emilio (or, for that matter, Preuss) felt no need to wager their lives against the common promises of human existence – the love of a spouse, a family of one's own, financial security, a home – in hope of eternity. Emilio's oeuvre of new routes, recorded for posterity, was, wittingly or not, a gamble on transcending the limitations of earthly life. His name, certainly, but more importantly his achievements, would be recorded in climbing guidebooks and on the tongues of generations of climbers as yet unborn. His climbs would test those who stretched their sinews and minds. To solo was to embody this autonomy from death in the present, and to make an ultimate expression of the ambitious goal he first took upon himself when he slipped Lucia's bracelet around his wrist beside her death bed on Via Bazzoni. Soloing at Emilio's limit could not be justified by the simple pleasures of climbing unencumbered by equipment. To suffer the terrifying fall and to die, barely halfway through life, but to know one had forever changed the path of what one loved the most, was to partake at the fountainhead of the obsessions of art, religion, philosophy and magic.

"I recognize, *a priori*, that solo climbing, on difficult walls is the most dangerous thing possible," Emilio wrote in 1937. "Only a few climbers have dared to try it and as history shows it usually ended badly, therefore I would not recommend it. What I feel [when I solo] is so sublime that it is worth the risk. I realize I have spoken a blasphemy and infringed upon beliefs and the commandments of Christ... But to live, you must risk something. You must dare." Sadly, he ends this confession that even the ancient proscription against suicide does not apply to the free soloist with the hollow and unlikely claim that "the Duce has showed us the way."[181]

After a few days, obsessing about the past and the physical urge to climb overcame Emilio's sense of martial duty. He changed out of his *alpini* uniform into his climbing trousers and jacket, packed a few pitons and a rope and told the hut custodian, the superb climber Bruno Detassis, that he planned to solo the Fehrmann Dihedral, a IV+ route on the 300-metre-high pillar of the Campanile Basso. It was easily justified as a reconnaissance for his excursion with his officer-clients. Detassis knew that Emilio had rarely soloed, even in Val Rosandra, let alone the Dolomites, although he was famous for his roped climbing.[182] Detassis begged him to bring the hut porter as a belayer, an offer Emilio declined.

With no belays or partner to slow him down, the Fehrmann Dihedral flowed into a single, continuous effort. On the summit of the Campanile, Emilio checked his watch. Three hundred metres of climbing had taken him only an hour and 15 minutes.

In the summit register, he read the signatures of the best climbers of the last 50 years. Hans Dülfer, Piaz, Otto Herzog, and new names too, like the young German Anderl Heckmair. He flipped backwards to the first few pages. There, dated July 28, 1911, on the third page, was the elegant Viennese German handwriting of Preuss himself. It gave Emilio goosebumps. "Extremely difficult," Preuss had written after the solo first ascent of the east face; "*Allein*." Alone.

Emilio had always felt alone, whether he was with friends or leading in a vertical maze of rock. In the solitude of his own mind he had conceived his big wall routes. On most climbs, his skill and drive isolated him from his partners. Now, he felt a wild urge to climb as Preuss had climbed, alone in the most existential sense, not on a trivial climb like the Fehrmann, but on one of Preuss's own routes.

Emilio climbed down the Via Normale towards the ledge that traversed over to the east face, scrambling past startled roped parties, excusing himself as if he was on a crowded sidewalk. He heard his name murmured, but was too excited to slow down and exchange greetings.

He took a deep breath before he traversed out onto the east face. More climbers had scaled his two-year-old route on the north face of the Cima Grande than had climbed the east face of Campanile Basso in the 22 years since Preuss soloed the first ascent. None besides Preuss had soloed the climb.

Preuss had woven back and forth on the face to find the best rock. Emilio added his own, straighter variation.

Halfway up, he found a small ledge and looked down between his feet. No rope. No partner. Hundreds of metres of air between his feet and the ground. Somewhere near here, Preuss had left a note to prove his claim to the face in 1911, and in 1927, Pino Prati, Rudatis's mystic apprentice, had fallen, torn out his protection pitons and the belay and pulled his partner, Giuseppe Bianchi, to their deaths. Shortly before Prati's death, Dario Wolf painted Prati with a skull and the Campanile Basso in the background. He called the picture *Gli amici*, or *Good Friends*. Acknowledging the presence of Pino's ghost, as well as Preuss's, Emilio placed some solid pitons, as if in offering to Pino.

Emilio might have wanted to apologize to Preuss as he hammered. Preuss had placed two pitons in his career, and then only to help a couple of novices avoid an unplanned bivouac. The world had changed, however, and Emilio knew there was no going back.

Soloing the Campanile Basso changed Emilio. For a moment, climbing wasn't about him, the CAI in Rome, the *sesto grado*, the gatekeepers in Cortina or the newspapers. It was about the breath of the ancient, dangerous, illimitable Alps, sombre, sweeping – a wildness that affirmed both life and death. That day, he knew he would, in his own way, continue the work of Preuss.

On the small summit, he met some of the climbers he had passed less than two hours before. They were astounded. Emilio would have preferred a request to be guided, but he was polite nonetheless. He opened the logbook for the second time that day and wrote in his achievement. It wasn't the first grade v+ solo, but it was the first solo of the east face.

As Emilio descended the Via Normale, he passed climbers from Trento making their way painstakingly towards the summit. He had taken piton climbing as far as he could, and he began to wonder how far he could take his new-found passion.

Other long solos followed, the hardest of which were the 450-metre Dülfer Crack on the Cima Grande, the Dülfer Dihedral on the Catinaccio d'Antermoia and the Preuss Crack on the Cima Piccola di Lavaredo, all of which were v+. Most of his solos were unrecorded, and Emilio found freedom in the lack of publicity and competitors.

The most articulate observer of Emilio's solos was one of his guiding clients, poet Antonia Pozzi. Pozzi had joined the Milan Section of the CAI in 1923, at age 11. Her life had material and social privileges, but she chafed against bourgeois norms of behaviour and took refuge in the hours she spent every day writing and revising poetry. Snow, wildflowers, laconic climbing companions and jangling iron climbing hardware were part of her internal poetic universe. Although her intellectual contacts included some of the leading figures of the interwar generation, including the poet Vittorio Sereni, the alpinist author Guido Rey and the anti-fascist intellectuals Paolo and Piero Treves, she rarely showed her verse to anyone.

Too shy to climb on her own, or even with friends, she relied on guides like Angelo Dibona and Oliviero Gasperi, with whom she formed deep bonds. When Emilio introduced himself, she was charmed by his smile, his taut, sunburned skin, the movie star's jawline, the sad eyes that made her believe that she shared something profound with him. Since her father had broken off her love affair with her tutor, Antonio Cervi, frequent periods of depression overwhelmed her. She could see that alpinism had made demands of Emilio, which he had accepted completely, similar to those poetry had made of her.

She hired Emilio both as a ski instructor and a summer guide, but he had no idea how deeply she observed him, nor the way his climbing gave her hope. After she watched him solo the Innerkofler Route on the Cima Ovest, Pozzi wrote that "the highest note was up there, a tiny point crucified on a black slab in the infinite silence." She lay "on the sharp pointed grass and pressed my heart against a boulder... If I could always remember that hour, life would be a continual victory."[183]

***

In early summer of 1936, when Emilio's tour in the army ended, Escher, as usual, was eager to quit the confines of Alexandria for the freedom of the European mountains and the company of her favourite guide. In June, Emilio and Escher set out from Trieste on their second Mediterranean rock climbing adventure. In Marseilles, they joined up with Yugoslavian guide Jova Lipovec and a Miss Mally, whom Emilio had guided on the Matterhorn in 1932. They sailed to Perpignan and disembarked on June 11 in Barcelona.

Their first stop was the granite towers of the Sierra de Gredos, where Spanish climbers had been active on 200-to-300-metre-high granite pillars since 1916. They made a first ascent of the west face of Galayos Primiero, added a second route to the Torre de los Galayos and climbed the Torreón de los Galayos. Their last climb in the area was an attempt on the 2591-metre Almanzor, the first long route on their itinerary. Emilio's leg pain, however, continued to be unpredictable, and they had to retreat before they reached the summit.

The last destination on the trip was the French Pyrenees. After a few easier climbs, on July 4, Emilio climbed a grade VI on the steep, alpine rock wall of the northwest face of Petit Encantat, likely with Escher and Lipovec. Unfortunately, whether or not Emilio knew it, the face had been climbed the year before by Spanish climbers Josep Boix, Josep Costa and Carles Balaguer.

As the party steamed homewards across the Mediterranean, elements of the Spanish military launched a coup against the elected government. On July 17, 1936, the Spanish Civil War broke out with clashes between government supporters and conservative rebels who chose General Franco as their leader. The rebels soon had the support of Hitler and, as a result, Mussolini. Many Italians admired Mussolini's conquests of Libya and Ethiopia as the fulfilment of the 19th-century dream of an Italian east Africa. Emilio's hostility towards the Germans made him suspicious of any kowtowing to Hitler. Emilio shared Mussolini's immature and cavalier attitude towards war, however, and likely did not join the majority of Italians, who disapproved of their dictator's decision to embroil Italy in the first full-blown European conflict since the Great War.

***

When Emilio returned from Spain, he continued to solo, but also returned to the kind of big wall projects that had built his reputation, although this time with less enthusiasm than before. Emilio always procrastinated before he attempted his projects, although he was invariably disappointed when others took advantage of his dithering to claim the first ascents.

Emilio's August 1936 climbs suffered from a Bohemian lack of logistical focus. In his letters to Casara, he complained that he had mislaid most of his climbing kit on his travels to lectures and his commutes between Misurina and Trieste, and asked Casara for 20 pitons, ten carabiners and a hammer. "Let me know if you can get these things," he wrote, "or I will try somewhere else... Call at the blacksmith of Vincenza, so he can send me the pitons I ordered."[184]

Emilio's loss of the north face of the Cima Ovest in 1935 had left him with a surfeit of emotions. The sense of accomplishment he felt after climbing a wall never came close to his intense disappointment when he was denied a climb by circumstances. To add his own route now would only be to admit his exclusion from the honour of the first ascent; besides, the north face of the Cima Ovest offered few other climbable routes.

The company of his mother – or, if it was during one of his frequent breakups with Alice, a new girlfriend – would often help Emilio overcome the initial pangs of heartbreak when he was beaten to a climb. The Cima Ovest was so visceral, however, that Emilio needed another physical route to replace it, preferably a route of note in the same group that made a logical trifecta with his other two great ascents there.

He settled on the northwest ridge of the Cima Piccola di Lavaredo. The northwest ridge, although not on the Cima Ovest, offered some geometrical satisfaction as a sort of bookend to his Spigolo Giallo on the other side of the north face of the Cima Piccola. "They appear as two enormous pillars," he said, "one 300 metres high, the other over 250, supporting the ruins of an ancient manor."[185]

The "base [of the northwest ridge of the Cima Piccola] is corroded and concave," Emilio wrote, "gloomy, always forgotten by the sun, corroded by old age. That northwest corner, the only one that directly connects the base of the mountain with the summit, particularly attracts the eye and calls out to you from a distance and is unforgettable. But how many, in the past, tried it, given the huge overhang at the base, and even more, the continuity of the overhanging line, rather than turn away their eyes and decline that invitation?" The northwest ridge of the Cima Piccola lacked the technical qualities Emilio admired most: firm rock and natural features that made a more or less vertical line he could follow to the top. His attraction to the climb had a kind of nostalgia for his days in the caves below the Carso; weirdly shaped roofs and almost subterranean shadows, a line going out as much as up, often on poor rock, by means of "the most difficult technique, that is, with double and triple rope on pitons and *staffe* and with pendulums."[186]

Once again, partners were a problem. Piero Mazzorana, a 24-year-old guide from Selva di Cadore, a hamlet 20 kilometres south of the main guiding enclave of Cortina, needed to build his reputation, and a new route with the great Comici was good, free publicity. A third climber was helpful on a big aid wall, at least to remove pitons and haul rucksacks, and Emilio asked Umberto Pacifico to come along.

Pacifico was the last of the GARS climbers to enjoy Emilio's patronage, if not his direct mentorship. His judgement and skill had, however, been impeded by the absence of his master. The other climbers from the GARS questioned Pacifico's judgement on the rock. The word in Trieste was that Pacifico was unready for a big new route. In response to other climbers' doubts rather than to his own, Emilio took Pacifico up a practice route on the Cadini di Misurina. Pacifico passed the test.

The next day, the trio started up the northwest ridge and climbed for 15 continuous hours. All of the pitches were difficult, and the rock was poor in places. The crux pitch overhung so much that they left the pitons in place so they could pull themselves in to the wall if they had to rappel. After a few more pitches, a rainstorm pinned them beneath an overhang for the night. In the morning, rockfall struck Mazzorana in the foot and injured him so seriously that they had to rappel.

Instead of making another attempt with Pacifico alone, Emilio gave Mazzorana a few days to heal. When they returned, the formerly ignored northern aspect of the Cima Piccola had drawn a party from Friuli, led by Gino Di Lorenzi. Their plan was to climb the north face, which was to the right of Emilio's line, but Emilio was furious. He considered the Friulan line, which did come within a few metres of his own in some places, an attempt to claim the first ascent of the northwest ridge.

Emilio decided that only a party of two could climb fast enough to ensure the first ascent. As the climbing above the roof was likely poorly protected and mostly free, Emilio had to choose his partner with care. He also had to consider the social and professional implications of his choice. Mazzorana needed the climb to build his professional reputation as a guide. Pacifico wanted the climb to improve his status on the cliffs of Val Rosandra. On the Cima Piccola, Emilio decided that Mazzorana needed the climb more than Pacifico.

Emilio and Mazzorana left a disappointed Pacifico in the hut and climbed quickly beyond their high-point. To Emilio's frustration, di Lorenzi's team simultaneously made good progress beside them. Even as Emilio led a hard, dangerous face later found to comprise some of the most demanding climbing yet done in the Tre Cime, he shouted angrily at di Lorenzi's team, accusing them of stealing his route.

Emilio and Mazzorana were still on the summit when di Lorenzi and his team arrived, half an hour later. When di Lorenzi tried to congratulate them, Emilio exploded. How could di Lorenzi expect him to be civil to a party who had practically tried to rob him of a wall he had climbed only after leading an incredibly challenging overhang and surviving an accident that injured one of his friends?

The outburst surprised di Lorenzi. Emilio, after all, had a reputation for graciousness. Di Lorenzi explained that they had intended to climb the north face, never the northwest ridge, and that their route was separate from Emilio's. Emilio stared at the ground for a moment and then apologized. He offered di Lorenzi all of the equipment in his rucksack to make up for his behaviour. Whether or not di Lorenzi accepted the gift is unrecorded.

Emilio's frustration had little to do with di Lorenzi. The unclimbed big walls of the Dolomites had become too crowded for Emilio, who, a few years before, had been able to make uncontested first ascents of some of the finest walls in the Alps. The Cima Piccola remained an obscure, little-travelled creation in Emilio's oeuvre and the development of Dolomites climbing. Subsequent parties found an easier way around the roof that Emilio considered the crux. The climb's history mirrored Emilio's own dissatisfaction and emotional turbulence on the climb.

When Emilio returned to the hut, he learned that Pacifico, angry with himself for not demanding a place on the Cima Piccola climb, had teamed up with fellow *Triestino* Giuliano Perugino to try another new route right away. Emilio rushed to the base of their climb to shout encouragement, but it was no use. They retreated at a section of rock that would not be climbed until 1947, and then only with the use of bolts.[187]

Although Emilio had forgiven di Lorenzi, whatever satisfaction he had gained from the northwest ridge lasted only a few days. Although it was a hard climb, it was also his last new route in the Tre Cime. For his next project, he chose a mountain on which he had not yet climbed a new route. The south face of the Marmolada di Penia was high on Emilio's list of unclimbed objectives. The face was not as overhanging as the Cima Grande's or Cima Ovest's north face, but it was 1000 metres high, with long, smooth and featureless sections that promised high-standard free climbing.

By late August, Emilio had guided only ten days since he had returned from Spain in July. He needed money, but his drive to climb new routes was more urgent. There was no time to entreat Casara to come to Misurina.

Since he was a boy, Emilio had believed that his outdoor adventures expressed his nationalism. The ultimate nationalistic institution, the army, had helped out with caving, his film and his climbing wall. In Emilio's mind, there was nothing untoward about asking Colonel Masini, the commanding officer of his *alpini* regiment, to provide climbing instructors to accompany him on the wall.

Masini promptly ordered two hapless mountain infantry instructors to accompany Emilio on this dangerous detail. Emilio's immediate impression of his conscripts was dubious. He used up three days of good weather that he could ill afford to waste so late in the season to train them on the crags of the Cadini di Misurina. On August 22, he ferried the officers, one by one, on the pillion seat of his motorcycle to Contrin, below the Marmolada.

Gino Soldà and his climbing partner Umberto Conforto had

booked a room in the same hotel in Contrin. Soldà was a guide and an Olympic cross-country skier with legendary physical fitness. That summer, with Franco Bertoldi, Soldà had made a new route on the 1100-metre-high north face of the Sassolungo. At VI+, it was one of the hardest climbs in the Dolomites.

Neither party shared their plans, but both knew that the race for the southwest face of the Marmolada was on. What Emilio did not know was that Umberto and Soldà had already climbed as high on the face as the Cengia Alta ledge system and had fixed ropes on the hardest sections.

Emilio asked his hotelier to wake him at four a.m. He planned to sneak out quietly and get ahead of the others, but Soldà and Conforto had risen at three a.m., and with their superior knowledge of the wall, they were already 200 metres up it when Emilio's team arrived at the face. There was no way to overtake them, so Emilio and his officers returned to the hotel. On August 26, Emilio wrote in his diary: "strong sorrow for the loss of the ascent."[188]

Humiliation was added to Emilio's sorrow when Soldà received the coveted Comitato Olimpico Nazionale Italiano (CONI) medal awarded by the CAI for the most daring ascent of the year. Emilio had not won the medal in 1933, when he had climbed the north face of the Cima Grande and the Spigolo Giallo. In 1934, Renato Chabod and Giusto Gervasutti won it for a trio of new routes in the Mont-Blanc group.

Climbers were often emotionally crushed by the disappointment of losing the medal in a year when they anticipated a victory. In 1935, Mary Varale, who had accompanied Alvise Andrich on the first ascent of the sustained south face of the Cimon della Pala, resigned from the CAI and quit climbing when the prize went instead to Raffaele Carlesso. She had brutal words for the judges: "In this company of hypocrites and buffoons I can no longer stay, I am sorry to lose the company of the dear comrades of Belluno, but I will not do anything in the mountains that can honour the Alpine Club from which I walk away disgusted."[189]

In 1937, the year Emilio soloed the north face of the Cima Grande, Ettore Castiglioni and Vitale Bramani won the medal for the first ascent of the northwest face of Switzerland's Piz Badile. In 1938, Cassin and Ratti had taken the prize for the first ascent of the northeast face of the Piz Badile. Naturally, this had been difficult for Emilio, whose climbs were always amongst the hardest efforts and who had craved honours ever since the Raspo cave rescue in the 1920s. He might have been passed over for reasons that were political or personal rather than athletic, but his chances of winning nonetheless diminished with the growing evidence that he was no longer the best climber in the Dolomites.

A week after Soldà and Conforto's victory on the Marmolada, 24-year-old guide Hans Vinatzer and Ettore Castiglioni climbed the hardest route in the Dolomites on the 1000-metre-high Punta Rocca, also on the Marmolada. After a day of hard climbing, Castiglioni shivered in his bivouac sack while Vinatzer slept as well as he could with nothing but old newspapers stuffed into his coat. The second half of the climb included some of the hardest free climbing ever done in the Alps. The Vinatzer-Castiglioni Route was not repeated until 1957. Emilio, like most active Dolomite climbers, would have known all about it through gossip from his friend Castiglioni, who was so taxed by the climb that he never hired Vinatzer again.

On September 8, Emilio returned to the Dito di Dio with expert client Sandro Del Torso and Piero Mazzorana, with whom Emilio had climbed his new route on the Cima Piccola. They made the first ascent of the Dito di Dio's 600-metre-high north face, a hard route that followed an almost perfect, vertical line. For del Torso, it was the climb of his lifetime. Emilio had already climbed the nearby northwest face with Fabjan seven years before and remained unenthusiastic. New routes on walls that had already been climbed bored him. Instead of enjoying the climbing on the Dito di Dio, he had two days on the route to brood on how much more he would have preferred to have made the first ascent of the pristine southwest face of the Marmolada.

Emilio had helped out Mazzorana when he chose him over Umberto Pacifico for the first ascent of the northwest ridge of the Cima Piccola, and he generously shared his guiding fees with him after the north face of the Dito di Dio. He unintentionally helped Mazzorana in another way. While Emilio stewed on the Dito di Dio, Mazzorana was polite and engaging companion. Afterwards, Mazzorana became the well-heeled Del Torso's favourite guide.[190]

Emilio thought so little of the Dito di Dio that he never mentioned it in his correspondence. Soon after his ascent, he wrote Casara to complain that he was running out of new walls to climb: "Meanwhile, the walls are taken by others. To me, every time a season of rock climbing passes, I am very melancholy and I feel I have done too little and I remain like a man whose hunger for the body of a beautiful woman can never be fully satisfied."[191]

Despite Emilio's ever-shortening list of projects, he procrastinated so much that the walls were often climbed by others first. He seemed almost to court the disappointment he felt at the loss of a first ascent.

His metaphor linking unfulfillable sexual desire to his remorse about unaccomplished climbs echoed the stresses in his relationship with Alice. She enjoyed rock climbing and the occasional ski trip, but her life was in the city, where she had a modest job and hoped to start her own adult life. Emilio wanted Alice but knew that he could not provide her with the normalcy that would be required to keep her.[192] Emilio, who had fulfilled climbing dreams few mountaineers would ever have been brave enough to voice, dwelled on his unquenchable desires.

Emilio's absences in the mountains had always upset Alice, and in April 1937, he planned his longest absence ever, a two-month-long trip to climb in Egypt with Anna Escher, her friend Dr. Gizman and the guide Jova Lipovec, who had been on the Spanish climbing trip. Alice could not compete against Escher's privilege. Escher's wealth allowed her to take Emilio away from home for months to entertain her in the mountains, and legitimized his absences as an essential part of his work. On April, 17, 1937, the day before Emilio was due to ship for Egypt on the SS *Galileo*, Alice broke off their relationship.

The ship called in Piraeus and Rhodes, and in the five days it took to reach Egypt, Emilio had time to himself to consider what to do about Alice, but as soon as he arrived in Alexandria, he was swept up into the exciting preparations for the desert adventure, which was to combine modern rock climbing with cross-country automobile exploration.

Their first objective was Itbāy, known to Europeans as the Red Sea Hills, a range of eroded volcanic rock peaks 350 kilometres south of Cairo. After the cars bogged down in the sand and had to be towed or pushed clear, they finally made it to a camp in a wadi beneath the red granite rock walls of Itbāy. The accounts of Western visitors were hard to reconcile with the canyons, rock faces and hills around their wadi campsite, but they settled on a new route on Gabel Sha'ib al Banat, at 2175 metres the highest mountain in mainland Egypt. Abu Harba had harder climbing, with long, unbroken rock walls, but the rock quality was too poor to inspire enough confidence to try a second climb.

Itbāy turned out to be something of a disappointment for climbing, and after a week, they made the long drive back to Alexandria, where Lipovec returned to Italy. Emilio, Gizman and Escher repacked for the train journey on the Sinai Military Railway to Wadi Feiran in the Sinai Peninsula, an area that had been extensively explored, if not by climbers, by prophets, monks, Arab hunters and the British Camel Corps.

On the granite mountains and walls of Sinai, they summited Um Shomer (2537 m), the second-highest mountain on the Sinai Peninsula and a beautiful peak with some steep face climbing on good rock. The northwest face of the Jebel Quattar provided a new 800-metre grade v. On Jebel Musa, they made the first ascent of the northwest face. On Jebel el Saru, they made the first ascent of the west face *direttissima*, which had sections of grade v.

In a couple of years, American rock climbers would climb Shiprock in Navajo territory in New Mexico, beginning an era of American desert rock climbing, but in 1937, Emilio and his friends were the first modern desert rock climbers. In an age obsessed with icy north faces, they explored the possibilities of pure rock climbing in wild settings, without the threat of rockfall or bad weather. An ethereal photo of Comici in an open shirt, a broad-brimmed sun hat and shorts, frozen in a balletic movement on a giant wind-carved feature, likely on Jebel el Saru, is a timeless image of rock climbing at its most balletic.

Emilio, who complained about approach hikes in the Alps, embraced the exotic challenge of desert approaches. On one occasion, however, he became separated from the rest of the group and was quickly lost in the unfamiliar desert terrain. An Arab he had helped down from a cliffside a few days before found him and brought him to safety.

Emilio had rescued refugees, stranded climbers and cavers trapped by floods. He had shielded his companions from rockfall with his body. The first person to rescue him was an Arab. After the rescue, Emilio grew a beard and wore little except shorts, boots and a turban; by the end of the trip, his skin was tanned deep brown. Unlike the Bedouins, though, Emilio maintained the privileges of being white – one of which was to dress like an Arab while ardently supporting a fascist regime that enforced brutal racist laws and committed acts of genocide against the Arabs in Libya and Black east Africans.

In Emilio's eyes, the Arabs were just part of the scenery. Their ongoing struggle with colonial powers was irrelevant to the sense of freedom he felt there. In Emilio's white, colonial gaze, what made the desert an Eden of rock climbing was the absence not of locals but of European climbers. Through the landscape of rock, sand, privilege and fantasy, he carried and nurtured his dream of climbing alone, on the wildest wall imaginable.

***

On the boat trip home to Trieste, Emilio convinced himself that the latest breakup with Alice was temporary and that she would at least meet him at the docks when he disembarked on May 17. She did not. On May 18 and 19, Emilio wrote in his diary, "A. does not come." On May 26, he noted that he "wrote her a letter."[193]

He took a guiding job in the Grignetta and lectured in Bergamo, but when he returned, he noted that "A. writes me but does not come."[194] In her letter, she revealed that she had fallen in love with another man. Emilio was desolate. "Saw A. in the Via Caducci with the other," he wrote. And then, "I wait for her outside her office at six and left as her good friend."[195] The underlined words might have been a warning to himself to accept Alice's decision, but they had little effect. The next weekend, he saw her in Val Rosandra. "How much bitterness," he wrote in a diary usually restricted to the most basic facts; "my greatest disillusionment."[196]

"I was ill and could not find peace or health," he wrote Casara; "that evil had brought me down badly, morally and physically."[197] Emilio was prone to bouts of depression, but this time, the illness crippled him. He might have picked up a virus in Egypt that worsened his typical symptoms, or his leg injury might have flared up, but whatever the cause, for a month and a half, he could not climb, guide, write or give presentations.

On June 28, an unexpected proposal from Casara arrived from Vicenza. Casara suggested that they attempt the north face of the Eiger. The north faces of the Grandes Jorasses, the Matterhorn and the Cima Grande di Lavaredo had all been climbed. Of the great north faces, only the northeast face of the Piz Badile and the most famous and sinister of all, the Eigerwand, remained unclimbed. The mere mention of that icy, dark 1800-metre-high wall overcame Emilio's symptoms.

In 1935, Germans Karl Mehringer and Max Sedlmeyer had died of exposure high on the face. In 1936, Germans Andreas Hinterstoisser and Toni Kurz and Austrians Willy Angerer and Edi Rainer had been trapped in bad weather above a traverse later named after Hinterstoisser. All but Kurz were swept off the face to their deaths by an avalanche. Kurz hung from his rope, out of reach of rescuers, until he died. Hitler, out of a predictable fascination with anything deadly and heroic, offered a prize to any German climbers who made the first ascent.

Most of the climbers who had attempted the Eiger were less talented and experienced than Emilio. Hinterstoisser and Kurz's biggest climb had been the fifth ascent of Comici's own route on the north face of the Cima Grande di Lavaredo. Not many Eiger climbers were any more expert at ice and snow climbing than Emilio, and the current preference for trying the climb in the summer made it mostly a rock climbing problem. Emilio was highly qualified for an attempt, and his enthusiastic response to Casara contrasted with his decreasing enthusiasm for objectives in the Dolomites:

> I am writing you urgently to let you know that if you intend
> to go to the Eiger there is not a moment to lose, because

the highly trained rope of [Giorgio] Pirovano, wrote to tell me that he has been training for more than a month with [Bruno] Detassis and that he was leaving that day for the Eiger, as are many other German, Italian, French Swiss, Yugoslavian, etc.... teams. Now I am overwhelmed by two obsessions, one that I cannot explain, and the Eiger. I would do anything to be there and I think if I was under the wall, I would even try it alone. Therefore, I beg you to make a decision and we will leave together, immediately. Maybe we do the Cima d'Auronzo for training, or we could go for a workout on the spot (in Grindelwald). If Carlesso came, it could also be a good thing, but two crazy people like us might succeed. I would carry only sleeping bags and bivy sacks for the bivouacs. The big question is how you can get Swiss money. Please call me by telephone asking for an urgent communication. I could leave by Saturday and be in Vicenza by noon with the equipment, if you want.[198]

Emilio's increasing dependence on climbing partners and friends who were also client-benefactors might have contributed to his idea that an attempt on the Eiger with Casara was a good idea. Like Preuss, he was the type of expert who thrived when he was the strongest and most experienced leader. Emilio would not have invited Carlesso, since they had fallen out, but Carlesso would have been a more suitable partner than Casara, who had no chance of scaling the hardest north wall in the Alps.

Emilio, however, soon had second thoughts about trying the wall with Casara. It was one thing to humour a client-friend on familiar mountains, and another to launch onto one of the hardest climbs in the world with a man who some considered a fantasist. Before Casara had a chance to respond, Emilio sent him a telegraph to cancel his proposal.

"Bad timing," Emilio wrote, "needless to come."[199]

After the Eiger's brief moment on Emilio's itinerary of projects, only the obsession he alluded to in correspondence, but neither revealed nor explained – but for which he seemed as yet, unready – remained on his list. Liberated from the climbing desires that had tortured him, Emilio haphazardly, and yet with a certain peace with himself, fell in with partners on routes they had selected, often against his advice. These climbs were typified by encounters with rockfall, avalanches, bad rock, storms, hapless partners and ghosts, and in Emilio's reports, comprise the most complete, personally integrated and even strangely tranquil periods of climbing of his life.

Emilio's first climb since Egypt, and the climb he would attempt with Casara in lieu of the Eiger, was the 1000-metre-high south face of the Cima d'Auronzo on the Croda dei Toni in the Sexten Dolomities. Casara had tried to get Emilio to attempt the wall for years, but Emilio thought it was ugly and doubted the quality of the rock.

From the start, it was a stressful excursion. The road to the Principe Umberto hut was closed for repairs, and they had to walk uphill for hours in the dark to reach the hut. Emilio, who often had trouble falling asleep, got little rest that night. The next day, they trudged uphill for a reconnaissance and to stow their gear for an attempt, but then the weather broke. The wet snow was tinged blood red, which seemed ominous to Emilio, although the source of the redness might have been the corroding equipment from the Great War strewn across the talus. They stowed their gear in a trench lined with old armour plates and waited for the clouds to thin and allow a glimpse of the wall. Emilio tried to sing himself to sleep with his favourite song of the moment, "Triste Domenica" (Gloomy Sunday), Rezső Seressa's so-called "Hungarian Suicide Song,"

> Sunday is gloomy,
> My hours are slumberless
> Dearest the shadows
> I live with are numberless
> Little white flowers
> Will never awaken you
> Not where the black coach of
> Sorrow has taken you
> Angels have no thought
> Of ever returning you,

Would they be angry
If I thought of joining you?

Casara, however, kept Emilio awake by speaking of what Emilio called "strange things" about Paul Preuss. As Emilio listened and watched the face, the clouds dissipated and he "saw the mythical silhouette of Preuss climbing up [Casara's chosen line] in front of us," he said, "all alone, with his unmistakable style," of which he had heard from Emmy. "Then the words [of Preuss] touched the core of my being, my eyes clouded and as if through a veil, the rocks became confused. When I saw clearly again, Preuss was gone."[200]

A cascade of rockfall triggered by snowmelt poured down the face. If they had been closer, or the rock had fallen while they were on the wall, they would have been killed. It was one of the many times in his climbing career that Emilio's intuition of the presence of danger was accompanied by the experience of ghosts.

The ghosts of Spinotti on the north face of the Riofreddo and Orsini on the Torre degli Orsi had urged Emilio upwards to justify their sacrifices. No blood had been shed to conquer the south face of the Cima d'Auronzo. There was no *vendetta*. Emilio could walk away with honour. Was the ghost a manifestation of Emilio's sense that given his partner, the rockfall and the bad weather, they might face serious consequences on this wall?

The sky was full of low clouds the next morning. They climbed anyway, because Casara did not know better and Emilio had been less cautious since his last breakup with Alice. Clouds darkened by the hour, but they went on. An exposed and unprotected traverse was as dangerous for Casara as for Emilio, but both climbed it quickly, conscious of the impending bad weather. Snow, accompanied by thunder, overtook them on the last half of the wall. Emilio climbed without protection. Time after time, he thought he was on the last pitch, only to find that the falling snow had hidden the mountain above.

On the summit, their hardware hummed from the electrical charge in the air. Emilio said his "face felt like it was being caressed by a horrible maiden, from underneath my clothes and up towards my hair. It was the electricity of the peak escaping through our bodies. The summit cairn made noises like sizzling, a big pot of boiling oil, or as if the stones were a hundred singing cicadas."[201]

To Emilio's horror, Casara did not seem to understand the risk of being killed by lightning. When Casara knelt to write a note for the tin can that served as the summit register, Emilio shouted at him to leave the summit at once.

On the descent, the air was thick with snow, and they shivered and fought to remain mentally focussed. A rappel sling on a rock spike began to become untied as Casara rappelled. Emilio shook off his torpor fast enough to replace the sling before Casara fell to his death.

After the Cima d'Auronzo, Emilio returned to Trieste to teach at the climbing school and try to mend things with Alice, who was single once again. Fabjan, who knew Emilio better than most, said that Emilio hung on to the relationship with Alice mostly because she was the first woman who walked away from him before he was done with her.[202] Emilio's inability to either abandon the relationship or provide the stability needed to maintain it doomed him to a cycle of breakups and rapprochements that were emotionally intense but settled nothing.

In 1937, Emilio's financial situation continued to embarrass him. He ran out of money and accepted a loan from his mother, a deeply shameful situation, since it had always been his intention to continue to support his family on Via Bazzoni, even when he lived in Misurina. In the entire month of August, he only found enough clients for five days of work, even when he reduced his fees by half. Tourists continued to ask for his autograph, but they hired less famous guides.[203]

Emilio's poverty as a guide coincided with his discovery that soloing appealed to his sense of *lontananza*, more than the piton-heavy approach to big walls that had made him famous. He did not give up on big wall climbing as he had come to know it, but he had already thought up a plan in which soloing and his big wall experience would complement each other. He told a climbing friend, Gianfranco Pompei, about his secret obsession: to bring Preuss's solo approach to a climb from his own oeuvre. And not just any climb, but the creation that had brought him both glory and pain: the north face of the Cima Grande.

It was an astounding vision. A solo would be greater, even, than the first ascent. No one had ever free soloed a grade VI, because few climbers could climb at that level without absolute confidence that they would not fall. Emilio planned to free solo most of the route, but he would have to use aid on the bottom half of the climb. It would take incredible strength to struggle with pitons and *staffe* without rope tension from a partner. Even with some aid on the lower half, the route would be dangerous without a proper belay. The upper half of the climb was easier, but still grade VI, and many parties still used some pitons for aid. Rescue anywhere on the route would take days to arrange. Even if he could rig a rope on some of the aid sections, for the majority of the route, a fall would kill him.

The plaudits for such a climb would be inevitable. There were few solo climbers in the Alps, and mostly they stayed on less steep routes with secure cracks or, in a few cases, ice routes. The only solo climb in recent years that had caught the public's attention was Gervasutti's 1936 Christmas Eve solo of the Matterhorn, partly because of its pious overtones. No one had soloed one of the great north faces, let alone a climber who had also made the first ascent of the same wall.

The intensification of climbing experiences by grades, and the implication that to pursue that difficulty was not just an option but both natural and the source of merit in climbing, had always been in harmony with Emilio's personality. Since the Campanile Basso, Emilio had adapted himself to an existence that offered rewards and risks few had savoured. The logic of his new life on the mountains led him, alone, directly to the north face of the Cima Grande.

The decision to solo the north face was also fuelled by Emilio's unresolved *vendetta* with the Dimais. Free soloing the pitch Giuseppe Dimai had led because he said that Emilio had been too weak to continue would prove not only Emilio's ability but his superiority. Even after Emilio had moved into a higher and more rarified field of climbing endeavours, he could not forget a slight to himself or his comrades, whether it came from rivals, a mountain, or even death itself, the power at the root of all of his quarrels with the world.

This quarrel with death, his oldest adversary, justified on its own the total risks of the climb. The mystics could speak of making friends with death, but Emilio was its sworn enemy, ready to take umbrage at its every incursion into his world. His solo would question death's rule over one of its least disputed realms, the north walls of the Alps.

***

By 1937, the north face of the Cima Grande had been climbed at least 30 times. Austrians Peter and Paul Aschenbrenner had made the second ascent a month after Emilio and the Dimais and discovered the abandoned drill on the bivouac ledge. Although the Aschenbrenners took the gear as a souvenir, no one seemed to have been scandalized by their discovery.[204]

The Aschenbrenners were so impressed with the first ascensionists that Peter said, "We will never be able to overcome greater technical difficulties."[205] Germans Andreas Hinterstoisser and Toni Kurz and Austrian Mathias Rebitsch had climbed it, and so had Italy's best: Hans Vinatzer, Mario Dell'Oro, Raffaele Carlesso and Riccardo Cassin. The oldest climber of the north face was Peter Aschenbrenner, who was born a year before Emilio; Heckmair and Dell'Oro were 30. The rest were in their 20s. Emilio was 36 and planned to solo what the others had done with partners.

The wall had become a barometer of climbers' skills. The first eight ascents had been made with at least one and sometimes two bivouacs. On the ninth ascent, German climbers Arthur Heilin and Joseph Reischman stormed the wall in 12 hours. By 1937, the record was five and a half hours. But to do the climb alone, at speed, was such a break with the wall's history to that point that Emilio brought his friend Gianfranco Pompei as a witness.

On September 2, 1937, Emilio arrived at the base at 11 a.m. He knew from the hut logbook that Germans Killian Weissensteiner and Hubert Höller had started out early that morning, and he wanted to give them time to complete the lower half of the climb, where they would be hard to pass. His calculation had been correct, and they were already 200 metres up the face when he arrived. Emilio would reach them when they were on the easier upper half of the route, where he could pass them if he needed to.

Emilio carried barely enough equipment for a day in Val Rosandra: a hammer, ten carabiners and pitons and a 20-metre rope he would tie in a loop to his waist and clip into any pitons he found. He carried a single *staffa* but planned to pull up on the pitons with his hands as much as possible. In case of retreat he had a thin rappel line with him. When he reached the Italian Bivouac, he would coil the ropes, clip his carabiners and pitons to them and throw it all off the wall. He would then be committed to free soloing the last 350 metres.

As Emilio arranged his equipment, the Germans dislodged some rocks that tumbled through the air before they broke on the talus five metres out from the wall. Emilio shrugged to reassure Pompei and started to climb. At the first aid pitch, he was still a little clumsy with his unfamiliar self-belay system and dropped a carabiner. He still had nine, but on this, the ultimate climb, there could be no more mistakes.

On the next pitch, he attached himself to a piton with a carabiner and tied in to both ends of the rope so that when he no longer needed the security of the piton, he could untie one end and pull the rope through and save time at the expense of a couple of pieces of hardware. He aid climbed on pitons for 20 metres, until he no longer needed the rope. He untied one end of the rope, but as he pulled it through, it twisted and jammed in the below carabiner. It was the second mishap of the climb.

Piton by piton, with his fingers pinched by the rope creaking and twisting in the carabiners, Emilio climbed down to the rope jam, freed it and climbed back up. On the next pitch, he let the ropes hang from his waist and free soloed, as he had done on the Campanile Basso. He felt free and secure, with good holds, on steep but firm rock. He sang as he climbed. When a foot slipped, he laughed. As frightening as it must have been for Pompei to watch, Emilio was solid.

A hundred metres below the bivouac ledge, he shouted to the party ahead to be careful not to drop any rocks because he was alone.

"Alone?"

There was a pause.

"We're Killian and Hubert. Who are you?"

"Comici!"

Another pause.

"We thought so!"[206]

Emilio had reached the most strenuous pitch of the climb, the overhanging 20-metre crack and the traverse where he had let Giuseppe Dimai take the lead. Emilio was disappointed to find fixed pitons in the crack, which had been pristine before the last time he climbed it. Without realizing it, Emilio and the Dimais had defeated not just the wall itself but the concept of the impossible in the Dolomites. Ironically, they had also made the former symbol of the impossible accessible to less extraordinary climbers by leaving pitons in place.

Emilio had observed the end of timelessness in alpinism. After Mont-Blanc and the Matterhorn had first been climbed, they remained more or less as they had been for a century. Reaching these summits required the same bravery and skills in 1930 as it had in 1850. After 30 ascents, the reign of the north face of the Cima Grande as a fearsome route was ending, largely because of the increasing number of fixed pitons that made the climb easier and safer for each subsequent party. Emilio and the Dimais had left 30 pitons on the wall; by 1937, there were more than 90. Emilio said he felt sorry for the mountain, but the ironmongery on the crux allowed him to make fast work of it.

He coiled the rope and slung it over his shoulders to free solo the traverse he had surrendered to Giuseppe Dimai on the first ascent. Now he would undo the humiliation of giving up the lead to Giuseppe in 1933. Emilio picked his way across the vertical wall alone, unroped, where the slightest error would send him hundreds of metres to his death on the talus. He later said that Giuseppe's traverse was, at best, no harder than grade iv.

At the Italian Bivouac, Emilio made some small talk with the startled Germans as he snacked on some sugar and chocolate. Then he coiled his ropes, clipped his carabiners and pitons to the coils and threw them off the wall. The bundle of manila and steel tumbled silently through the air for many seconds before it crashed into the talus, 30 metres away from the wall.

The Germans were shocked, but Emilio was calm. He had already free soloed three climbs at least as long and difficult as the rest of the route without incident. He left a note to prove he had been on the ledge and free soloed out ahead of the others. It can be dangerous to follow other climbers on limestone walls, since no matter how careful they are, they could drop rocks on climbers below. A soloist could also become a dangerous projectile. The Germans, however, trusted Emilio's reputation too much to bring up these objections. They set out after Emilio had climbed about 30 metres.

When Emilio soloed, he instinctively avoided holds that looked suspiciously friable and carefully tugged even solid-looking holds before he weighted them. But to climb on alpine limestone is to accept the limits of knowledge and to proceed on faith. Fifty metres above the bivouac, he reached a ledge where he could stand with both his feet and view the rock above. From his stance, he could see at least one overhang where most climbers still used aid.

Without any warning, the ledge slipped off of the mountain. He slapped his free hand on the closest hold, gripped hard, and scrabbled for purchase in his basketball shoes on the dusty scar where the ledge had been. With his heart beating fast, he saw the ledge plummet past the Germans and burst into fragments against the bivouac ledge. Then he saw Pompei, a tiny figure on the ground, walking into the path of the rockfall to retrieve his rope and carabiners. He screamed for Pompei to run, but his voice was muffled by the wind. As if by a miracle, the stones peppered the scree around Pompeii and left him unharmed.

Emilio climbed down through air that smelled of crushed rock, checking every hold more carefully than before. A white scar marked where the rock had struck the ledge beside the Germans, but to Emilio's relief, they were both unharmed. Emilio apologized, and although he had no real way to control it, risked a promise that there would be no more broken holds. The fact that a few minutes ago his solo attempt had almost cost his life, the lives of the Germans and the life of his friend on the ground remained unsaid. Emilio would not allow himself to turn back, so his life depended on climbing the last 350 metres as calmly as if the rock had never fallen.

Emilio did not record his state of mind on the upper wall but elsewhere spoke of a trance-like state when he soloed. "I like [soloing] immensely," Emilio wrote. "I have not tried anything more beautiful [than the north face of the Cima Grande]. If these moments brought me joy, it means that they also messed me up and dazed me. It is beautiful, very beautiful to climb everything free, on a wall that overhangs. To see between your legs that emptiness and feel that you can dominate it with your abilities alone. When I am alone, I always look down to inebriate myself with emptiness and I sing with joy. If I do not have the breath to sing because I am on a difficult passage, then the song remains, silently inside my head."[207]

His client Antonia Pozzi was the greatest poet of the psychological and spiritual landscape of climbing between the world wars. Her reflections on Emilio's climbing in a poem dedicated to him offer her insights into Emilio's preoccupations while he was "messed up" and inebriated with emptiness on the final 350 metres of the north face of the Cima Grande.

Ascent

Your hand blooms on the rock
We are unafraid of the silence.
The immense womb,
The valley elides fear
Distant avalanches
Are light smoke
On black walls,

Your fingers on
The stone
Reach upwards
For the white edge of the sky
We are not afraid of the desert

Let us go up to Cima Sorapis
Where we will be alone
And exposed
On the crystal altar.[208]

An hour and a quarter after he had left the Italian Bivouac, Emilio slipped out of the shadows of the north face and stood in the sunshine on the summit. He was the first to reach it that day.

He took the summit register out of the steel box bolted to the rusty cross. Inscribed on its pages were the entry he had made after the first ascent of the wall he had climbed alone, the names of the rivals and friends who had climbed it since, the climbers from all over the world who had scaled this, the proudest rock pillar in the Dolomites; the communion of the climbing living and dead. He flipped ahead to a blank page and added a note unprecedented in the history of climbing. He had soloed the north face of the Cima Grand in three hours and 15 minutes.

He closed the book and laid his head on his rucksack to have a nap. An hour later, the first party of the day on the Via Normale arrived on the summit. Emilio was easily recognized by climbers throughout the Eastern Alps. They asked him whether he had climbed the north face.

"Yes."

"Then where is your partner?"

"I climbed it alone. It's a very beautiful route. Have you done it?"[209]

He still heard them babbling when he lay down again on his rucksack.

It was the hardest solo ever done. The master of aid climbing was now also Preuss's obvious successor. Emilio had become the first climber to solo one of the classic north faces, and remained the only climber to make both the first ascent and first solo ascent of any of them. Free soloing had just been the way that Preuss usually climbed. With Emilio, it became a sport and a style unto itself, albeit one open only to the very best climbers.

His climb would have seemed to have transcended all doubts about his mastery of the north face of the Cima Grande. A few days afterwards, Emilio was back on the summit of the Cima Grande with guiding clients. When he flipped to the new page on the summit register, someone had scratched out his note about his solo climb and scribbled in the margin, "Exaggeration!" Someone else had written "*Bumm*," Tyrolean slang for crazy.

Summit registers and hut logbooks had always tempted climbers to anonymous insults and compliments. Sometimes, the insults backfired. When the Germans wrote in the summit register of the Civetta that the northwest face was "no food for Italians," they galvanized

Italian climbers to improve. Emilio could have scratched out or ignored the slight. Predictably, he chose to treat the comments as a serious affront.

Emilio suspected the Dimais or some other rival who anticipated his reaction to be the culprit.[210] Instead of ignoring the insult, Emilio announced that if the anonymous detractor identified himself and offered a wager, Emilio would solo the face again and shave 30 minutes off his time.

Although he could have made up the time merely by avoiding the mishaps with the stuck rope and the loose rock, the dare exposed a petty, self-defeating side of Emilio. His solo had been in the finest traditions of alpinism. He could have weighed the two words in the logbook against the numerous letters and telegrams he had received from all over the world praising his solo, and dismissed the scribblers as unworthy of his attention. The solo was so far ahead of anything yet done, it would remain unrepeated for 24 years.[211] There was no need to boast that he could do even better.

Emilio was also embarrassing himself politically by taking umbrage. He had praised the partnership of the rope, but now, he seemed to prefer his own company in the mountains. His attitude fell outside of the fascist narrative in which mountaineering was a metaphor for literal battle precisely because, on the mountain, comrades strove together, not alone, for victory. "Only some forms of camaraderie," wrote Evola, "forged during wartime on the battlefield, may bring about, like the experience of the mountain, this active sense of solidarity... this is virility without ostentation..."[212]

Emilio's reaction reminded Manaresi and Berti of his unwelcome complaints about the Dimais, his inability to let any slight go unanswered and his combination of fame and self-absorption. To the fascist intellectuals of the CAI, Emilio's dare was more proof of his proletarian lack of gentlemanly polish. The climbers who saw Emilio as a self-promoter, a modern soul with little feel for traditions or community, were too sophisticated to write silly comments in a logbook, and in many cases too old to climb the Cima Grande. When Emilio cited the whole climbing world as potential authors of the comment, he had created an impasse for himself. No score could be settled against his anonymous detractors.

Emilio's last new routes of 1937 were partly to pay back Gianfranco Pompei for his help with the Cima Grande. Together, they climbed a new grade VI on the north face of the striking but short pillar near Misurina know as Guglia Giuliana and the easier, 300-metre south ridge of Il Mulo, a sub-peak of the Cima Ovest.

In early autumn, Emilio's leg injury flared up once again. His mother had come down with chronic mastoiditis, an infection of the skull behind the ear, and before the fall weather came, he retreated to Trieste to rest his leg and attend to her. "Everyone on earth must suffer," Emilio wrote Casara from Trieste, "and many people are more miserable than I am. What I really cannot stand and what causes me terrible pain is the pain of a mother, and my dear mother... These mothers suffer a lot but do not complain."[213] Emilio found in his mother something like the *Mater Dolorosa*, or Mother of Sorrows, of Catholic piety, ever present in her temple on Via Bazzoni, where her son might, at any time he needed, find succour.

Here was a source of Emilio's *lontananza*: Regina's love was beyond anything that could ever be known with climbing partners or lovers. Her love kept him apart from others and devoted to her. The ultimate test of the mother's love, the event for which she prepared both herself and her son, was their inevitable separation. In the story of the passion of Christ, that separation was through death and resurrection. For many traditional Italian women, it was through the slightly less awesome but nonetheless distressing process of the son's marriage to a woman who would replace her. Losing Emilio to a wife seemed less likely every year, now that he was in his mid-thirties, but he had chosen another love in life, and one with much more literal potential to take him from her.

Emilio knew that his love affair with climbing might add to his mother's sorrows. His solos were more dangerous than the climbs that had won him his fame. Deaths in climbing depressed him, partly because he considered each one a *vendetta* that must be settled against, or at least, on, the mountain. He knew that the fallen were mostly as strong as he was. He knew he could die too. Emilio, however, with his tears, ghosts, depressions and worship of his suffering mother, accepted the potential cost of his dreams and felt powerless to resist them.

To the poet Vergil, *ante ora parentum* – a parent watching the death and burial of their own child – was the apotheosis of anguish; the climbing community, however, had become inured to the deaths of its young. Accidents happened in a few incomprehensible and almost unreportably violent moments. They had become so common that climbers developed language and symbology to slow down death in the mountains enough to beautify and comprehend it in elegiac language. Emilio had had cause to use these words many times.

In 1937, Italians were beginning to see the difference between Mussolini's speeches about the glories of Italian expansion and the complicated realities of foreign adventures. The war in Ethiopia, although declared an unequivocal victory by the party, ground on, with guerilla attacks by the Ethiopians and massacres of prisoners by Italian troops. Mussolini's unpopular support of General Franco brought Italian fascism more and more in line with Nazism, to the chagrin of fascists like Emilio who were decidedly anti-German. Both campaigns drained the government's funds at a time of economic crisis and resulted in thousands of Italian casualties.

"Gloomy is Sunday, with shadows I spend it all," ran the lyrics to Emilio favourite song. In 1937, two of the beacons of his life – climbing and Mussolini – faltered. Then he lost a third. After his Cima Grande solo, Alice visited him in Misurina, where they had their last fight. In the morning, she left abruptly for Florence, far from both the mountains and Trieste. Emilio never saw her again.

CHAPTER EIGHT

BLOOD THAT DREAMS OF STONE

In late 1937, Emilio wrote an emotional and eerie account of the first ascent of the south face of the Cima d'Auronzo. In the past, Emilio's writing had reflected seasons of ambitions and worries about how he might be seen by his readers. In the opening paragraphs of this piece, Emilio set the tone for an extraordinary piece of work: "Readers of this article who are mainly interested in my mountaineering will find little interest in my sufferings and the state of my nerves, but I write of these things because of their close relationship to my work... I fear that this piece will gain criticism, because I may be too sincere, and will hide nothing because it will bring me no honour."[214]

In the Cima d'Auronzo piece, Emilio achieved a new level of psychological insight and frankness about himself, his psychological experiences, his partner Casara and the risks they took on the wall. Casara decided that the benefits of publishing a report on a first ascent he had made with Emilio outweighed the potential embarrassment of Emilio's frankness about his poor performance. He submitted Emilio's article to Berti and promised Emilio that it would be published, not as a short article in the *Rivista Mensile* but in the CAI's vaunted annual journal. He submitted the piece on Emilio's behalf, and they waited for a response.

Writing frustrated Emilio, and he blamed how long it had taken him to finish the piece on his lack of education. His insecurity was deepened by the CAI's exclusion of mountain guides from membership, first in the academic section and then in the national club. Members were required to have spent the last four seasons climbing as amateurs, which was obviously impossible for mountain guides. The goal was to maintain the control of the club by urban, educated social elites and to exclude lower-income mountain-based climbers from decision-making in the climbing community. A CAI member from

Trieste tried to introduce a motion to make an exception for Emilio, but Manaresi quashed it.[215]

Although Emilio expressed grudging respect for Berti and the editors of the CAI, the constructive criticisms of friends and sometimes harsh judgements of editors stung him. In the mountains, he had done brilliant things without the benefits of learning; in the publishing world, the academics remained his masters.

After months of silence from Berti about his Cima d'Auronzo article, Emilio complained to Casara, who had encouraged him to write more. Casara had no option but to wait on Berti's pleasure. By mid-March of 1938, Emilio was skeptical that the piece would ever be published and commented that publication could "take years," and asked Casara to get his manuscript back.[216]

Berti tried to deflect Emilio's reaction to the delay of his article with a compliment. Although Berti acknowledged that the Cima d'Auronzo piece was "the best piece of alpine literature he had ever read," he said it was not right for the CAI.[217] He suggested that Emilio submit it to the literary journal, *La Lettura*, a middlebrow literary magazine published by *La Domenica del Corriere*, roughly comparable to the American *New Yorker* magazine. Some would have seen Berti's assessment as a handsome compliment. Emilio, however, did not subscribe to a hierarchy of cultural values in which a literary magazine was a more exalted platform for his work than a mountaineering journal.

Berti's motivation not to publish Emilio's piece was most likely aesthetic. Berti's readership expected climbers to portray themselves as gentle and poetic yet tough under pressure. Their views on nature were meant to be pastoral and appreciative and more important to them than climbing controversies and techniques. Modern exceptions like Rudatis and Buzzati had, to some degree, circumvented these norms, but only by strenuously intellectualizing climbing and making it awkwardly nationalistic.

Emilio's writing mirrored the physical and psychological strain of modern climbing: sleepless nights in slings, climbing hundreds of metres of overhanging rock, penduluming off bad pitons, falling off and tearing out pitons, being pummelled by falling rock, free climbing overhangs and avenging the deaths of his climbing partners on the walls that had killed them. Although Emilio was not a literary aficionado, he took the challenge of recording all of this straight-on and avoided literary flourishes and clichés. For his trouble, the Cima d'Auronzo piece was rejected during his lifetime and only published a year after his death, not in an Italian magazine but in the *Austrian Alpine Journal*.[218]

His next piece, "La falciata della morte" ("The Scythe of Death"), was even more extraordinary. The short work of creative non-fiction was based on Emilio and Osiride Brovedani's close call with rockfall on a 650-metre-high wall on the Pomagagnon, north of Cortina.

Brovedani was one of Emilio's most extraordinary partners.[219] Although he was a *Triestino* of working-class background, he was not the typical GARS climber, happy to escape to the mountains or Val Rosandra on the weekend and shuffle off to a modest job in Trieste on Monday morning. Brovedani had made a fortune after he acquired a franchise to make Fissan pasta. He started in a tiny rented basement workshop, but by 1938, he was a self-made 44-year-old pasta tycoon and factory owner.

Brovedani was also a self-educated polymath who could discuss the ideas of Rudatis and Evola, trends in modern painting and the latest innovations in heavy machining. He was the first person Emilio had met from his own working-class background whose intellectual horizons equalled those of bourgeois elites like Rudatis and Casara, despite his lack of an expensive and socially inaccessible university education. By 1938, Brovedani only climbed recreationally, but he lived a stoic lifestyle and kept fit. He could have afforded to hire Emilio as a guide, but either he climbed well enough or Emilio liked him too much to charge him.

Emilio and Brovedani were climbing on Pomagagnon in the Eastern Dolomites in 1938 when a 150-metre long section of a ridge overhead broke off. The rockfall was so enormous that the dust cloud came down to the valley and photographers in Cortina captured it on film. The shockwave from the falling rock was so strong that Emilio and Brovedani thought they would be obliterated, but a ridge directed the landslide away from them.

After the climb, they investigated the huge, sickle-shaped track of fresh rockfall at the base. Rock dust in the air settled on their clothes and made them look like ghosts. When more rock clattered down the wall, they ran for shelter at the base. As he scrambled towards safety, Emilio had a vision of his corpse being taken away by the Cortina mountain rescue team. He imagined the mourners at his funeral and cursed himself for ignoring a nagging intuition that he should renew his life insurance policy.

Although Emilio climbed a grade vi the next day, he had a strange experience that night. "I turned to go to bed and got a glimpse of my naked body in the long closet mirror," he wrote. "Honestly, I almost never look in the mirror, especially when I am naked. My lean legs were thinly swathed in muscle and my chest was disproportionately large and cobbled with muscles that suggested a horrible, apocalyptic vision of death in the form of an anatomical study. I was horrified, but a moment later, on the other hand, I saw myself as handsome. I did not seem to be myself. To make sure I was not asleep, I felt my chest and legs and arms and saw myself as a beautiful, dark, suntanned, true masterpiece of nature."[220]

Whether Emilio intended to publish the piece is unclear. The *distacco* people sometimes observed in Emilio kept him a man apart, even in his moments of joviality and fellowship. He was sometimes a mystery to his friends and, as this passage reveals, at times an enigma even to himself.

In March, 1938, Emilio took a three-week job as a ski guide for Anna Escher and her sons. They started out in Tržič in Yugoslavia and moved on to Kleine Scheidegg in Switzerland in early April. From the famous hotel patio at Kleine Scheidegg, Emilio could see the unclimbed north face of the Eiger. Less than a year before, just the prospect of attempting the face had healed the symptoms of his paralyzing depression. He made no mention of it now. A winter-conditions attempt, even with the best partners, was out of the question at the time, but the fact that Emilio did not even mention the wall suggests that he was more at peace with himself than he had been in 1937.

"I'm a real mountain guide," he wrote Casara, "not the academic alpinist who came to you for some reason. That man is my shadow."[221]

***

While Emilio struggled with his vocation as a writer, he had less difficulty expressing his climbing style and ideals through the popular modern medium of photography. He had made the first film that presented real-world high-level modern climbing skills to the crowds at the movie theatres. Photographers, under Emilio's direction, made several series of action photographs of Emilio climbing cracks and overhangs, rappelling, belaying and hammering pitons, all mostly in Val Rosandra. It was one of the first comprehensive photographic catalogues of climbing techniques, and it supplied posterity with the most referenced visual images of Emilio.

Emilio leans into the wall and braces with a shoulder when he belays a second, he thrusts his hips in any direction that maintains a low centre of gravity, he avoids moving off bent arms and uses both the inside and outside edges of his feet. He drops his knee to get his foot on an otherwise unreachable hold. When he is aid climbing, he looks kinetic, swinging or leaning off of a carabiner, always with at least one hand or foot on the rock itself and usually a tip-toe in his *staffe*. Sometimes he grimaces in concentration, but usually he is smiling and having fun. The photographs, along with his film, make Emilio one of the first rock climbers who can still be seen in action, proudly showing off his tricks just as he had to his partners.

In January 1938, Emilio presented his movie at a film festival in Turin. The organizers asked him to promote it with a climbing demonstration. He provided the festival with a plan for an elaborate artificial climbing wall, but all they could produce in time for the event was a couple of blank, unclimbable slabs of granite masonry a few metres high. A chisel was produced to try to make holds, but in the end, Emilio had no choice but to reduce his demonstration to rappelling and prusiking the rope. "Very sad," Emilio said. "The audience applauds you, as if after an acrobatic number... I am almost ashamed to leave the house."[222]

Emilio's film did not win a prize. In France and Germany, alpine documentaries were popular, but in Italy, most mountain films were still set on the Alpine Front in the Great War.[223] In both Italian and German mountain films, the mountains were not a place for modern recreation but a stoic refuge from modern life. Emilio's film invited his viewers to witness athletic pleasure on the rocks and was too light for most critics' tastes and, not coincidentally, the mood in climbing.

In the summer of 1938, climbers focussed on two of the Alps' most deadly walls, the Walker Spur on the north face of the Grandes Jorasses in the Mont-Blanc range, and the north face of the Eiger. Both walls were arduous and committing and had already claimed the lives of climbers.

In late July, an Austrian-German party of Anderl Heckmair, Wiggerl Vörg, Fritz Kasparek and Heinrich Harrer made the first ascent of the north face of the Eiger. In four days of brilliant climbing, Heckmair, who had also climbed Emilio's route on the north face of the Cima Grande di Lavaredo, led the way to the top of the biggest and most dangerous face in the Alps.

Italians Cassin, Ugo Tizzoni and Gino Esposito had planned to climb the north wall of the Eiger but arrived in Grindelwald just as news reached town that Heckmair's party had made it to the top. Undeterred in their quest for a prize of the highest order, they went straight to Chamonix. Despite their inexperience in Europe's highest mountains, they made the first ascent of the Walker Spur, arguably an even harder climb than the Eiger. For Esposito and Cassin, who had made the first ascent of the northeast face of the Piz Badile in Switzerland in 1937 with Vittorio Ratti, the Walker was their second great north wall. It was also the last of the north walls to be climbed. The trio received the CONI medal of honour for their climb in a solemn presentation from Mussolini himself. All three wore blackshirts and full fascist uniforms for the occasion.[224]

It was a glorious summer for the alpinists of fascist Italy and their ally, Nazi Germany. Even for climbers leery of fascism, the climbs of 1938 suggested that something extraordinary was going on in countries that could field such daring and tough young men. Emilio, however, had no part in either of these efforts.

In the spring of 1938, Hitler took over Austria in the Anschluss to create a massive single German state on Italy's hard-won northern border. Hitler did not inform Mussolini of his intentions in advance. As soon as the Germans arrived in Vienna, the Nazis proceeded to parade Jews through the streets, steal their property and force them to clean public toilets and wash the streets.

Emilio had never been sympathetic to Germans, and several of his climbing partners, including Riccardo Deffar and Osiride Brovedani, came from Jewish backgrounds, as had his hero, Paul Preuss. When he learned of recent events in Vienna, his first thought was not of politics but of Emmy. He wrote to Casara and asked if he had heard from her. Casara responded: "Always the eternal Emmy. Empires fall, Austria falls, the world changes, but the Emmys are always the same, whether they sleep on a rock, a motorcycle or a comfortable bed."[225]

Casara's response was a cruel or at least ignorant appraisal of the dangers threatening a woman to whom he had confessed his love. Like many Europeans, Casara unwittingly but surely and effortlessly slipped into anti-Semitic tropes when he spoke of how Jews would weather the Nazi takeover of Austria because they were "eternal" and had a pest-like capacity for survival.

Like many naive Italian fascists, Emilio believed, despite growing evidence to the contrary, that anti-Semitism would never be officially encouraged by the party. Mussolini, however, revealed his own anti-Semitic beliefs when he adopted racial policies parallel to Hitler's. In 1938, he banned Jews from owning large businesses and attending state schools and universities. Books with Jewish authors were removed from libraries. The CAI had already banned Jews from its huts and trails, and although the policies were not enforced as strictly as they were by the German Alpine Club, many sections posted notices prohibiting Jews in their huts. At first, some Italian fascists had resisted racial measures. On November 18, 1938, opposition to party-led racial laws became illegal. Nazi-style legislation came into effect, banning intermarriage between Jews and non-Jews and excluding Jews from government jobs. After 16 years of fascism, in which the party had gained control over all aspects of national and local life, there was little that anyone could do to stop this final step in the direction of Nazism. Tragically, the Julian section of the CAI had not taken a passive role in this development. The section banned all Jews from their activities and properties six months before it was required by law.[226]

Emilio withdrew from hard climbing, the only pursuit which had gained him any attention from his superiors in the party. For now, his political fantasies were lived out in his capacity as an army reservist rather than in the increasingly xenophobic, racist and violent *squadristi*. The army had liberated Trieste not with racial laws, secret arrests, oppression or even combat of any kind but with parades, marching bands, drunken bonfires and crowds singing the "Marcia Reale." Emilio's love of Italy had its most bittersweet, enduring outlet in his childlike, unreciprocated love of the army. As he marched in regimental parades and mounted colour guards at fancy events for party bosses, sometimes even nostalgically costumed as an *alpini* from the Great War, Emilio could imagine himself not just as an armed member of a political party but as one of the same liberators who had ended the 500-year nightmare of Austrian rule over his beloved hometown.

***

Emilio had played the guitar and mandolin and sung since he was a boy. He loved the emotional folk songs of Italy, despite the fact that Mussolini had tried to suppress mandolin and folk music because they led to unmanly emotional displays.[227] Mussolini approved of the piano, an instrument that he could play passably well.[228] The piano was an expensive instrument-cum-furnishing of bourgeois households that was closely associated with self-cultivation through the mastery of serious classical music. There was no piano in number six Via Bazzoni, but Emilio loved to listen to gramophone recordings of Bach and Mozart, hummed the tunes as he climbed and dreamed of being able to play them himself.

In the late 1930s, Rita Palmquist, a Danish climber and a pianist who had performed in Italy, Russia and France, moved to Passo Sella in the Dolomites. She hired Emilio as a guide, and Emilio, in turn, hired her as his piano instructor.

Palmquist found in Emilio an eager if unconventional pupil. In addition to a modicum of talent, she wrote that his big hands resembled those of Franz Liszt, the 19th-century concert pianist noted for his magnetic attractiveness to women. Emilio's actual performance, Palmquist said, was complicated by his history and psychological

makeup; one of his stated motivations was to play for his convales-
cent mother. Palmquist recalled "the reserve with which we decided
to make music together and how painful our first musical contact
was." Emilio struggled to read sheet music.[229] When he found a few
bars of Bach that reminded him of the sound of a piton being struck
home, he could not stop humming it.

After one frustrating session, Emilio rose, closed the dust cover on
the piano and said, "You have witnessed the most splendid symbol of
my spiritual life. A closed door. You see, I have worked hard to develop my body, my muscles. I managed to do so, but at the detriment
to my inner life. A few years ago, I thought I would be a writer, but it
was an illusion. In the spiritual realm, there is a closed door for me."[230]

Palmquist was deeply moved by this insight into a man who rarely
revealed the secrets of his inner life. She thought that they would
never play together again, but Emilio rarely gave up on a challenge,
and he came back after climbing the next day and attempted to play
the same score again.

Like most students, Emilio focussed on the simpler melodies of
Handel and Vivaldi, but Palmquist heard something dissonant and
tragic in his renditions, resonant with 20th-century music. "This
man," Palmquist said, "who some accused of turning climbing into a
mechanical thing, was, in fact, deeply sensitive."[231]

Emilio was as unconventional in his approach to the piano as he
had been with climbing. He believed that he could avoid hours of
practice if he could somehow assume the correct spiritual attitude
towards the music. When he heard a talented young student play
Mozart's Concerto in D Major, he was overwhelmed with the desire
not to practise more but to achieve a more childlike spiritual state,
which he considered necessary to mastering the piece.

Emilio preferred to come to grips with the basics of a piece and then
move on to another composition rather than wait to perfect each
score. The method allowed him to rapidly accrue a basic grasp of a
broad range of techniques, and to Palmquist's amazement, he could
soon tentatively pick his way through some of Beethoven's more intricate piano sonatas.

Nonetheless, his lack of technique vexed him. "I am like a dog who can smell a caged hare," he told Palmquist. "The cage is my ignorance and the hare is the beauty of the music." Emilio could not take music on the bourgeois terms of Palmquist and other aficionados. He tried to dissect the complex scores by singing the different parts to himself as he climbed. He struggled to guess the tonal values of hammer blows on pitons and compared scales to different groups of mountains. He believed that the obstacle in his soul that blocked his musical development must be removed in the setting of daily life, rather than on the piano bench.

Emilio never had the opportunity to spend hours studying or practising anything indoors. Sitting at a keyboard "in a drawing gown and slippers," as his friend and fellow guide Jova Lipovec described the alternative to the life of a mountain guide, simply did not exist for Emilio. If there was any way upwards in society, it was through either climbing or the burgeoning, well-financed and lucrative world of skiing.

***

Emilio had worked as a ski instructor for most of his winters in the mountains. Although he was not talented enough to be a serious ski racer, he had put together a small instructional booklet for his students.[232] In 1938, an advertisement appeared in the Vicenza newspaper for the Emilio Comici Ski School in Misurina. Those who assumed that the hotel had branded their ski school after Comici only because he was a famous climber underestimated his qualifications as teacher. Although he was no champion, he was a popular instructor, skilled enough to amuse his students by darting amongst the tourists on the slopes above Misurina.

Emilio's relatable skill level helped him become a popular and empathetic instructor, and many of his students returned year after year. Antonia Pozzi skied at Emilio's school in the winters of 1937 and 1938. Unbeknownst to him, she continued to imagine his psychological and spiritual motivations for climbing and to place them within her poetic gaze. In 1937, she wrote her greatest climbing poem about Emilio:

Lakes of amazement are wide open

in the evening, in your eyes,
between lights and sounds:

flowers of madness open slowly
on the waters of your soul, mirrors
of the great spires crowned with
clouds.

Your blood, that dreams of stones
it's in the room,
an incredible silence.[233]

In 1938, darkness was falling on Pozzi. Her friends had fled or held out hope that fascism would not prevail. Her lover, Antonio Cervi, would never return to her. She wished she faced only the mountains of stone and ice that were Emilio's destiny. Poetry, the *palestra* in which she had tried to become strong enough to overcome her *sesto grado* of shyness, entangling privilege, fragility, loneliness, had failed her. In the fall of 1938, Pozzi visited the 13th-century abbey of Chiaravalle della Colomba in Milan. She swallowed a bottle of barbiturate pills and lay down in the cold moonlight.

The next day, her parents found a note in her pocket.

"I would like them to bring me down [from the mountains,]" she wrote, "a nice boulder and plant rhododendrons, edelweiss and mountain mosses every year. Thinking of being buried here [in the Grignetta] is not even dying, it's going back to my roots. Every day I feel them grip more tenaciously inside me. My mother, the mountains."[234]

Emilio's reaction to Pozzi's death is unrecorded. When her poetry, including the poems dedicated to Emilio, was published in 1939 and hailed as a triumph of Italian letters, he appears not to have taken note.[235]

In the fall of 1938, Emilio was appointed head instructor at the ski school in Selva di Gardena in South Tyrol. The Cortinesi guides may have been happy to see him go, but Emilio would have been sad to leave his handful of friends in Misurina for German-speaking Selva, which was further away from Trieste than Cortina. The position was seasonal and the pay was comparable to what Emilio made running his ski school in Misurina, but it was the first permanent job Emilio had had since he left the Magazzini Generale in his 20s.

CHAPTER NINE

AT THE ANGEL'S GRAVE

In 1939, world events set in motion the process by which Emilio was finally promoted by the fascist regime. On April 1, 1939, General Franco announced that after three years of war and the support of Italy and Germany, he had defeated the Republican forces. A week later, the Italian army crushed the tiny armed forces of Albania and added that nation to its new Roman empire.

The mood of the moment between Spanish and Italian fascists was celebratory and expansive. Franco sent Ramón Serrano Suñer, the ultra-fascist minister of the interior, who was married to Franco's wife's sister, to Italy to express thanks for military assistance. Serrano Suñer's handler was to be the Italian foreign secretary, Guido Buffarini Guidi, a rotund bon vivant and right-wing fascist who was extravagantly corrupt, even by fascist oligarch standards.

After a round of state dinners, parades and military demonstrations, Buffarini took his guest to his fiefdom in the Dolomites, which netted him enough money to support his Jewish mistress in Switzerland. The alpine entertainments planned by Buffarini included a climbing demonstration by Emilio, who was referred to by the papers in this context not as a new Roman superman but as a "human fly," a term Emilio had always disliked.[236] Perhaps Emilio's experience climbing in Spain added to his suitability for the occasion. His guiding partner in Spain, Jova Lipovec, was also a strong climber with Spanish climbing experience, but as a Slav, was unlikely to have been asked to perform for a foreign dignitary.

Buffarini was no climber, but he was impressed by Emilio's skill. He was, however, disappointed that a man who could scale rocks like Emilio had not received some sort of role (if not the kind of lucrative preferment Buffarini himself enjoyed), and vowed to do something about it. Inquiries ensued, and the modest post of prefectural commissioner was settled upon as appropriate. With the approval of Manaresi, who was despised in South Tyrol for his role in the repression of the German-speaking population, and who was also the official most likely to be concerned with any preferment of Italy's best climber, Emilio received notice of his new position in late April 1940.[237]

Despite a myth to the contrary, Emilio was never a *podestà*, the highest-ranking local official appointed by the fascist government to govern his community by edict and arrest any dissidents.[238] The will of a *podestà* was done by prefectural commissioners like Emilio.[239]

Podestà held their well-paid positions for five years, during which time there were plentiful opportunities for graft and bribes. Prefectural commissioners held part-time, one-year positions with tiny stipends and constant oversight from their *podestà*. It was not a prized position reserved for important figures.

Prefectural commissioners, especially in Tyrol, were notorious for supplementing their incomes through corruption and bribes.[240] Emilio, however, rented a small room in his friend Tomaso Giorgi's flat in Santa Cristina because he could not afford his own apartment. The army had requisitioned the little car he called Topolino (the Italian name for Mickey Mouse), which he had used to drive clients from Cortina to Misurina. He rode his battered old motorbike to the *podestà*'s headquarters in Bolzano when summoned. At least his uniform included jackboots to protect the old leg wound from the exhaust pipe. He kept his job as director of the ski school and guided a little in the summertime.

Emilio had had every opportunity in life, beginning with the Trieste Gymnastics Society and moving on to the xxx Ottobre, the *squadristi* and the army, to have become an outstanding and stringent fascist. Nonetheless, his moodiness, slightly preening individualism, tendency to complain when others were praised and he was not, dislike of the party's German allies and lack of anti-Semitism made him a rather lacklustre candidate for any more responsible position than that of prefectural commissioner.

On his rounds, Emilio strode through Selva di Gardena in his jackboots. His tall black prefectural commissioner's hat with its silver-plated tin eagle was hot in the summer sun, but as with his boots and gloves, he was required by regulation to wear it.[241] His uniform was supposed to inspire fear and admiration as he went about the village on his quest to inspire – or failing that, enforce – fascist fervour.

Buffarini had procured Emilio a hardship post, since Selva, like most of South Tyrol, was predominantly anti-fascist, Catholic and German-speaking. Emilio's duty was to enforce, by police action if necessary, Italian urban-based fascism in an ethnically South Tyrolean German village. The whole fascist system of local governance was deeply unpopular in the countryside. "Throughout Italy," wrote Tyrolean German-speaker Dr. Eduard Reut-Nicolussi, "the substitution of Fascist Podestas [sic] in the place of elected communal representatives was introduced, and thus were all communes given over as lawful Fascist prey."[242]

The villagers' resistance to Emilio's authority took many forms. Even goat-keeping could be an anti-fascist statement. The regime and Mussolini himself abominated goats, the most common and versatile alpine barnyard animal. Numerous attempts to control the goat population were promulgated and flouted.[243]

The adult population illegally avoided the fascist ceremonies of the *Sabato Fascista*. Girls and boys were required to attend activities run by the Opera Nazionale Balilla that were aimed at political indoctrination and paramilitary training. A propaganda film of a Balilla march of about 200 boys in Selva di Gardena shows a disciplined event, but since the entire population of the village was about 1,100, most of the boys would have been brought in from outside.[244] Many parents in Selva regularly made excuses for their children not to attend Balilla, which peasants believed undermined Catholic values.[245]

The source of the population's resentment was the government's opposition to the majority German culture.[246] The fascists appointed senator Ettore Tolomei to invent Italian place names to replace the German names common in the Tyrol. Speaking German, singing German songs and teaching German to children were all as commonplace as they were illegal. Emilio's job included enforcing the ban on German and passing on information about those who broke it to the police. A range of fines and prison sentences awaited malcontents who defied Italianization.

In June 1939, German-speaking Tyroleans were given the choice to either become *Optaten* and leave forever for the German Reich, or stay and become *Dableiber* (adapted from the German verb "to stay"). Some 165,000 German-Tyroleans became *Optaten* and left Italy. The 65,000 who remained behind were oppressed by the Italian government and accused of treason by the *Optaten*.[247] Eighty per cent of the population of Selva di Gardena abandoned their homes for relocation to areas controlled by Nazi Germany.

Emilio blamed the villagers' mediocre fascism and lack of Italian patriotism not on the government's policy of ethnic cleansing but on their German heritage and the commonly held but untrue belief that only weak-willed and craven Tyrolean Germans had remained behind.

The Vicenza Section of the CAI worried that military conscription left them with no choice but to hire a German Tyrolean as a hut custodian. Emilio advised them not to worry and hire "one of the German pretenders... One is from Ortisei and one from Santa Cristina, both locals, which is good, because they will worry about their reputations and do a good job. Maybe it will give them a chance to prove that they want to be Italian. If they do, we'll praise them."[248]

One of the paradoxes of fascism, and indeed of human nature, is that the same man who could write the haunting lines in "The Scythe of Death," and be compared to an angel as he climbed, could also indulge in such absurdities at the expense of his innocent fellow citizens.

***

In May and June 1940, Hitler defeated France and forced the British expeditionary forces to evacuate from Dunkirk. On June 10, Mussolini made good on his 1939 Pact of Steel with Hitler and declared war on Britain and France.

On June 21, 1940, several Italian divisions, including Emilio's beloved Ninth Alpini, invaded France over the Little Bernard and Cenis passes. Italian forces were under-armed, and many were killed by the French patrols to whom they had sold their weapons during training manoeuvres. French fortresses mercilessly shelled the Italians and received little fire in return.

If the French had not been forced to surrender by Hitler on June 25, they might have had time to annihilate the Italian invaders completely. In the four-day battle, a few dozen French soldiers were killed. About 650 Italian soldiers died, 2,150 were taken out of the battle by frostbite and more than 600 went missing in action, most of whom deserted.

Emilio, however, was not called up, either because a 39-year-old corporal already doing an administrative job was not a prime candidate for combat duty or because the officers he had once guided were doing him a favour. Emilio felt left out. Like many Italian fascists, he believed that the alpine invasion had played a decisive role in the defeat of France. Despite the Italian embarrassment in the Alps and the extensive German victories of 1939, Emilio believed the German soldier to be an inferior fighter, given to pilfering and malingering. He was not surprised when a villager appealed to him to intervene with the German army command. Their son, who had chosen to leave the Tyrol and had been conscripted by the German army, was imprisoned for stealing firewood from a Polish farmer. Emilio grudgingly filled out an appeal for the youth's release that was, in all likelihood, ignored.[249]

Emilio was more optimistic than ever for Italy's imperial future and hoped to participate in an offensive role in future campaigns. In the atmosphere of suppressed excitement brought on by reports of Italian armies amassed in Albania on the Greek border, Emilio volunteered for the paratroopers, a futile gesture given his age.

To most Italian fascists, Italy remained the senior partner in the axis, but Emilio must have had his doubts when he was forced to collude in German rapaciousness in Selva. In addition to human genetic stock, the Germans insisted on removing from the Tyrol any "objects [of German cultural significance], whether they belong to the state or church or are private property," including "furniture, old wall panels, cupboards, tile warming stoves, household wares, art objects, materials for making traditional clothing, tombstones, archives, church registers." All of the wooden carvings traditional to Selva di Gardena were considered by German folklorists to be "Germanic."[250] When the SS Ahnenerbe cultural staff ordered Emilio to do so, he had to facilitate the removal of these goods, by force if necessary, and without monetary reparations to the owners.

Emilio's passion for climbing waned as his political involvement increased. With no access to his most effective outlet for inner conflicts, his depression became fatalism. "I did not find anything beautiful" in the Dolomites, he said. "Although it is clear that my destiny is in the mountains, it is impossible for them to bring me peace. They will only get me in the end."[251]

Compared to the brilliant alpine summer of 1938, weather in 1939 had been poor. Emilio's only new route of consequence had been the second Campanile di Popera with Arturo Dalmartello, a good grade v but a moderate route for Emilio. In 1940, Emilio stopped climbing for two months, the longest such period of his adult life. At the end of the season, he made his single noteworthy climb of that summer, the first ascent of the Salame del Sassolungo, a smooth, unclimbed 350-metre tower in the Sassolungo massif that was shaped like a salami.

Casara suggested the climb. Over the course of his friendship with Emilio, Casara had shown generally poor judgement in suggesting new route projects. A host were too pedestrian for Emilio; some, like the south face of the Cima d'Auronzo, were so dangerous that Emilio avoided them or only climbed them with dread. A few were considered impossible by experts, like the overhang on the north face of the Campanile di Val Montanaia, which Emilio made an excuse not to attempt every time Casara suggested it. Other climbs Casara proposed, like the north face of the Eiger, were simply too hard for an amateur. The steep, clean, climbable Salame del Sassolungo was the exception.

In mid-August, the hard climber Ercole "Ruchin" Esposito from Milan had tried the route and retreated, which increased the face's appeal as a challenge. On August 28 and 29, Comici and Casara climbed the north face of the Salame del Sassolungo in two days. The climb had 15 pitches on good rock, many of which were grade vi. The route would have made any other climber famous in itself, but it remained a largely ignored footnote in Emilio's illustrious record.

On the summit, Comici left a note in a tin can with the following inscription: "28-29 August 1940 –XVIII – First ascent from the north, in 29 hours from the beginning of the climb, with bivouac: difficulty of the sixth grade. For Italo Balbo, alpine, aviator, *quadrumviro* of the Fascist Revolution."[252] After the north face of the Cima Grande, Emilio had thanked Mussolini and praised his revolution. He dedicated his only wartime new route to Mussolini's greatest fascist rival.

Balbo had been an *alpino* in the Great War and an aviator who had risen to the position of marshal of the Italian air force. He was so popular that Mussolini forbade the newspapers to mention him more than once a month and shipped him away to Libya to be his governor-general.

Balbo opposed the race laws imposed against Jews by Mussolini in 1938. He was also the highest-ranked fascist to decry Mussolini's choice to back Hitler and warned Mussolini that the Italians would "end up shining the Germans' shoes." Balbo's plane was shot down by Italian anti-aircraft guns in 1940, supposedly by accident, although there was a rumour that it had been done deliberately, under Mussolini's orders. The British sent a plane to drop flowers on his funeral in Tobruk.

Balbo was also popular abroad and had been on the cover of *Time* magazine. To foreigners and many Italians, he represented a less brutal form of fascism. Did the choice to name the tower after Balbo reflect a glimmer of Emilio's disappointment with Mussolini's Italy? The authorities would have said so, but by the time anyone of political importance read the notice, it was too late to do anything about it.

***

Emilio took Saturday, October 19, 1940, the day before the *Sabato Fascisti*, off, and not to go climbing. Climbing was far from his mind, as were guiding and lecturing. "I have no desire to give lectures," he wrote. "I believe that now, in time of war, they are a bit out of place."[253]

He loved the autumn in the valley, when the hay had been gathered in and the fields were golden bowers in the deep, green woods. The high mountains were now always laced with snow and the clouds that lingered white and opaque. By late October, the tourists had departed, along with the need to keep track of them for the police. Summer had been fine, despite the lack of climbing. Photos show him off-duty and shirtless, sometimes in his climbing pants or even in swimming briefs. There are guitars and open bottles of wine. He and his friends look a little drunk.

He had his favourites among the villagers. He referred to a couple of Italian boys being raised by their poor grandparents as "his sons," in the manner of a village priest. He visited them at dinner on occasion to play with the boys and enjoy polenta. Emilio was genuine in his concern for the downtrodden, but in Selva, his concern could not extend to ethnic Germans.[254]

On October 19, a luncheon party was planned at the house of Dr. Fissore, the village doctor. Guests included Emilio's friend and landlord, Tomaso Giorgi; Gianni Mohor, a climber from Trieste; and a local girl named Lina Demetz. Emilio was a single man now. Alice was finally in his past, and his naturally sad demeanour inspired his friends' well-intentioned efforts to introduce him to eligible young women.

Lunch dragged on into the afternoon, and when the wine was all gone, Fissore broached the idea of a visit to the *palestra* at Vallunga, which Emilio himself had developed and equipped with pitons. Mohor wanted to climb, and Fissore said he would bring his shotgun and they could try to shoot some birds. Emilio was not in the mood to shoot or climb, so he brought his guitar.

At Vallunga, Fissore and Giorgi climbed while Emilio played a few songs for Lina. When he folded his jacket into a pillow for a nap, Lina begged him to take her climbing instead. He protested that he had no equipment. She insisted, and he finally got up and rifled through Mohor's pack and found a few slings and some five-metre lengths of rope he tied together to make a line long enough to climb short pitches, so long as he did not use any protection.

Ten metres above the belay on the third pitch, Emilio decided that a smooth, five-metre-long dihedral above was too holdless for a beginner like Lina. He told her that the climb was over, and as she was on a wide ledge, she should untie so he could double up their improvised rope for a rappel.

He ran the rope over a solid rock spike and checked that both ends made it to Lina. Mohor, on the adjacent climb, shouted for some advice about the direction of his route. Emilio gripped both strands of the rope, put his feet against the wall and leaned off the rope to point out Mohor's route. He heard the rope tear apart. The broken ends of the rope were still in his fist as he fell 30 metres and hit the ground so hard that he bounced, fell, and smashed his head hard against a rock.

Lina screamed. Emilio stood up, with blood running down his face and neck, and then he fell again. Fissore rushed over with his gun and shot it twice in the air to signal for help. Another climber, Antonio Mussner, came to help, but it was no use. Emilio Comici was dead, with a broken piece of manila rope clenched in his hand. It looked fine and new on the outside, but its centre was black with rot.

***

For three days, the coffin of Leonardo Emilio Comici lay open beneath the gothic altarpiece in the church of Santa Maria Assunta in Selva di Gardena. The undertakers had dressed Emilio's body in his climbing jacket with his guide's badge and bandaged his head to hide the wound. In a gesture whose meaning is lost in the forgotten protocols of fascism, someone lay a *podestà*'s cap, with a peak even higher than the prefectural commissioner's, on his coffin.

Giorgio Brunner, who had climbed with Emilio since the 1920s, came from Trieste. Alone in the church, he touched Emilio's hand. In his head, he heard Emilio complain to him that his life had been too short and that Brunner should do all of the things that Emilio could not. Brunner balked at the idea of having to complete the climbing career of the greatest *sestogradiste* in Italy. He compromised with Emilio's spirit and promised to make sure Emilio's achievements were celebrated in a book.

The day of the funeral was cold and grey. The alpini honour guard from the ninth regiment wore their capes and feathered hats. The *podestà* brought a colour troop of Carabinieri policemen to march solemnly beside the coffin. The Balilla kids were in uniform, but they fooled around, despite the solemnity of the occasion. Guides and climbing friends wore their coiled ropes and climbing boots. Some acted as pallbearers, some lined the path of the procession like soldiers at a military funeral. A young climber walked in front of the coffin with a spray of edelweiss and the climbing rope that would have kept Emilio alive if he had brought it to the *palestra* at Vallunga. Few villagers are visible in the photos of the procession, which, after all, was purely ceremonial, as the cemetery was adjacent to the church.

Alice Marsi had come from Florence and stood at the edge of the grave in her worn fur coat, her blonde hair impiously uncovered. Beside her stood Emmy Hartwich-Brioschi in her fashionable Viennese hat and outfit. She clasped a handbag with both hands and for the first time in decades did not use a cane. It was not Emmy's first time at the graveside of a great climber in a small mountain town. In 1913, she had wept at the graveside of her lover Paul Preuss. Mountaineering had first denied these women the place they had craved in their lovers' hearts, and then had taken those lovers away forever.

In a photo at the graveside, Emilio's father stands behind them. Emilio's mother is not visible in the picture and likely had been too ill and overcome with grief to make the trip. Local guides Hans Vinatzer and Toni Demetz attended. Berti came from Vicenza, Stefenelli from Trento. Fabjan travelled from Rome, where he was working for the national sports program. Piero Mazzorana came up from Selva di Cadore.

There were absences. Anna Escher lived amongst the enemy in the British protectorate of Egypt, which was now under attack by the Italian army. Casara had fallen out with Emilio's other friends and stayed in Vicenza.

At the graveside, they sang the "Stelutis alpinis". The composer, Friulan Arturo Zardini, had composed it when he was a refugee from the Great War in Florence, far from the Alps. Since its first performance in 1920, it had become the unofficial funeral hymn of fallen *alpini* troops and climbers.

> If you come up
> here among the rocks,
> where they buried me,
> there is a clearing full of edelweiss:
> it was soaked in my blood.[255]

It was the perfect choice. Emilio had always loved a sad song.

CHAPTER TEN
WHAT COLOUR ARE THE DOLOMITES?

The first person to go through Emilio's papers and his desk was his piano teacher, Rita Palmquist, who lived close by in Passo Sella. His letters and books, to which he had intended to return later that afternoon, remained in disorder. She distributed them among his friends, who, for now, were more preoccupied with their grief than with their friend's personal effects. Emilio's letters, diaries and other materials were divided among a handful of his friends spread throughout Italy, his family and the CAI.

The first steps towards a legacy were symbolic conquests of landmarks and institutions. Climbers renamed the Zsigmondy hut the Rifugio Comici. Zsigmondy was a hero of the guideless climbing movement in Vienna in the late 19th century, and although Emilio would not have admired him for that, at least he would have liked the idea of supplanting an Austrian. The rock school in Val Rosandra was renamed the Comici School. The Salame del Sassolungo that Comici had tried to claim in the name of Italo Balbo was renamed after Comici himself.

Giorgio Brunner made good on his promise to commemorate Emilio and formed a committee of five to collate and edit a book about him. Casara was not invited to join the editing team, but he was allowed to submit an essay on the north face of the Salame del Sassolungo. The five editors lived in different parts of Italy, and wartime disruptions to communications, postal service and travel made for slow work.

Manaresi blessed the project, although his blessing contained a guarantee of censorship. The CAI apparatus in Rome finally gave Emilio the gold medal for the relatively unimportant Salame climb. Emilio was dead. He could not remind them moodily about how they had held it back for the Civetta, the Cima Grande, the great solos. In death, Emilio was promoted from his earthly role as a troublesome and self-absorbed party member to a paradigm of fascist masculinity: strong, resolute, manly, never doubting his Duce. Dead, Emilio became "the acme of the virile qualities of the Latin race regenerated by fascism."[256] Manaresi wrote the preface, and, not surprisingly, the north face of the Cima Grande, over which Emilio had quarrelled with partners and his party superiors, was not included in the articles commissioned by the editors. In life, Emilio had tried to disrupt the way that educated, powerful men redacted his work and reputation. Post-mortem, the same men had free rein. In the end, Manaresi drew their materials together and published *Alpinismo eroico* (*Heroic Alpinism*) in 1942. For a year of shortages and famine, it was a remarkably thick book, and full of photo plates. It was a collation of Emilio's writings and those of his friends.

Casara set to work separately on his own book, *L'arte di arrampicare di Emilio Comici*, mostly using anecdotes and his personal correspondence, although he was accused of redactions in favour of his myth of Emilio as "The Angel of the Dolomites."[257] The name was based on Emilio's compassion towards other climbers and his grace on the rock. But the first climber to have been nicknamed after a supernatural being was Tita Piaz, the Devil of the Dolomites. Despite Piaz's claim that he had a demonic appearance, he had earned the name by hard and dangerous climbing. A true anarchist, Piaz survived the prisons of Emperor Franz Joseph, King Victor Emmanuel, Mussolini and Hitler. Emilio and Piaz were both poor kids who became climbers, and both pushed the definition of what was acceptable on the rock. But when it came to politics, they were opposites.

Emilio was not the only fascist amongst the greats of Italian climbing between the wars. Cassin, Gervasutti, Chabod, Ratti, Carlesso and many others embraced fascism openly, albeit to varying degrees. Although few climbers shared Emilio's idealism about the party, it offered him few rewards.[258]

Emilio might have changed his politics had he lived until July 1943, when the government decided to oust Mussolini. The ouster, after all, was engineered by jaded long-time PNF loyalists like Dino Grandi, Galeazzo Ciano and Pietro Badoglio. Even Angelo Manaresi and

Emilio's old commander Colonel Masini joined the anti-fascists out of a revulsion Emilio would have shared for the Nazi invasion of Italy in 1943. By then, Masini's Ninth Alpini regiment had fought in Greece and Russia, where most of the soldiers Emilio trained in elegant climbing on the *palestra* at Castello Jocteau had been killed or captured. The unit was disbanded in Udine in 1943. Soldà, Cassin and Ratti joined the resistance. Ettore Castiglioni became a partisan and helped anti-fascists flee to Switzerland. He died of exposure after escaping incarceration by Swiss border guards who had taken away his clothing and equipment.

If Emilio had lived until 1943 and retained his position as prefectural commissioner in Selva di Gardena, he would have lost his job when the Nazis occupied the Tyrol. The Germans fired all of the fascist *podestà* and their commissioners and made the Italian fascist party illegal. Emilio's anti-German views and his enthusiasm for the ethnic cleansing of Tyrolean Germans would have made life under the Nazis difficult and dangerous.

Even after the Trieste section of the CAI hung signs forbidding Jews in its huts, Emilio had fretted over the predicament of his Jewish friends, not as if racism was a core program of his beloved party (which, after 1938, it was), but as if it was some kind of unintended oversight by a regime he saw as benevolent. What would Emilio have thought when the Nazis built concentration camps in both Trieste and Bolzano?

In the summer of 1944, Osiride Brovedani, whose mother was Jewish, was arrested after being accused of listening to *Radio Londres*, the allied Italian radio broadcast written by Antonia Pozzi's literary friends. As the train headed north towards the camp, Brovedani looked out a crack in the boards of the locked cattle car full of Jewish *Triestinos* and saw the Montasio. "I will see you again, divine Montasio, companion of all my summer climbs" he wrote. "My eyes were veiled with tears when we passed through Valbruna; the Jôf Fuart stood out clearly with the summit illuminated by the sunset... I said goodbye to the Mangart."[259]

Brovedani was interned in Bergen-Belsen, Dora and Buchenwald concentration camps, a fate shared by the brilliant 23-year-old Jewish rock climber and partisan Ezio Rocco, who was shot in one of the camps. Several young climbers from the xxx Ottobre who formed the "Bruti" (Brutes) of Val Rosandra worked in the resistance as they continued to climb. Would Emilio have remained unmoved when, after the German occupation of Trieste, his climbing partner Piero Slocovich became a partisan, along with a dozen poorly armed and organized members of the GARS? Teenage climber and partisan Glauco Sabadin (who used the code-name "Whymper") died of typhoid fever fighting in Istria. Giulio Della Gala was betrayed to the Nazis by his climbing partner, tortured and hanged. Eighteen-year-old partisan Luciano Soldat, also betrayed by a climbing partner, stayed in Trieste instead of running into the hills so that his parents would not be punished. He was hanged by the Nazis. The talented climber Dario Ceglar was deported to Buchenwald, where he was killed. Emilio's climbing partner Riccardo Deffar was also killed in the camps.[260] Slocovich, like Brovedani, survived the camps.

Spiro Della Porta Xidias, a member of the Bruti, said that Emilio had become a kind of patron saint of struggling *Triestino* climbers, even those in the resistance. Emilio, said Xidias, "rose above all baseness... his smile is accentuated and gradually fades into a great light, a light that is total and restores strength and courage and dissipates the darkness in my soul."[261] Like a medieval saint's, his power was rooted not in the facts of his life but in the hope those in need found in his image and memory.

Although the climbers of Val Rosandra might have forgiven him, if Emilio had survived the war without changing his political views, he would have been vulnerable to vigilante justice by the survivors of the fascist terror. In Selva di Gardena in May 1946, former partisans tortured and then burned to death five former fascists. Emilio's patron Guido Buffarini Guidi, who had colluded in the murder of 335 civilians in the Ardeatine Massacre in Rome, was captured as he fled to join his Jewish mistress in Switzerland. He was tried in Milan by an "extraordinary court of justice," tied to a schoolchild's desk and shot.

Julius Kugy was arrested by the fascist police in 1941 on suspicions of Slavic sympathies but released shortly afterwards. He died in 1944, after having spent the last years of his life secretly aiding Slovene partisans, a final luminous act of Mitteleuropean nostalgia for the cosmopolitanism of Austria-Hungary.

Unlike many fascists, Emilio maintained friendships with Slavic climbers like Jova Lipovec. The climbing scene in Val Rosandra was a haven of tolerance between Italians and Slavs. These considerations would have counted for little when, in 1944, the Yugoslav People's Army of Marshal Tito occupied Trieste. Over 40 days, Tito's armies murdered hundreds of citizens they judged to be guilty of fascism and filled the mouth of the Bus de la Lum cave with their corpses.

On May 14, 1941, Emilio's long-suffering mother, Regina, died. Less than a year later, on March 18, 1942, her husband, Antonio, passed away. Neither lived to see the end of the regime that had shaped their lives for almost two decades.

In the late 1940s, life in Italy to returned to a semblance of normalcy, and the survivors of war and fascism rebuilt their lives. Fabjan became an important figure in Italian Olympic athletics and an organizer of the 1960 Rome Olympics. Fausto Stefenelli became an academic and a respected environmentalist. After surviving three concentration camps, Osiride Brovedani returned to Trieste and his wife and fellow climber Fernanda. In the camps, he had lost his enthusiasm for providing Italians with their national staple. He shifted his focus to selling baby powder, which made him a billionaire.

Angelo Dimai died in a climbing accident in 1946. After that, his brother Giuseppe never climbed extreme rock again. Giuseppe held to the ancient guide's wisdom of avoiding risks unnecessary to his profession. He died peacefully in Cortina in 1985 as the respected patriarch of his vocation.

Escher survived the war and continued to visit the Alps every summer into her 90s, by which time she had acquired a little Volkswagen Beetle for her travels. The extraordinary Emmy Hartwich-Brioschi survived the Holocaust and ended up in Nice when the war ended. Alice Marsi left the stage of alpine history after her photo was taken at Emilio's graveside.

Casara authored several films and books on mountain subjects, most notably on Paul Preuss. Domenico Rudatis, the arch-elitist intellectual and esoteric philosopher of the sixth grade, decided, after the war, to put his energy into refining the television set, the technical innovation most often blamed for post-war populism, consumerism and cultural mediocrity. He moved to New York in 1952 and filed a patent for a new form of colour television set in 1958.[262] Although he never climbed again, he continued to write about his favourite subject, the *sesto grado*.

Cassin went on to become one of the greatest climbers of his generation, with expeditionary firsts in Alaska, the Himalayas and Peru to his credit, in addition to many important alpine routes. He lived to be 100 and died in his bed.

***

In the 1950s, the breathless Italian press moved on to covering new achievements, like the Italian first ascent of K2 in 1954 by Achille Compagnoni and Lino Lacedelli. The photographers also had a new, charismatic, photogenic alpinist in Walter Bonatti, whose unprecedented solos, like the southwest pillar of the Dru, were followed up with expeditionary triumphs like the first ascent, with Carlo Mauri, of Gasherbrum IV (7295 metres) on a 1969 expedition led by Cassin.

Emilio Comici became the most prominent name in most general accounts of Italian climbing between the world wars. Only the specialist literature on Italian climbing dwelled in any detail on the wild free climbs of Hans Vinatzer, Attilio Tissi's ability to climb at the hardest levels without protection and the hard climbs of Alvise Andrich, Celso Gilberti, Luigi Micheluzzi, Gino Soldà and a host of others. Cassin, Esposito and Tizzoni's ascent of the Walker Spur became the only exception to this relative silence.

The longevity of Emilio's reputation among climbers is partly attributable to the popularity of two of his greatest routes. The north face of the Cima Grande and the Spigolo Giallo became popular classic itineraries. Beginning in the 1950s, however, Emilio's reputation was partly kept alive by those who saw him as one of the most culpable heirs in a succession of individuals who relied on technology to diminish and then defeat nature. In this narrative, in the first decade of the 20th century, Hans Dülfer introduced tension traverses, planned aid manoeuvres, pre-inspection on rappel and the liberal use of pitons, and on one occasion even carried, but did not use, a drill to make a hole for a piton. Emilio Comici took up the torch in the 1920s and attacked hitherto impossible problems like the north face of the Cima Grande with pitons, fixed ropes and the technique of climbing from piton to piton.

Beginning in the late 1950s, examples of what critics considered ruthless big wall climbs appeared at least every few years. Lothar Brandler, Dieter Hasse, Jörg Lehne and Siegfried Löw's June 1958 *direttissima* on the north face of the Cima Grande was the first climb on the wall to rely on bolts and was seen as the logical next step for those who, for better or worse, followed Emilio's example. In 1959, Italian climber Cesare Maestri claimed the first ascent of the ice-encrusted granite tower of Cerro Torre in Patagonia, but his partner, Toni Egger, died on the descent, and many doubted Maestri's account. Maestri returned in 1970 and used a gas-powered compressor to drill over 400 bolt holes in the mountain's southeast face to the reach the summit. It was the most brutal settlement of a climbing *vendetta* in history.

The backlash against Maestri, his means and ethics was immediate. Reinhold Messner, a young Tyrolean climber and friend of Rudatis, condemned the use of bolts as *"l'assassinio dell'impossibile,"* which British magazine editor Ken Wilson translated as "the murder of the impossible."[263]

Some climbers looked for precedents to Maestri's deed and found Emilio culpable. British big wall climber Doug Scott described Emilio as a talented climber but also a preening narcissist who loved having his photograph taken shirtless or in what he calls "velveteen jumpers," and who unscrupulously deployed technology to overcome climbs.[264]

Emilio, however, never used bolts, and if he had used them, he would not have been the first. Laurent Grivel in the Alps and David Brower in the United States, neither of whom are associated with breaking climbing traditions, had beaten Emilio to that honour, such as it was.

The climbs that continued Emilio's ideas were not Maestri's Cerro Torre epic but the northwest face of Half Dome in 1957, and the Nose of El Capitan in 1958. When California rock climbers took on the big granite walls of Yosemite with large stores of ropes and pitons, aid climbing and high-level free climbing, they mostly claimed for their inspiration the naturalist John Muir, who did not climb, and the eccentric Swiss-American rock climber John Salathé, who never climbed in Europe. The great American climber Royal Robbins listed Emilio Comici as a model, but only after Walter Bonatti.[265] The Comici-Dimai on the Cima Grande, the Cassin-Ratti on the Cima Ovest and a few other Italian climbs of the 1930s and '40s, however, were the only existing templates, anywhere in the world, for the climbs of the golden age of Yosemite big wall climbing. Emilio and his colleagues never truly got the acknowledgement that was their due for inspiring it.

***

A month after his funeral, a wooden statue of Emilio was placed beneath the wall at Vallunga, almost out of sight, close to where Emilio fell. It depicted a tall climber with a grim visage: the masculine Roman hero that Manaresi wanted the public to see.

A quiet little side street in Trieste, north of the Farneto Park, was named Via Emilio Comici. It is bounded on one side by a limestone wall and a green border of pine trees and on the other by apartments with stuccoed walls and strong shutters to block the Bora wind.

In Val Rosandra, Emilio was memorialized by a pillar of stones on the crest of the Cippo Comici, a shield of Carso rock. From the monument, you can look down the river valley, past the outcrops where Emilio first climbed, to the eastern edge of Trieste, and the sea. Below, the water that bore down into the Carso to carve the limestone cliffs sparkles among the stones.

Sailors had once come to these cliffs to build shrines overlooking the Adriatic so that Maris Stella, Our Lady of the Sea Star, would watch over them as they sailed. It became, in Emilio's day, a place for climbers whose gaze was not down to the wine-dark sea that had beckoned the wayward of other generations, but upwards, where, in the white rocks and the blue sky, they saw the Civetta, the Cima Grande, the Sorapiss and the Marmolada.

Although only climbers ever surveyed the valley from this place,

Emilio's nickname supplies the imagination with an angel roosting on the cliff edge.

Scripture says that mortals are, by their nature, "a little lower than the angels..."[266] The sad, driven kid from the docks who climbed so well and looked out for his friends was lower in the imagined celestial hierarchy than the archangels in the glittering, Byzantine apse of St. Giusto's Cathedral in Trieste, or the angels of mercy rescuing alpinists and lost, ill-clad shepherdesses on the lurid covers of *La Domenica del Corriere*. His mourners could not deny him his angelic status simply because of his politics. After all, most of them had shared those beliefs while Emilio lived. Perhaps they should have known better.

It seems more appropriate to find new meaning in the angelic title than to simply ignore it. An angel, after all, could fall, warn or unleash plagues as well as bless. Emilio's life was a warning as well as a reassurance. Self-absorbed, skilled, obsessive, attuned to the supernatural, a visionary in his field of climbing, a fascist, there was no greater proponent of the search for difficulty as it was defined first by tradition and secondly by the new techniques and a grade system in which the highest beauty was the hardest climb. "I embrace you," Emilio wrote to his friends, "in the sixth grade."

Climbers respected Paul Preuss and the purists but did not follow them. Leonardo Emilio Comici led generations of climbers to the biggest rock walls in the world. Did he lead us into, or out of, a paradise of innocence? We still have to learn that, whether we are inclined to reject technology when we climb or to accept it, all disputes with the mountain need not be settled; to leave some of our beliefs and reasons, prices we are willing to pay, and strategies of last resort on the ground. "When we reach the sixth grade," Tita Piaz warned us, "we will find that we have not entered the kingdom of heaven."[267]

Dino Buzzati, the great literary navigator and philosopher of Italian alpinism in the mid-20th century, reflected that mountains defy our urge to impose permanent order upon them, whether through language, politics or technology. "What colour are the Dolomites?" he wrote. "Are they white? Yellow? Grey? Mother of Pearl? Ash-coloured? Reflections of silver? The pallor of the dead? The complexion of roses? Are they stones or are they clouds? Are they real, or is it a dream?"[268]

During Emilio's adult life, the Dolomites were none of these evocative hues; they were black, the colour of fascist ardour and sacrifice. His climbs and his spirit were shaped by Italian fascism and the choices he made to accommodate himself to it, but they cannot be reduced to expressions of his politics. Emilio drove big wall climbing and free soloing to new levels and expanded the sense of what was possible on rock walls far beyond what climbers assumed were the limits of human endeavour when he started climbing in 1925. Emilio was just a sullen, poor, uneducated kid from the docklands of Trieste, but in the words of the refined poet Antonia Pozzi, his very blood dreamed of the rock. Few observed him as deeply and dispassionately as Pozzi did in her poem "For Emilio Comici":

> The boats dazzle on the burning glass.
> Where did you leave your clothes,
> the faces
> of the girls, the oars?
> Tonight, at the bivouac
> white clouds
> will break mutely on the stone:
> so far from the thud of the waves
> on the dock of Trieste.
> No Moon
> will thaw gardens, nor shine on
> women laughing at a streetlight,
> or warm your hair,
> but you will only see
> your rope
> encased in ice
> and your hard heart
> among the pale spires.[269]

Pozzi understood that Emilio was a man apart, if not an angel. That very distance at the heart of his being, which made life so hard for him, gave him the ability to contribute so much to alpinism.

NOTES

1 Cited in Mark Thompson, *The White War* (New York: Basic Books, 2010), 120.

2 Scipio Slataper, *My Carso*, trans. Gerald Moore (Trieste: Edizioni Università di Trieste, 2002), 98.

3 Severino Casara, *L'arte di arrampicare di Emilio Comici* (Milan: Hoepli, 1957), cited hereafter as AA, 12.

4 Spiro Dalla Porta Xidias, *I Bruti di Val Rosandra* (Bologna: Capelli, 1952), cited hereafter as *Bruti*, 68. Xidias later became an important biographer of Comici, partly because he was the first to have access to Emilio's diaries, and partly because he was an insider of the Trieste scene and had conversations with Emilio's friends, like Fabjan, Stefenelli and Brunner, in the 1950s and '60s, after the need to protect their talented leader had passed.

5 Napoleone Cozzi, Alberto Zanutti and Nino Carniel, *Albo, Estate, 1907* (self-published: Trieste, 1909), 34.

6 Livio Isaak Sirovich, *Cime irredente* (Turin: Vivalda, 1996), 158–59.

7 The Italian term *palestra*, which translates literally as gym, when applied to climbing can mean either a crag developed for rock climbing or an artificial climbing wall.

8 René Moehrle, "Fascist Jews in Trieste: Social, Cultural and Political Dynamics 1919–1938," *Quest: Issues in Contemporary Jewish History* 11 (October 2017), 3.

9 Rita Palmquist, "Emilio Comici e musica," in Antonio Berti, Giorgio Brunner, Giordano Fabjan, Pietro Sagramora and Fausto Stefenelli, eds., *Alpinismo Eroico* (Milan: Hoepli, 1942), cited hereafter as AE, 200–2. There is also an abridged edition (Turin: Vivalda, 2012) with an excellent introductory essay by editor Elena Marco. All citations hereafter are from the 1942 edition, which gives full bibliographical information on the first place of publication of articles from the *Rivista Mensile del Club Alpino Italiano* and other periodicals.

10 Mario Carli, *L'italiano di Mussolini: Romanzo dell'era fascista* (Verona: Manadori, 1930), 56–58.

11 *Camicie nere* (blackshirts) and *squadristi* were interchangeable terms. By the time Emilio joined the blackshirts, after 1923, the group had evolved from bands of right-wing vigilantes into the Milizia Volontaria per la Sicurezza Nazionale (MVSN), a paramilitary organization roughly parallel to the

SS in Germany, which answered directly to Mussolini. Emilio belonged to the Sixth Zona (Venezia Giulia) of the MVSN.

12 Johannes Mattes, "Underground Fieldwork: A Cultural and Social History of Cave Cartography and Surveying Instruments in the 19th and at the Beginning of the 20th Century," *International Journal of Speleology* 44, no. 3 (2015), 251–66.

13 Duilio Durissini, "Abissi: scuola de altezze," *AE*, 188.

14 Xidias, *Emilio Comici: Mito di un alpinista* (Belluno: Nuovi Sentieri, 1988), cited hereafter as *EC*, 19.

15 Gruppo Speleologico Geo CAI Bassano, "Storia della speleologia," http://www.geocaibassano.it/storia-speleologia.

16 Rodolfo Battelini, *Abisso Bertarelli, nelle sue emozionanii e tragiche esplorazioni* (Trieste: Capelli, 1926), 47.

17 Julius Kugy, "Ricordando Emilio Comici,"*AE*, 194.

18 Sirovich, 111 ff.

19 Julius Kugy, *Aus dem Leben eines Bergsteigers* (Munich: Bergverlag Rudolf Rother, 1925). Translated as *Alpine Pilgrimage* (London: John Murray, 1934).

20 Julius Kugy, cited in "The Honourable Julius Kugy," SummitPost, https://www.summitpost.org/the-honourable-julius-kugy/326920.

21 Paul Kaltenegger, "Dr. Julius Kugy," trans. Hugh Merrick, *The Alpine Journal*, 1965, 88.

22 Antonio Berti, *Le Dolomiti Orientali: Guida turistico-alpinistica* (Milan: Treves, 1928), cited in Marco Armiero, *A Rugged Nation: Mountains and the Making of Modern Italy* (Cambridge: White Horse Press, 2011), 100.

23 Armiero, 88.

24 Domenico Rudatis, *Das Letzte im Fels*, translated from the Italian by Emmeli Capuis and Max Rohrer (Munich: Gesellschaft Alpiner Bücherfreunde, 1936), 19–20.

25 *Bruti*, 34–45.

26 Giani Stuparich, "Scuola di roccia," *Pietà del sole* (Florence: Sansoni, 1942).

27 Roberto Santachiara and Wu Ming 1, *Point Lenana* (Rome: Einaudi, 2013), cited hereafter as *PL*, 195.

28 Emilio Comici, "Tecnica e spiritualità dell'arrampicata," *AE*, 148–49.

29 Comici, "Sorella di Mezzo Terza Sorella, pareti Nord-Ovest," cited hereafter as "Sorella," *Rivista Mensile* (this periodical is cited hereafter as *RM*) (1930), 293; *AE*, 36.

30 Guido Rey, *Peaks and Precipices: Scrambles in the Dolomites and Savoy*, trans. J.E.C. Eaton (New York: Dodd, Mead, 1914), 129–30.

31 *EC*, 85.

32 Ibid.

33 Kugy later wrote a frank account of the hardships of early 20th-century guiding, *Anton*

Oitzinger, *Ein Bergführerleben* (Graz: Leykam Verlag, 1935), translated as *Son of the Mountains* (London: Thomas Nelson and Sons, 1938).

34 *PL*, 95.

35 Riccardo Cassin, *Fifty Years of Alpinism* (London: Diadem, 1981), 15.

36 "Sorella," *AE*, 32.

37 Comici, "Cima di Riofreddo delle Madri dei Camosci, parete Nord" (cited hereafter as "Riofreddo"), *RM*, 1930, 156, *Österreichische Alpenzeitung*, 1932, 52, *AE*, 23.

38 Angelo Manaresi, "Un grande maestro, un purissimo eroe," *AE*, 5.

39 "Riofreddo," *AE* 25.

40 Ibid., 26.

41 Gino Buscaini, *Alpi Giulie Italiano e Slovene* (Milan: CAI Milano, Touring Club Italiano, 1974), 43.

42 *AA*, 31.

43 Emilio Comici, "Torre Dario Mazzeni," *RM* (1930) 158, cited hereafter as "Mazzeni," *AE*, 49.

44 Armiero, 13.

45 Dino Buzzati, "'Direttissime' sulla Civetta," *Corriere della Sera*, October 22, 1934, *I fluorilegge della montagna*, Lorenzo Viganò, ed. (Milan: Mondadori, 2010), cited hereafter as *Montagna*, vol. 2, 26.

46 Julius Evola, *Meditations on the Peaks*, trans. Guido Stucco (Rochester, VT: Inner Traditions, 1974), 34.

47 Domenico Rudatis, "Civetta: palestra di ardimenti," *L'illustrazione veneta*, 1929, cited hereafter as "Rudatis, 'Civetta.'"

48 Vittorio Varale, Reinhold Messner, Domenico Rudatis, *Sesto Grado* (Milan: Longanesi, 1971), cited hereafter as *SG*.

49 Domenico Rudatis, correspondence with Vittorio Varale, April 19, 1930, Biblioteca Civica di Belluno, Fondo Varale.

50 Luigi Piccioni, *Domenico Rudatis e la Storia dello sport dell'arrampicamento*, 2, https://arrampicamento.wordpress.com/2014/02/24/la-storia-dellarrampicamento-uno-straordinario-quasi-inedito/. Rudatis considered Cassin and Gervasutti "Western" alpinists, because of their interest in big alpine peaks in the Western Alps, and despite Cassin's record in the Dolomites.

51 Eric Roberts, *Welzenbach's Climbs* (Seattle: Mountaineers, 1980), 98 ff.

52 Evola, 37. In a post–Second World War essay in *Meditazioni*, Evola cites Carlo Anguissola d'Emet citing a paragraph supposedly authored by Emilio Comici: "A real climber cannot be somebody who does not love, understand and pursue the fifth or sixth degree." The sentence, which was often quoted, is likely apocryphal. Evola's use of the quotation, however, is to show his approval of the sentiment.

53 Fritz Schmitt, "Emil Solleder," *Bergsteiger* 6, no. 84 (1984), 62.

54 Giovanni Angelini, *Civetta* (Belluno: Fondazione Giovanni Angelini, 2009), 18.

55 Rudatis, "Civetta."

56 Schmitt, 62.

57 Richard Hechtl, "Hundert Jahre Felsklettern: Die Geschichte eines gesellschaftlichen Phänomens," (DAV, Bayerland, 2003), 70, http://www.alpen verein-bayerland.de/module _requirements/geschichte/ hundert_jahre_felsklettern/ pdf/001-214%20Hundert%20 Jahre%20Felsklettern.pdf.

58 *SG*, 11.

59 Alessandro Pastore, "L'alpinismo, il Club Alpino Italiano e il fascismo," *Sport und Faschismen/ Sport e fascismi*, 2004, no. 1, 68.

60 Ibid., 85.

61 Rudatis later recognized Emilio Comici's importance in climbing history. See *SG*, 1 ff..

62 Armiero, 149.

63 *AA*, 41.

64 Cassin, 34.

65 "Riofreddo," *AE*, 23.

66 Kirsten Barnes and Nicholas J.S. Gibson, "Supernatural Agency: Individual Difference Predictors and Situational Correlates," *The International Journal for the Psychology of Religion* 23, no. 1 (2013), 42–62.

67 *SC*, 44.

68 "Riofreddo," *AE*, 28.

69 Ibid., 29, 30–31.

70 Ibid., 31.

71 Ibid., 21.

72 "Atto costitutivo della 'Scuola di roccia di Val Rosandra,'" April 14, 1933, https://www.scuoladialpinismo .eu/storia-scuola-alpinismo -emilio-comici.

73 Pastore, 69.

74 "Circolare," October 1 (year unrecorded), https://www.scuola dialpinismo.eu/storia-scuola -alpinismo-emilio-comici; "1929– 2019, Gli Anni di Scuola," *Alpi Giulie* 113, no. 2 (2019), 52–61.

75 "Apunnti Sulla Scuola Nazionale di Alpinismo," October 3, 1936, https://www.scuoladialpinismo .eu/storia-scuola-alpinismo -emilio-comici.

76 That summer, Casara began a one-sided correspondence with Emmy, to whom he was soon confessing his love, despite their both being married; she never reciprocated in her copious surviving polite responses. Personal Correspondence of Severino Casara, November 23, 1931, Biblioteca della Fondazione G. Angellini-Centro Studia sulla Montagna, Belluno.

77 Severino Casara states that Emmy met Emilio on top of the Dito di Dio and, after looking over the edge and watching him make the first ascent of the north face with Fabjan, said he climbed like Preuss (Casara, 40). The author agrees with Xidias that this is likely a story made up by Casara, partly because of the difficulty of watching anyone climb the north face from the summit and also because of Emmy's

questionable fitness for the standard route on the Dito di Dio in 1929 (*EC*, 49).

78 Moehrle, 4.

79 Dino Buzzati, "Severino Casara: Il caso degli strapiombi nord mise a rumore le Dolomiti," *Corriere della Sera*, January 13, 1948, *Montagna*, 27–31; Alessandro Gogna and Italo Zandonella Callegher, *La verità obliqua di Severino Casara* (Turin: Priuli and Verlucca, 2009).

80 *AA*, 39.

81 Felice Benuzzi sent his young German girlfriend to stay with Emilio in Misurina so that Emilio could test her climbing skills and thus her suitability as a bride for Benuzzi. After the test, Emilio wrote Benuzzi "'The girl will do quite well in the mountains" and sent her on her away. *PL*, 143.

82 Armiero, 18.

83 Cortina was renamed Cortina d'Ampezzo after the Great War but was typically still referred to as Cortina.

84 "Riofreddo," *AE*, 35–36.

85 "Sorella," *AE*, 36.

86 Ibid., 35.

87 Ibid., 44.

88 "Mazzeni," *AE*, 46.

89 Ibid., 46.

90 Ibid., 47.

91 Ibid., 50.

92 The Zsigmondy hut beneath the north face of the Croda dei

Toni was destroyed in the Great War; in 1928, it was rebuilt and renamed the Mussolini hut. In 1945, it was renamed the Comici-Zsigmondy hut, a name still in use at time of writing.

93 The peak is also known as the Zwölferkofel. The feature Emilio, Fabjan and Slocovich climbed was named Croda Antonio Berti after Berti's death in 1956.

94 Emilio Comici, "Cima di Mezzo della Croda dei Toni, parete Nord-Ovest," *RM* (1931), cited hereafter as "Croda dei Toni," 115. *AE*, 53.

95 Ibid., 59.

96 *PL*, 111.

97 Pastore, 69.

98 Pietro Crivellaro, "Nel CAI fascista irrompe lo sport," *Montagne* 360 (April 2013), 54.

99 Rudatis: "Lo sport dell'arrampicamento," *Lo sport fascista*, cited hereafter as *Sport*, 3 (1930), 33–39; "Dall'alpinismo tradizionale all'affermazione sportive," *Sport* 4 (1930), 108–15; "L'ascesa dello sport dell'arrampicamento sino all'alba del nostro secolo," *Sport* 5 (1930), 30–42; "Di scalata in scalata verso il limite del possibile," *Sport* 7 (1930), 34–45; "L'apogeo della tecnica d'arrampicamento," *Sport* 8 (1930), 18–31; "L'estrema progressione dell'arrampicamento," *Sport* 12 (1930), 32–42.

100 Riccardo Cassin, "Italian Climbing Between the Wars," *Alpine Journal* (1972), 151.

101 *EC*, 34.

102 Emilio Comici, "La Civetta, direttissima italiana: Parete Nord-Ovest," *RM* (1931), 799, and *Annuario Club Alpino Accademico Italiano* (1931), 268, cited hereafter as "Civetta, direttissima," *AE*, 70.

103 Ibid.

104 Ibid., *AE*, 71.

105 A search of contemporary English climbing literature revealed no sources for the simile. Edward Whymper, whose *Scrambles Amongst the Alps in the Years 1860–1869* (London: John Murray, 1871) was available in Italian translation and quoted by Emilio, preferred to make straight routes to summits, and chastised guides and other climbers for not doing so, but made no mention of the role of the water drop in route choice.

106 "Civetta, direttissima," *AE*, 72.

107 Albert Frederick Mummery, *My Climbs in the Alps and Caucasus* (London: T. Fisher, 1895), 162.

108 "Civetta, direttissima," *AE*, 75.

109 Cassin, 47–48.

110 "Civetta, direttissima," *AE*, 79.

111 *AA*, 41.

112 "Sorella," *AE*, 44.

113 According to German climber Hans Steger, for most of his climb, Emilio had thought he was on the Solleder-Lettenbauer, which would give him a reason to avoid comparisons between the two routes on the northwest face of the Civetta. The distance between the two routes for most of the wall makes Steger's claim unlikely.

114 Doug Scott, "The Great Pioneers of the Eastern Alps, Part 2: The Mid 'Twenties to 1939," *Mountain* 34 (April 1974), 31. Scott's is the last in-depth treatment of climbing in the Eastern Alps in English, at time of writing. Scott outlined the careers and achievements of climbers in the Eastern Alps who were little known to English-speaking climbers, including Steger, Micheluzzi, Carlesso, Solleder and Comici, whom he sees as an era-ending figure.

115 *EC*, 77.

116 Armiero, 144.

117 *EC*, 94.

118 *EC*, 92.

119 Armiero, 135.

120 Kerwin Lee Klein, "A Vertical World: The Eastern Alps and Modern Mountaineering," *Journal of Historial Sociology* 24, no. 4 (December 2011), 534.

121 Alessandro Gogna, "Angelo Dibona" (2013), Club Alpino Italiano website, http://www .caisem.org/pdf/csc_2013/ Angelo_Dibona.pdf.

122 Emilio Comici, "La via eterna primo giro completo della Cengia degli Dei," cited hereafter as "Cengia degli Dei," *AE*, 60.

123 *EC*, 80.

124 *AA*, 196.

125 The investigation was undoubtedly influenced by a malicious rumour not only that Casara was

a liar but that his cowardice and his numerous adoring comments on Emilio's physique indicated that he was a homosexual, a serious crime in fascist Italy.

126 Cassin, 11.

127 Lida de Polzer, "I Bazzoni: Racconto incompleto della storia di famiglia, pieno in cambio di notizie che non interessano nessuno," website of the Astronomical Observatory of Trieste, http://www.oats.inaf.it/bazzoni/doc/storiabazzoni.pdf.

128 Cassin, 22.

129 AA, 44.

130 AA, 44.

131 Cassin, 34.

132 Dino Buzzati, "Strapiombi," La Lettura, August 1933, cited in Montagne, 15.

133 Frank Smythe, The Spirit of the Hills (London: Hodder, 1935), 112.

134 J. Monroe Thorington, "Das Letzte im Fels, by Domenico Rudatis," American Alpine Journal, 1937, 98.

135 EC, 98.

136 EC, 99.

137 Named after the American climber Miriam O'Brien Underhill, a client of the Dimais who was married to the American mountaineer Robert Underhill.

138 AA, 44.

139 AA, 44.

140 EC, 95–103. The Longeres hut was bombed in the Great War, rebuilt and named Principe Umberto after the crown prince of the Italian royal family. In July 1957, it burned down; the hut rebuilt on the site is named the Auronzo hut.

141 Buzzati, "Cima Grande di Lavaredo," La Domenica del Corriere, 37 (1935), cited hereafter as "Buzzati, 'Cima Grande.'"

142 Buzzati, "Cima Grande."

143 Comici, "Anticima della Piccola di Lavaredo, Spigolo Giallo Sud," RM (1934), cited hereafter as "Spigolo Giallo," 524, AE, 81.

144 Ibid.

145 Ibid.

146 "Spigolo Giallo," AE, 83.

147 EC, 101.

148 EC, 101.

149 Buzzati, "Cima Grande."

150 SC, 43.

151 Personal letter, Angelo Manaresi to Emilio Comici, April 4, 1934. Sass Balòss blog, https://sassbaloss.wordpress.com/2018/05/25/emilio-comici-e-la-lettera-al-presidente-generale-del-cai/.

152 In 1929 Aimone de Savola-Aosta, the nephew of the Duke of the Abruzzi, led an expedition not primarily concerned with mountaineering, to explore the upper Baltoro glacier, near to K2. In the same year, a small trip with three Italian climbers visited eastern Greenland.

153 Brunner was not a typical working-class Val Rosandra climber disposed by poverty and a childhood under occupation towards fascism. Xidias suggests that a

family fortune protected Brunner from the consequences of repudiating the party. See Giorgio Brunner, *Un uomo va sui monti* (Bologna: Alfa, 1957).

154 General Carlos Ibáñez del Campo, who called himself the "Chilean Mussolini," had been recently ousted, but his followers were still highly influential in the cabinet and anticipated (correctly) their leader's return. Chile was blockading arms shipments to neighbouring Bolivia, which was at war with Paraguay in the Gran Chaco region. Mussolini wanted to increase his influence and prestige by instating cordial relations between two conservative states, shoring up the failing, German-trained Bolivian army and selling Italian military hardware to the landlocked Bolivians, which would have to be delivered through Chilean territory.

155 Evelio A. Echevarria, *The Andes* (Augusta, MO: Joseph Reidhead, 2018), 280–85.

156 In 1934, for instance, he spoke only to the local sections of the CAI in Venice, Milan, Rome, Genoa, Bergamo and Vicenza.

157 AA, 10. Casara says that Emilio's usual fee was 250 lire, of which 100 lire was spent on the train ticket and 100 on lantern slides. The remainder would be easily spent on meals and accommodation.

158 Emilio Comici, "Tecnica e spiritualità dell'arrampicata," *AE*, 146.

159 Emilio Comici, "Arrampicata in Grecia" (1934), *AE*, 86–87.

160 Ibid., 94.

161 Ibid., 96.

162 Museo Nazionale della Montagna – CAI Torino, *Cinema delle Montagne* (Turin: Utet Libreria, 2004), 121.

163 *Cinema delle Montagne*, 89.

164 Jacqueline Reich, *Maciste Films of Italian Silent Cinema* (Bloomington: Indiana University Press, 2015), 241.

165 Giuseppe Inaudi, "Emilio Comici e la Scuola Centrale Militare di Alpinismo di Aosta," *AE*, 162.

166 *EC*, 208, 218.

167 *AA*, 44.

168 *EC*, 87.

169 Ibid.

170 In *EC*, Xidias accuses Casara of having made up the story about Bruna's ghost, and references Emilio's diary (a document unavailable to Casara) to show that the event could not likely have occurred when Casara claimed it had. Allowing for some exaggerations and inaccuracies by Casara, including the date of the event, the story is more or less in harmony with Emilio's other experiences of the supernatural.

171 *EC*, 93.

172 Benito Mussolini, *My Autobiography*, trans. Richard Washburn Child (Mineola, NY: Dover, 2006), 11.

173 *SC*, 58.

174 *AA*, 34.

175 In the 1930s, Cassin mixed nationalism and fascism with his

climbing. The season before, in 1934, he named the new route he had climbed on the Cimone della Bagozza with Aldo Frattini, Luigi Pozzi and Rodolfo Varallo "xxvii Ottobre – Achille Starace." Starace was a colourful, floridly corrupt, right-wing militant fascist party secretary and soldier. October 27 was the anniversary of the fascist March on Rome.

176 Cassin, 60.

177 AA, 50–51.

178 Inaudi, 228.

179 *Il Popolo*, October 18, 1932, 1.

180 Emilio Comici, "Alpinismo Solitario," cited hereafter as "Alpinismo Solitario," AE, 133.

181 Ibid., 141.

182 EC, 159.

183 Marco Dalla Torre, *Antonia Pozzi e la montagna* (Assago: Ancora, 2009), 97.

184 AA, 55–56.

185 Emilio Comici, "Spedizione alpinistica in Spagna," AE, 98–99.

186 Ibid.

187 Umberto Pacifico made one significant but short route, the Spigolo Pacifico on the Castelletto Inferiore, in 1941, and then retreated to his first love, Val Rosandra. He eventually became the head of the mountaineering school, based on his reputation for a love of the Carso and patience with ambitious young climbers.

188 EC, 140.

189 "Mary Varale, 'la signora di Milano,'" *Qvota 864: Quaderni di Vita di Montagna* website, http://qvota864.it/mary-varale.html.

190 After the first ascent, Giuseppe Novello tore the page out of a hut register describing Emilio, Sandro del Toro and Piero Mazzorana's first ascent of the north face of the Dito di Dio in 1936, and added his name to the list of first ascensionists. When Novello's page became public after his death, a rumour that Novello had been on the first ascent was born. "Il mistero del Dito di Dio," *GognaBlog* (personal blog of Alessandro Gogna), February 9, 2019, https://www.gognablog.com/il-mistero-del-dito-di-dio/.

191 SC, 58.

192 EC, 221.

193 EC, 145.

194 Ibid.

195 Ibid.

196 Ibid., 146.

197 "Mazzeni," AE, 50.

198 AA, 62.

199 "Cengia degli Dei," AE, 62.

200 Emilio Comici, "Cima d'Auronzo, Südwand," Österreichische Alpenzeitung 67 (1941), AE, 108.

201 Ibid., 111.

202 EC, 221.

203 AA, 67.

204 E-mail from Reinhold Messner to David Smart, August 6, 2019: "P. Aschenbrenner (1933) found the things on the end of the big

difficulties. There is no doubt that Comici left them on the last Bivy-Place."

205 EC, 103.

206 "Alpinismo Solitario," AE, 141–42.

207 AA, 67.

208 Antonio Pozzi, "For Emilio Comici," cited in David Smart, "Blood that Dreams of Stones: Antonia Pozzi, Climbing Poet," *Alpinist* 68 (winter 2020), 98.

209 "Alpinismo Solitario," AE, 145.

210 EC, 162. Casara reported that the news of Emilio's solo of the north face of the Cima Grande "fell on the heads of his detractors like an axe" and silenced any serious criticism. It is more likely that the Cortinesi guides did not care, or thought his solo an unnecessary flourish, but there is no evidence that they wrote the derogatory comment in the summit register.

211 Belgian climber Claude Barbier made the second solo ascent of the north face of the Cima Grande, in 1961.

212 Evola, 35.

213 AA, 70.

214 Emilio Comici, "Cima," AE, 104.

215 PL, 137.

216 SC, 80–81.

217 SC, 80–81.

218 Österreichische Alpenzeitung 67 (1941), 104.

219 Emilio Comici, "La falciata della morte," AE, 114.

220 EC, 37.

221 AA, 83.

222 SC, 78–79.

223 See entries for 1920 to 1940, *Cinema delle Montagna*, 49–172.

224 Official CAI Presidenza Generale letter, "Medaglie al Valore Atletico anno XV," Angelo Manaresi to Riccardo Cassin. June 14, 1938, *GognaBlog*, https://www.gognablog.com/wp-content/uploads/2017/10/Montagna-uomini-idee-3-6.jpg.

225 AA, 77.

226 "Anche il Centro Alpinistico epurato dei soci ebrei" Notice, *Il Piccolo*, November 17, 1938. Sirovich, tavola XVII.

227 Goffredo Plastino and Joseph Sciorra, *Neapolitan Postcards* (London: Rowman and Littlefield, 2016), 192.

228 Fabio Presutti, "The Saxophone and the Pastoral: Italian Jazz in the Age of Fascist Modernity," *Italica* 85, no. 2/3 (summer/autumn 2008), 273.

229 Rita Palmquist, "Emilio Comici e la musica," AE, 200.

230 Ibid.

231 AE, 203.

232 Emilio Comici, *Con me, a scuola a sci* (Milan: Hoepli, 1945).

233 Smart, "Antonia Pozzi," 101.

234 Dalla Torre, 100.

235 Antonio Pozzi, *Parole* (Milan: Mondadori, 1939).

236 PL, 230.

237 Il Prefetto della Provincia di Bolzano, "Certifica che il Signor

Comici Leonardo Emilio,"
Bolzano, April 23, 1940.

238 *PI.*, 232.

239 Carlo Rossi, "Local Government in Italy under Fascism," *American Political Science Review* 29, no. 4 (August 1935), 658.

240 Eduard Reut-Nicolussi, *Tyrol unter dem Bell* (Munich: 1929) published in English as *Tyrol under the Axe of Italian Fascism*, trans. K.L. Montgomery (London: Unwin Brothers, 1930), 253–54: "the [prefectural] commissioners… rivalled each other in patriotic lavishness to Italian societies, travel associations, memorials, and charitable foundations. The Fascist administration announced the town of Bozen as a perpetual member of the Dante Alighieri Society, presented a thousand metres of land to an Italian Kindergarten Union, allotted to the Italian lessee of Bozen theatre, on account of his losses during the Italian representations, an annual supplement of 100,000 lire, together with the expenses of lighting, fitting-up, advertising, theatre staff, such as dressmakers and hairdressers, etc. They further gave a thousand lire for the Italian war memorial on Monte Grappa and many hundred thousands to Italian War Unions, Invalid Days, receptions of students out of every imaginable Italian town, and members of the Royal Household. As all set in for the communal officials, with numberless banquets… at the cost of the townsfolk."

241 Casara's observation that Emilio "went about his job in climbing pants and a T-shirt" was based on his visits during Emilio's off-duty days.

242 Reut-Nicolussi, 250.

243 Armiero, 134.

244 Istituto Luce Cinecittà YouTube channel, "Giovanni balilla in un Campeggio presso S. Cristina in Val Gardena" (1936), https://www.youtube.com/watch?v=Q6IU9nBA040.

245 Reut-Nicolussi, 69, 273.

246 Ibid., 273.

247 Reinhold Messner, "Sudtirolo e nazionalsocialismo," *Messaggero Veneto* 02 (2006), 14, http://ricerca.gelocal.it/messaggeroveneto/archivio/messaggeroveneto/2006/02/14/NZ_21_MON3.html?refresh_ce.

248 *AA*, 23–24.

249 Ibid., 23.

250 James R. Dow, *Heinrich Himmler's Cultural Commissions: Programmed Plunder in Italy and Yugoslavia* (Madison: University of Wisconsin Press, 2018), 13.

251 *AA*, 95.

252 Sirovich, 312.

253 *EC*, 178.

254 "Riofreddo," *AE*, 22.

255 Dante Alighieri Society, "Stelutis Alpinis," http://danteact.org.au/dante-musica-viva/repertoire/stelutis-alpinis/.

256 *AE*, 132.

257 *EC*, 208. Franz Rudowsky, editor of the *Österreichische*

Alpenzeitung (*Austrian Alpine Journal*), was the first climber to compare Emilio's climbing style to an angel's.

258 *PL*, 106.

259 Sirovich, 326.

260 Ibid., 326–38.

261 *Bruti*, 76–77.

262 Rudatis, "Color Television System, U.S. patent number 3,053,931, 1958," *Official Gazette of the United States Patent Office* (Washington: United States Government Printing Press, 1962), vol. 7612566.

263 Reinhold Messner, "L'assassinio dell'impossibile," *RM*, October 1968; Ken Wilson, "Cerro Torre: A Mountain Desecrated," *Mountain* 23 (September 1972).

264 Scott, 29.

265 Bernadette McDonald and John Amatt, eds. *Voices from the Summit: The World's Great Mountaineers on the Future of Climbing* (New York: National Geographic Society and Banff Centre for Mountain Culture, 2000), 190.

266 Psalms 8:4–5 (King James Version).

267 Buzzati, "Mezzo secolo di scandalo sulle più aeree Dolomiti," *Corriere d'informazione*, Nov. 26–27, 1947, cited in *Montagna*, vol. 2, 17.

268 Buzzati, *Montagna*, vol. 2, 10.

269 Antonia Pozzi, "For Emilio Comici," Smart, 98.

INDEX